EPHESIANS, PHILIPPIANS, COLOSSIANS AND PHILEMON

for EVERYONE

20TH ANNIVERSARY EDITION WITH STUDY GUIDE

NEW TESTAMENT FOR EVERYONE
20TH ANNIVERSARY EDITION WITH STUDY GUIDE
N. T. Wright

Matthew for Everyone, Part 1
Matthew for Everyone, Part 2
Mark for Everyone
Luke for Everyone
John for Everyone, Part 1
John for Everyone, Part 2
Acts for Everyone, Part 1
Acts for Everyone, Part 2
Romans for Everyone, Part 1
Romans for Everyone, Part 2
1 Corinthians for Everyone
2 Corinthians for Everyone
Galatians and Thessalonians for Everyone
Ephesians, Philippians, Colossians and Philemon for Everyone
1 and 2 Timothy and Titus for Everyone
Hebrews for Everyone
James, Peter, John and Judah for Everyone
Revelation for Everyone

EPHESIANS, PHILIPPIANS, COLOSSIANS AND PHILEMON
for
EVERYONE

20TH ANNIVERSARY EDITION WITH STUDY GUIDE

N. T. WRIGHT

STUDY GUIDE BY MICHAEL KIRKINDOLL

WESTMINSTER
JOHN KNOX PRESS
LOUISVILLE • KENTUCKY

First published in Great Britain in 2002 by the
Society for Promoting Christian Knowledge
36 Causton Street
London SW1P 4ST
www.spckpublishing.co.uk

Copublished in 2004 by the Society for Promoting
Christian Knowledge, London, and Westminster John Knox Press,
100 Witherspoon Street, Louisville, KY 40202.

20th Anniversary Edition with Study Guide
Published in 2023
by Westminster John Knox Press
Louisville, Kentucky

23 24 25 26 27 28 29 30 31 32—10 9 8 7 6 5 4 3 2 1

Cover design by Allison Taylor

Library of Congress Cataloging-in-Publication Data

Names: Wright, N. T. (Nicholas Thomas), author. | Kirkindoll, Michael.
Title: Ephesians, Philippians, Colossians and Philemon for everyone / N. T.
   Wright; study guide by Michael Kirkindoll.
Other titles: Paul for everyone
Description: 20th anniversary edition with study guide. | Louisville :
   Westminster John Knox Press, 2023. | Series: New Testament for everyone
   | Summary: "This expanded edition contains Wright's updated translation
   of the biblical text, a new introduction, and a study guide designed for
   use in Bible study classes and individual reflection. Helpful summaries
   and insightful questions assist group leaders, study participants, and
   solo learners to encounter these early Christian letters in exciting and
   enriching new ways"-- Provided by publisher.
Identifiers: LCCN 2023031452 (print) | LCCN 2023031453 (ebook) | ISBN
   9780664268787 (paperback) | ISBN 9781646983438 (ebook)
Subjects: LCSH: Bible. Ephesians--Commentaries. | Bible.
   Philippians--Commentaries. | Bible. Colossians--Commentaries. | Bible.
   Philemon--Commentaries.
Classification: LCC BS2650.53 .W75 2023 (print) | LCC BS2650.53 (ebook) |
   DDC 227/.07--dc23/eng/20230731
LC record available at https://lccn.loc.gov/2023031452
LC ebook record available at https://lccn.loc.gov/2023031453

Most Westminster John Knox Press books are available at special quantity discounts when purchased in bulk by corporations, organizations and special-interest groups. For more information, please e-mail SpecialSales@wjkbooks.com.

For
Julian and Miranda
remembering the great mystery
of Christ and the Church
(Ephesians 5.31–32)

CONTENTS

CONTENTS

PHILIPPIANS

COLOSSIANS

CONTENTS

PHILEMON

INTRODUCTION TO THE
ANNIVERSARY EDITION

It took me ten years, but I'm glad I did it. Writing a guide to the books of the New Testament felt at times like trying to climb all the Scottish mountains in quick succession. But the views from the tops were amazing, and discovering new pathways up and down was very rewarding as well. The real reward, though, has come in the messages I've received from around the world, telling me that the books have been helpful and encouraging, opening up new and unexpected vistas.

Perhaps I should say that this series wasn't designed to help with sermon preparation, though many preachers have confessed to me that they've used it that way. The books were meant, as their title suggests, for everyone, particularly for people who would never dream of picking up an academic commentary but who nevertheless want to dig a little deeper.

The New Testament seems intended to provoke all readers, at whatever stage, to fresh thought, understanding and practice. For that, we all need explanation, advice and encouragement. I'm glad these books seem to have had that effect, and I'm delighted that they are now available with study guides in these new editions.

N. T. Wright
2022

INTRODUCTION

On the very first occasion when someone stood up in public to tell people about Jesus, he made it very clear: this message is for *everyone*.

It was a great day – sometimes called the birthday of the church. The great wind of God's spirit had swept through Jesus' followers and filled them with a new joy and a sense of God's presence and power. Their leader, Peter, who only a few weeks before had been crying like a baby because he'd lied and cursed and denied even knowing Jesus, found himself on his feet explaining to a huge crowd that something had happened which had changed the world for ever. What God had done for him, Peter, he was beginning to do for the whole world: new life, forgiveness, new hope and power were opening up like spring flowers after a long winter. A new age had begun in which the living God was going to do new things in the world – beginning then and there with the individuals who were listening to him. 'This promise is for *you*,' he said, 'and for your children, and for everyone who is far away' (Acts 2.39). It wasn't just for the person standing next to you. It was for everyone.

Within a remarkably short time this came true to such an extent that the young movement spread throughout much of the known world. And one way in which the *everyone* promise worked out was through the writings of the early Christian leaders. These short works – mostly letters and stories about Jesus – were widely circulated and eagerly read. They were never intended for either a religious or intellectual elite. From the very beginning they were meant for everyone.

That is as true today as it was then. Of course, it matters that some people give time and care to the historical evidence, the meaning of the original words (the early Christians wrote in Greek), and the exact and particular force of what different writers were saying about God, Jesus, the world and themselves. This series is based quite closely on that sort of work. But the point of it all is that the message can get out to everyone, especially to people who wouldn't normally read a book with footnotes and Greek words in it. That's the sort of person for whom these books are written. And that's why there's a glossary, in the back, of the key words that you can't really get along without, with a simple description of what they mean. Whenever you see a word in **bold type** in the text, you can go to the back and remind yourself what's going on.

There are of course many translations of the New Testament available today. The one I offer here is designed for the same kind of reader: one who mightn't necessarily understand the more formal, sometimes even ponderous, tones of some of the standard ones. I have tried naturally, to keep as close to the original as I can. But my main aim has been to be sure that the words can speak not just to some people, but to everyone.

Let me add a note about the translation the reader will find here of the Greek word *Christos*. Most translations simply say 'Christ', but most modern English speakers assume that that word is simply a proper name (as though 'Jesus' were Jesus' 'Christian' name and 'Christ' were his 'surname'). For all sorts of reasons, I disagree; so I have experimented not only with 'Messiah' (which is what the word literally means) but sometimes, too, with 'King'.

This book includes the four short letters Paul wrote from prison: Ephesians, Philippians, Colossians and Philemon. His own personal circumstances make these especially poignant, and give us a portrait of a man facing huge difficulties and hardships and coming through with his faith and hope unscathed. But what he has to say to the young churches – and, in the case of Philemon, to one man facing a hugely difficult moral dilemma – is even more impressive. Already, within thirty years of Jesus' death and resurrection, Paul has worked out a wonderful, many-coloured picture of what Jesus achieved, of God's worldwide plan, and of how it all works out in the lives of ordinary people. So here they are: Ephesians, Philippians, Colossians and Philemon for everyone!

Tom Wright

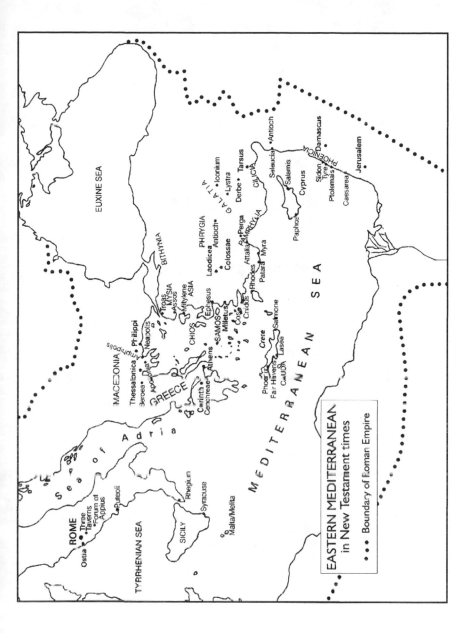

EASTERN MEDITERRANEAN in New Testament times

• • • • • Boundary of Roman Empire

EPHESIANS

EPHESIANS 1.1–3

Blessings on the Sovereign God!

¹From Paul, one of Messiah Jesus' apostles through God's purpose, to the holy ones in Ephesus who are also loyal believers in Messiah Jesus: ²may God our father and the Lord Jesus, the Messiah, give you grace and peace!

³Let us bless God, the father of our Lord Jesus, the Messiah! He has blessed us in the Messiah with every spirit-inspired blessing in the heavenly realm.

The most successful tourist attraction to appear in London in recent years is the 'London Eye'. From a distance it looks like a giant Ferris wheel, but this is no fun-fair ride. For a start, it's far, far bigger: it rises to 450 feet above the River Thames. Its 32 capsules can each hold 20 people, and it takes them half an hour to rotate the full circle. Plenty of time to have a wonderful view of all central London, with its historic buildings and palaces, its cathedrals and abbeys, its parks and gardens, with Big Ben and the Houses of Parliament in the foreground. The London Eye is, in fact, not only a wonderful sight in itself, visible from many points in the capital. It is the place from which you can get the best possible view of London. To do any better, you'd have to go up in an aeroplane, and indeed it is operated and run by one of the airline companies.

The letter to the Ephesians stands in relation to the rest of Paul's letters rather like the London Eye. It isn't the longest or fullest of his writings, but it offers a breathtaking view of the entire landscape. From here, as the wheel turns, you get a bird's-eye view of one theme after another within early Christian reflection: God, the world, Jesus, the church, the means of salvation, Christian behaviour, marriage and the family, and spiritual warfare. Like someone used to strolling around London and now suddenly able to see familiar places from unfamiliar angles – and to see more easily how they relate to each other within the city as a whole – the reader who comes to Ephesians after reading the rest of Paul will get a new angle on the way in which his thinking holds together.

Two questions need to be looked at as we begin. First, was the letter really by Paul himself? Many careful scholars have doubted it. It's clear that some of it is written in quite a formal way, without the rapid-fire, almost street-level debating style Paul uses in some of the other letters. On the other hand, some scholars have established their image of Paul on the basis of a particular way of understanding Romans and Galatians, and have then felt that Ephesians can't be by the same person,

3

because it doesn't support that point of view. Some have taken a compromise position, and said that though Paul may not actually have written it himself, it may have been written by an assistant under his direction. My own view, which I will follow in going through the letter here, is that, once we understand Paul's thought in the way I think we should, there is no difficulty about holding together what he says here with what he says in the other letters. The writing style is indeed a little different, but Paul wouldn't be the first or the last writer to use different styles when different occasions demand it.

The second point follows from this: who was the letter really addressed to? This question comes up in the very first verse of the letter, because in three of the best and earliest manuscripts of Paul we possess (from the third and fourth centuries) the words 'in Ephesus' are missing.

All sorts of theories have been suggested to explain this. The best, I think, is that this letter was originally intended as a circular to various churches in the Ephesus area. It was written while Paul was in prison, then taken round here and there. A copy might well have remained in the possession of the church in Ephesus, and someone later on might have assumed that it was written *to* Ephesus rather than from there.

Since in Colossians – which is very similar to Ephesians in many ways – Paul says that he's sending a letter to Laodicea which will be passed on to them, it's clear he did indeed sometimes write circular letters. The present letter might even be that 'letter to Laodicea', though we can't now be sure of that. And at the start of chapter 3 of the present letter, Paul seems to be talking to various people who don't know him and his work first-hand – which would hardly have applied in Ephesus itself, where he spent a long time. If we suppose that he intended the letter to go to several young churches within a hundred miles or so of Ephesus, we shan't go far wrong.

Most of Paul's letters start, after the initial greeting, by telling the church what he's praying for when he thinks of them. He will come to that later on in this first chapter (verses 15–23). But pride of place in the opening of this letter goes to a long and quite formal prayer of thanks and praise to God. This opening prayer lasts, in fact, from verse 3 all the way to verse 14. Though we can break it up into quite short sentences (and here we've broken it into two separate sections) it is really a continuous stream of worship, and we should think of it like that. Before Paul will even come to a report of his specific prayers, he establishes what is after all the appropriate context for all Christian prayer, reflection and exhortation: the worship and adoration of the God who has lavished his love upon us.

Who is this God, then? Why is he to be worshipped and adored in this way?

Paul's answer, which he never gets tired of repeating and which we should never take for granted as we hear it, is that the true God, who deserves and should receive our glad worship, is the father of the Lord Jesus, the king, the **Messiah**. He is not the same as the gods and goddesses of the pagan world. He isn't just a divine force, a vague influence or energy loosely known as 'the sacred'. He is the God who made the world, and who has now made himself known in and through Jesus. As far as Paul is concerned, any picture of God which doesn't now have Jesus in the middle of it is a distortion or a downright fabrication.

The entire prayer, all eleven verses of it, is woven through and through with the story of what God has done in Jesus the Messiah. He has blessed us in the king (verse 3); he chose us in him (verse 4), foreordained us through him (verse 5), poured grace on us in him (verse 6), gave us redemption in him (verse 7), set out his plan in him (verse 9), intending to sum up everything in him (verse 10). We have obtained our inheritance in him (verse 11), because we have set our hope on him (verse 12), and have been sealed in him with the **spirit** as the guarantee of what is to come (verses 13–14).

We shall look at all this in more detail in the next section. But what strikes us most about this astonishing bird's-eye view of the whole divine plan of salvation is the way in which Paul, almost relentlessly, sees that everything the one God has done he has done in and through Jesus the Messiah.

In particular, he has acted *for us* 'in him'. When Paul speaks of us as being 'in **Christ**' (I have used 'Christ', 'king' and 'Messiah' almost interchangeably, to bring out his full meaning), the centre of what he means is that, as in some Jewish thought, the king represents his people, so that what happens to him happens to them, and what is true of him is true of them. Think of David fighting Goliath (1 Samuel 17). David was *representing* Israel; he had already been anointed as king, and it wasn't long after his victory before people realized that he was the one who would lead Israel into God's future. So with us: Jesus has won the decisive victory over the oldest and darkest enemy of all, and if we are 'in him', 'in the king', 'in Christ', we shall discover step by step what that means.

Above all, as we do so, we learn to worship the God who has done it all 'in him'. As we read Ephesians today, to be strengthened and encouraged as Christians for the new tasks that lie ahead, we should remember that all genuine Christian life and action flows out of worship. True worship of the true God cannot help telling and retelling, with joy and amazement, the story of what this God has done in Jesus the Messiah. Enjoy the view. You won't get a better one.

EPHESIANS 1.4-10

The Choice and the Plan

⁴He chose us in him before the world was made, so as to be holy and irreproachable before him in love. ⁵He foreordained us for himself, to be adopted as sons and daughters through Jesus the Messiah. That's how he wanted it, and that's what gave him delight, ⁶so that the glory of his grace, the grace he poured on us in his beloved one, might receive its due praise.

⁷In the Messiah, and through his blood, we have deliverance – that is, our sins have been forgiven – through the wealth of his grace ⁸which he lavished on us. Yes, with all wisdom and insight ⁹he has made known to us the secret of his purpose, just as he wanted it to be and set it forward in him ¹⁰as a blueprint for when the time was ripe. His plan was to sum up the whole cosmos in the Messiah – yes, everything in heaven and on earth, in him.

Have you noticed how sometimes you have a story in the back of your mind which keeps peeping out even when you're talking about something else?

Imagine you've come back from work and the train has been late again. You stood for half an hour on the station platform getting cold and cross. Then when it arrived it was so full of people you had to stand, uncomfortably, all the way home.

But when you tell your family about the trip you find you're also telling them a larger story. Everybody knows that the trains aren't running properly because the present government has allowed them to get worse and worse so that they can have an excuse to introduce a new scheme of their own. But there's an election coming soon, and then you'll be able to vote out this government and put in another one that might at last get you a decent train service.

So as you talk about your anger over this evening's train ride, you are talking as well about your anger with the present government. And as you talk about how things could be better with the train you normally catch, you are talking as well about how good things are going to be with the new government. There is a larger framework, a larger story, within which your own smaller stories become more interesting and important.

Paul's great prayer at the opening of this letter is a celebration of the larger story within which every single Christian story – every story of individual conversion, **faith**, spiritual life, obedience and hope – is set.

Only by understanding and celebrating the larger story can we hope to understand everything that's going on in our own smaller stories, and so observe God at work in and through our own lives.

The prayer itself falls into three sections, though each one is tied so closely to the others, and overlaid with so much praise and celebration, that sometimes it's difficult to see what's going on. Verses 4–6 are the first paragraph, following the introductory word of praise in verse 3. Verses 7–10 are the second, and verses 11–14 round the prayer off. Let's look at them in turn.

Verses 4–6 celebrate the fact that God's people in the **Messiah** are *chosen by grace*. This is, perhaps, the most mysterious thing of all. God, the creator, 'chose us in him', that is, in the king, 'before the world was made'; and he 'foreordained us for himself'.

Many people, including many devout Christians, have found this shocking, or even unbelievable. How can God choose some and not others? How can being a follower of Jesus Christ be a matter of God's prior decision, overriding any decision or freedom of our own?

Various answers can be given to this. We have to be careful here. Paul emphasizes throughout this paragraph that everything we have in **Christ** is a gift of God's grace; and in the next chapter he will declare that before this grace reached down to us we were 'dead', and needing to be 'made alive' (2.5). We couldn't lift a finger to help ourselves; the rescue we needed had to come from God's side. That's one of the things this opening section is celebrating.

The second thing, which is often missed in discussions of this point, is that our salvation in Christ is a vital stage, but only a stage, on the way to the much larger purpose of God. God's plan is for the whole cosmos, the entire universe; his choosing and calling of us, and his shaping and directing of us in the Messiah, are somehow connected with that larger intention. How this works out we shall see a little later. But the point is that we aren't chosen for our own sake, but for the sake of what God wants to accomplish through us.

This alerts us to the other hidden story which Paul is telling all through this great prayer. It is the story of the **Exodus** from Egypt. God chose Abraham, Isaac and Jacob to be the bearers of his promised salvation for the world – the rescue of the whole cosmos, humankind especially, from the sin and death that had come about through human rebellion. When Paul says that God chose *us* 'in Christ' – the 'us' here being the whole company of Christians, Jews and **Gentiles** alike – he is saying that those who believe in Jesus are now part of the fulfilment of that ancient purpose.

But the story, of course, doesn't stop there. In verses 7–10 Paul tells the story of the cross of Jesus in such a way that we can hear, underneath

7

it, the ancient Jewish story of Passover. Passover was the night when the angel of death came through the land of Egypt, and the blood of the lamb sprinkled on the doorposts rescued the Israelites from the judgment that would otherwise have fallen on them. The word often used for that moment was 'redemption' or 'deliverance': it was the time when God went to Egypt and 'bought' for himself the people that had been enslaved there. Now, again in fulfilment of the old story, the true 'redemption' has occurred. Forgiveness of sins is the real 'deliverance' from the real slavemaster. And it's been accomplished through the sacrificial blood of Jesus.

Telling the story like this – the story of Jesus the Messiah, and the meaning of his death, told in such a way as to bring out the fact that it's the fulfilment of the Exodus story – is a classic Jewish way of celebrating the goodness of God. Worship, for Christians, will almost always involve *telling the story* of what God has done in and through Jesus. From the beginning, such storytelling built on the stories of God's earlier actions on Israel's behalf. The prayer will now conclude by moving forwards from the Christian version of the Exodus to the Christian version of the promised land.

Take some time, as you ponder Paul's prayer, to reflect on what it meant for him, in prison, to write in praise of the God who has set us free. Then open your heart in prayer on behalf of those who today still long that what God did in Christ might become a reality in their daily lives.

EPHESIANS 1.11–14

The Inheritance and the Spirit

[11]In him we have received the inheritance! We were foreordained to this, following the intention of the one who does all things in accordance with the counsel of his purpose. [12]This was so that we, we who first hoped in the Messiah, might live for the praise of his glory. [13]In him you too, who heard the word of truth, the gospel of your salvation, and believed it – in him you were marked out with the spirit of promise, the holy one. [14]The spirit is the guarantee of our inheritance, until the time when the people who are God's special possession are finally reclaimed and freed. This, too, is for the praise of his glory.

Not far from where I was born there is an ancient castle. It stands imposingly, high above the banks of a river, defying anyone to attack it. These days, the likely attacks come from bank managers and tax-collectors rather than marauding raiders; so the owners have taken steps to use it profitably. The castle has become a wonderful spot for tourists to visit – and for movies to be made. Many historical films have included it, at least in the background. Part of the famous Harry Potter film series was shot there.

It is still, though, a family home. The same family – one of Britain's ancient noble lines – has lived there for many centuries. It has been handed on from father to son. Or, in some cases, from brother to brother. Not long ago, the Duke who lived there died quite suddenly, in early middle age, and had no son or daughter to inherit. In a flash, his brother found himself thrown into the spotlight. All unexpectedly, he had received an inheritance which changed his life for ever.

He and his wife rose to the occasion. If they were going to have an inheritance like that, it was worth doing something with it. As I write, plans are being put into effect to make the castle gardens among the most spectacular in the country.

These days, an inheritance is often simply money – or something that can quickly be turned into money. But very often in the ancient world, and particularly in the Jewish world, an 'inheritance' consisted, like the castle and its grounds, of land that was not to be got rid of.

The basic inheritance that God had promised to Abraham, Isaac and Jacob was the land of Canaan. All the time that the Israelites were enslaved in Egypt, this was the hope that kept them going: the hope that, whatever the turns and twists of the plot in the long-running story, God himself would eventually give them the 'inheritance': not a gift of cash, but the ideal land, the land flowing with milk and honey.

Part of the meaning of the **Exodus**, therefore, was that they were now free to set off and go to claim their inheritance. They wandered in the wilderness for 40 years, led this way and that by the pillar of cloud by day and fire by night. The presence of the Holy One in their midst was dangerous – you would be foolish to grumble or rebel, as some of them found to their cost – but it was the guarantee that they would get there in the end. And they did.

Now Paul tells this part of the story over again, as the conclusion of his long opening act of worship and praise. Only this time, of course, it's the new Exodus, the new inheritance and the new wilderness wandering. As often in his writings, he sees the church in the **present age** as doing again what Israel did in the desert: coming out of the slavery of sin through God's great action in Jesus the **Messiah**, and on the way to the new promised land.

But what is this new promised land? What is the promised inheritance?

The standard Christian answer for many years and in many traditions has been: '**Heaven**'. Heaven, it has been thought, is the place to which we are going. Great books like John Bunyan's *Pilgrim's Progress* have been written in which the happy ending, rather than an inheritance suddenly received from a relative, is the hero reaching the end of this worldly life and going off to share the life of heaven. But that isn't what Paul says, here or elsewhere.

The inheritance he has in mind, so it appears from the present passage and the whole chapter, is the whole world, when it's been renewed by a fresh act of God's power and love. Paul has already said in verse 10 that God's plan in the Messiah is to sum up everything in heaven and earth. God, after all, is the creator; he has no interest in leaving earth to rot and making do for all eternity with only one half of the original creation. God intends to flood the whole cosmos, heaven and earth together, with his presence and grace, and when that happens the new world that results, in which Jesus himself will be the central figure, is to be the 'inheritance' for which Jesus' people are longing.

At the moment, therefore, the people who in this life have come to know and trust God in Jesus are to be the signs to the rest of the world that this glorious future is on the way. Equally, the sign that they themselves have received which guarantees them their future is the **holy spirit**. The spirit is to the Christian and the church what the cloud and fire were in the wilderness: the powerful, personal presence of the living God, holy and not to be taken lightly, leading and guiding the often muddled and rebellious people to their inheritance.

But the spirit is more than just a leader and guide. The spirit is actually part of the promised inheritance, because the spirit is God's own presence, which in the new world will be fully and personally with us for ever. (That's why, in some New Testament visions of the future, such as Revelation 21, heaven and earth are joined together, so that 'the dwelling of God is with humans'.) The spirit marks us out, stamps us with God's official seal, as the people in the present who are guaranteed to inherit God's new world.

We see this in verse 14 in particular. The word Paul uses for 'guarantee' here is a word used at the time in legal or commercial transactions. Suppose I wanted to buy a plot of land from you, valued at 10,000 dollars. We might agree that I would pay you the first 1,000 dollars as a 'down payment', guaranteeing the full sum to come in the future when the details were complete. The spirit is the 'down payment': part of the promised future, coming forwards to meet us in the present.

As this commercial metaphor takes over in verse 14 (the cheerful mixing of metaphors is, I think, one of several signs that this is indeed Paul's work), the implication is that we have placed something we own, or are meant to own, in a pawnshop, and now need to 'redeem' it as our own possession. We shall indeed do this, Paul declares; and the spirit is the sign that we shall one day possess it fully.

Everything, of course, is done 'to the praise of God's glory'. Look back over the story which Paul has told as an act of worship. God has taken the initiative; God has done what was necessary, at great cost to himself, to buy us back from the slavery of sin; God has given us the spirit as a sign and foretaste of the whole renewed cosmos which awaits us as our inheritance. Discovering that you are to receive an inheritance like that should change your whole life. How can you not join in the hymn of praise?

EPHESIANS 1.15–23

Knowing the Power of the King

15Because of all this, and because I'd heard that you are loyal and faithful to Jesus the master, and that you show love to all God's holy people, 16I never stop giving thanks for you as I remember you in my prayers. 17I pray that the God of Messiah Jesus our Lord, the father of glory, would give you, in your spirit, the gift of being wise, of seeing things people can't normally see, because you are coming to know him 18and to have the eyes of your inmost self opened to God's light. Then you will know exactly what the hope is that goes with God's call; you will know the wealth of the glory of his inheritance in his holy people; 19and you will know the outstanding greatness of his power towards us who are loyal to him in faith, according to the working of his strength and power.

20This was the power at work in the Messiah when God raised him from the dead and sat him at his right hand in the heavenly places, 21above all rule and authority and power and lordship, and above every name that is invoked, both in the present age and also in the age to come. 22Yes: God has 'put all things under his feet', and has given him to the church as the head over all. 23The church is his body; it is the fullness of the one who fills all in all.

'So how strong is it?'

My friend was showing me his new telescope. It was set up in an upstairs room, looking out towards sea.

'Well, take a look.'

I had been scanning the horizon with my own small binoculars. There were a couple of ships going by. A few small fishing boats closer in. Nothing much else. I put my eye to his telescope and couldn't believe what I saw.

The two ships I had seen – suddenly they were so close that I could see their names on the side, and people walking to and fro on the deck. But that was only the beginning. Out beyond them, where my binoculars had registered nothing at all, were several other ships: large and small, military and commercial, including a cruise liner. The telescope seemed to have the uncanny power of making things appear out of nowhere.

Power is one of the great themes of Ephesians. Perhaps this is because Ephesus itself, and the surrounding area, was seen as a place of power. Certainly in social and civic terms the city was powerful, and was set to become more so. It was a major centre of imperial influence in Paul's day. The Roman emperors were keen to establish and maintain places where their rule could be celebrated and enhanced.

But it was also a centre of religious power. All sorts of cults and beliefs flourished, and frequently they focused on power: the power of what we might call magic, power to make things happen in the world, to influence people and events, to gain wealth or health or influence for yourself and to bring about the downfall of your enemies. Their world, in other words, was dominated by the 'principalities and powers', the various levels of rulers and authorities from local magistrates up to internationally recognized gods and goddesses, and all stages in between.

For Paul, the greatest display of power the world had ever seen took place when God raised Jesus from the dead (verse 20). Nobody had ever been raised bodily from the dead, before or since. (If anybody today imagines that when the early Christians said Jesus had been raised from the dead, they meant that he had simply been exalted to **heaven**, they should think again. That wouldn't have been an extraordinary display of power, but rather the normal expectation of many, both Jews and non-Jews.) This power of the creator God at once sets itself apart from, and establishes itself as superior to, all the 'powers' that people might ever come across. The risen Jesus, in fact, is now enthroned, on the basis of this power of God, over the whole cosmos. And at the centre of Paul's prayer for the church in the area, which he now reports, is his longing that they will come to realize that this same power, the power seen at Easter and now vested in Jesus, is available to them for their daily use.

Far too many Christians today, and, one suspects, in Paul's day, are quite unaware that this power is there and is available. They are like I was with my friend: until I looked through his powerful telescope I simply didn't know what was out there. If someone says, 'Well, I don't seem to have much power as a Christian', or, 'I can't see the power of Jesus doing very much in the world', that simply shows that they need this prayer of Paul. Paul doesn't imagine that all Christians will automatically be able to recognize the power of God. It will take, as he says in verse 17, a fresh gift of wisdom, of coming to see things people don't normally see. And this in turn will come about through knowing Jesus and having what Paul calls 'the eyes of your inmost self' opened to God's light.

God has already begun to work in them powerfully, as their loyal **faith** and love indicates (verse 15). So Paul can pray with confidence that God will now add this increase in wisdom and knowledge, especially in showing them two things: the inheritance, in all its glory – in other words, the vision of the renewed cosmos of which we spoke in the previous section; and the power of God which will bring it about in its proper time.

That power, the power which raised Jesus and which will transform the whole world and flood it with his glory, is in fact already available for us (verse 19). This doesn't mean we can become conjurors, performing spectacular tricks to impress people. Many of the things which God's power achieves in us, such as putting secret sins to death and becoming people of prayer, remain hidden from the world and even, sometimes, from other Christians.

But when he speaks of **Christ** as exalted over all possible rulers and authorities, we know that he means what he says. The local magistrates and officials; provincial rulers and governors; kings, princes and the emperor himself: all are subject to King Jesus. They are all put 'under his feet', he says. This is a quote from Psalm 8, a favourite of the early church. It speaks of God's purpose for humankind: that we should be sovereign over the whole creation. This is what has been accomplished in Jesus the **Messiah**. He is the truly human being, before whom all the world must bow.

And King Jesus has, as his hands and feet, his agents within the present world, the church. It is 'his body, the fullness of the one who fills all in all'. If only the church would realize this, and act accordingly!

EPHESIANS 2.1–7

Warning Signs on the Wrong Road

[1]So where do you come into it all? Well, you were dead because of your offences and sins! [2]That was the road you used to travel, keeping in step with this world's 'present age'; in step, too, with the ruler of the power of the air, the spirit that is, even now, at work among people whose whole lives consist of disobeying God. [3]Actually, that's how all of us used to behave, conditioned by physical desires. We used to do what our flesh and our minds were urging us to do. What was the result? We too were subject to wrath in our natural state, just like everyone else.

> [4]But when it comes to mercy, God is rich! He had such great love for us that [5]he took us at the very point where we were dead through our offences, and made us alive together with the Messiah (yes, you are saved by sheer grace!). [6]He raised us up with him, and made us sit with him – in the heavenly places, in Messiah Jesus! [7]This was so that in the ages to come he could show just how unbelievably rich his grace is, the kindness he has shown us in Messiah Jesus.

Many years ago, I was staying for a few days in Cape Town, South Africa. Among the people I wanted to meet was an elderly man who lived on the edge of the city, in one of the outer suburbs. We arranged by telephone that I should drive out, in a rented car, and have supper with him and his wife.

He gave me detailed instructions on how to find him. Unfortunately, when I set off it was dark, and raining, and I managed to get on the wrong expressway. Or, rather, it was the right expressway, but I was going in the wrong direction on it. Since he had told me to go for ten miles or so before looking for the signs to turn off, I didn't worry until I'd gone at least twelve or fifteen miles and none of the signs were making sense. Eventually I turned off the road and asked at a garage. They hadn't heard of the district I was looking for, never mind the street. I was totally in the wrong part of the city. Only gradually, when we studied the map, did I realize my mistake. I had been driving confidently, believing I was doing the right thing, but with every minute I had been going further and further away from where I wanted to be.

The story ended happily, with very kind hosts and a very late supper. But it illustrates the severe point that Paul is making in the first three verses of this chapter. We live in a world where human beings, left to themselves, not only choose the wrong direction, but remain cheerfully confident that it is in fact the right one. Indeed, people regularly point out, as evidence of its being the right one, how confident they are on the subject. It is, after all, a fine road, much travelled and in good repair.

It has been, in particular, very popular to argue that the desires and aspirations that people find deep within themselves are obviously God-given and are for that reason to be followed. This is so particularly in discussions of sexual morality. ('This is how God made me, so he must want me to live like this.') But a moment's thought simply on human grounds, never mind a biblical viewpoint, shows how flawed that thinking is. Many people have deep desires which, unless held severely in check, lead to disaster. Some are by nature highly aggressive. Some appear to be naturally dishonest. Sometimes an entire section of the population senses deeply that it must behave in a certain way, even though their neighbours find it deeply offensive and threatening.

From a Christian perspective, these obvious responses can be taken a stage further. When God acted in Jesus the **Messiah**, he not only revealed himself fully; he revealed fully what genuine human life was like – and it turns out to be deeply self-sacrificial. Simply following the desires of the physical body, and equally of the mind, will lead you to ruin. (Note how in verse 3 the 'flesh' and 'mind' are both seen as sources of danger: Paul doesn't for a moment suppose that the mind is morally 'higher' than the body.) The problem is, though: even if you recognize this, what can you do about it? If you are already 'dead' as a result of all this – already heading the wrong way down the road, with no hope of turning off, let alone turning back, and apparently no brake on the car to enable you to stop – what hope can there be?

Before you look at Paul's answer, look at the full dimensions of the problem. In verse 2 he shows that there are forces which pull you, lure you, compel you to go in the wrong direction.

First, there is the **present age**: the way the world is now is not the way God intends it to be in the **age to come**. What seems right, especially to those who are simply 'going with the flow' of the world around them, actually isn't.

Second, there is the 'ruler of the power of the air'. This seems to be a way of referring to the **satan**, the devil, and a way of suggesting that his deadly ideas, his schemes for defacing God's beautiful creation and particularly his image-bearing human creatures, are, as we say, 'in the air'. You can sense their power 'in the atmosphere' of a place, of a room full of certain people, of a city or college or shop. The satan is a spirit, at work among people who see no need to behave any differently.

Perhaps the most devastating thing Paul points out here is that 'we' – in other words, the Jews – were no different in principle from **Gentiles** in this respect. When he says 'you' in verses 1 and 2, referring to the non-Jewish world, this doesn't mean that he's leaving a loophole for Jews to say, 'Ah, but we're different'. As in Romans 2.17–24, when this possibility comes up he firmly rejects it.

So what's the answer? Well, if the problem is that the settled and habitual behaviour of the whole human race leads them on the fast road towards death – the ultimate destruction of their humanness – the answer provided by God is a way through death and out into a new sort of life entirely. This, of course, is achieved through the death and **resurrection** of Jesus, the king. How do these events affect other people? Because, as throughout chapter 1, Paul sees the people who belong to Jesus as being somehow 'in' him, so that what is true of him is true of them. He has been raised – and so have they! He has been installed in glory, in the heavenly realms – and so have they! This is the secret truth of the life of all those who belong to Jesus.

The main thing Paul wants to stress about all this is the sheer, almost unbelievable, magnificent kindness of God. In four short verses he says this in several different ways. God is rich in mercy; he loved us with a great love; his sheer grace has saved us; his grace is rich beyond all telling; he has lavished kindness upon us. Whenever anyone says, or implies, that God is after all a bit stingy, or mean, or small-minded, look at these verses and think again.

Of course, lots of people who are heading at speed in the wrong direction want to think of God like that – just as people who are enjoying their drive don't like it if someone tells them they're going the wrong way, and that they're about to pass the last chance to turn off and head back again. But the crucial factor here, as always, is Jesus himself. Take away his resurrection, and for all anybody knows the road to death is the only road there is. Put it back in the picture, though, and you realize two things. First, there is another way. Second, you are urgently summoned to turn round and follow it.

EPHESIANS 2.8-10

Grace, Not Works

[8]How has this all come about? You have been saved by grace, through faith! This doesn't happen on your own initiative; it's God's gift. [9]It isn't on the basis of works, so no one is able to boast. [10]This is the explanation: God has made us what we are. God has created us in Messiah Jesus for the good works that he prepared, ahead of time, as the road we must travel.

In the mid-1970s a country vet in a small town in northern England suddenly became world-famous. James Herriot, quite suddenly and in midlife, wrote books that sold in huge quantities around the world. Herriot (whose real name was Alfred Wight) lived in the town of Thirsk, in Yorkshire, England. His delightful stories of people and animals in the local farms and villages brought pleasure to millions, not least through *All Creatures Great and Small*, the television series based on his work.

In one of his books, Herriot tells how he planned to take his wife out for a small celebratory dinner at a restaurant some distance from their home. On the way, due to a mishap, he lost his wallet, and found himself at the end of the meal without the means to pay. However, to his complete astonishment, the waiter told him that the bill had already been paid. Unknown to Herriot, his senior partner had telephoned the restaurant and told them to charge the meal to him instead. It was his personal gift to the couple.

The astonishment, and relief, of that moment are a small pointer to the flavour of this passage about the grace of God. We can, perhaps, only understand the force of what Paul is saying when we step firmly into the world he has sketched in the first three verses of the chapter. Often, today, people don't believe there's much wrong with the human race, and with themselves in particular. As a result, they don't see very much need for God's grace. Perhaps, they think, God might help me out in a tight corner here or there, but basically I can get along fine without him. All that God then has to offer, it seems, is a kind of spiritual enhancement of ordinary life, a gentle enrichment of what's already there rather than a radical rescue from imminent disaster. It is as though Herriot, in paying for his meal himself, discovered that his partner had paid to have music played during the dinner.

But Paul's **gospel** is all about grace that is more than mere enrichment. It gives life to the dead. It is God's free, undeserved gift. In these three little verses he has summed up his entire view of how this grace works and what it does. This is very close to what he says about **justification** in Romans and Galatians, though it's here condensed into a tight, shorthand statement. It's important, though, that we look at the particular things he's saying here. Paul never simply fine-tunes doctrines in the abstract; he's always addressing a particular topic.

Paul speaks in Romans, Galatians and Philippians of being 'justified' by **faith**; here, in verse 8, he speaks of being 'saved' by grace. 'Justification' and 'salvation' are not the same thing. 'Justification' has to do with people belonging to God's family. It answers the question as to how they are marked out as members of it. 'Salvation' has to do with people being rescued from the fate they would otherwise have incurred. It answers the question as to how that rescue has taken place, and who is ultimately responsible for it. When Paul speaks of justification, the thing which marks people out is their faith. When he speaks, as here, of salvation, the responsibility is God's, i.e. it comes about through 'grace'.

He speaks of 'salvation' here, not 'justification', since the topic of the chapter at this point is not how God's people in **Christ** are marked out, but how they are rescued from sin and death. At the same time, he glances at the other question: you have been saved, he says, *by* grace and *through* faith. Faith is not something that humans 'do' to make themselves acceptable to God. Nothing we can do, unaided, can achieve that. If there were such a thing, it would become a matter of our own initiative, and the people who had this ability would be able to hold their heads up in pride over those who didn't. On the contrary. Because it's all a matter of God's gift, there is no room for any human being to boast.

This, of course, pushes the question one stage further back. Why then do some people believe, and not others? The only hints Paul gives of an answer to this question are already set out in chapter 1 (verses 4–6). As part of God's eventual plan to draw together the life and purpose of the whole creation in Jesus the king, those who believe do so because they are the ones in whom he has begun the process of lavishing his love upon the world.

When Paul speaks of justification by faith, not by works of the **law**, the point he is making is that the community of God's people is marked out by their faith in Jesus as the risen Lord, not by the various things (**sabbath**, food laws, **circumcision**) which were badges of membership in the ethnic people of Israel. This concern is closely related to the present passage. He is going at once to speak in verses 11–22 of the coming together of Jew and **Gentile** in the **Messiah**. But the emphasis throughout these verses is on the contrast between the state of the human race as described in verses 1–3 and the state of the human race as God in his generous love has decided to remake it. The 'good works' which he mentions in verse 10 are not, therefore, the same as the 'works of the law' which he rules out as part of justification in Romans, Galatians and Philippians. They are the way of life which he will describe more fully in chapters 4–6 of the present letter. They are the road which Christians must now travel in the right direction, after the disastrously wrong journey described earlier.

Verse 10 is one of Paul's central statements of how Christians are at the centre of God's new creation. We are, he says, God's workmanship. This word sometimes has an artistic ring to it. It may be hinting that what God has done to us in King Jesus is a work of art, like a poem or sculpture. Or perhaps, granted what he goes on to say, we are like a musical score; and the music, which we now have to play, is the genuine way of being human, laid out before us in God's gracious design, so that we can follow it.

We can read this verse in two ways. Paul may have meant that the 'good works' are the new way of being human, the way which conforms to the standards God always intended, the way which is the same for all Christians alike. Or he may have meant that God has a specific and unique purpose for each individual. Since he certainly believed this about his own vocation (see, for instance, 3.8–13), it's likely he believed that it was true of all other Christians as well. But the present verse focuses more particularly on the moral behaviour which is expected of all of us.

What happens to people's moral and spiritual lives if they don't grasp the fact that our entire life, never mind our salvation, is God's undeserved gift? If that sounds too abstract a question, a story which makes it very vivid and personal is found in Luke 7.36–50. You might like to read and ponder that story alongside this short passage of Paul.

EPHESIANS 2.11–16

Two into One Will Go

[11]So then, remember this! In human terms, that is, in your 'flesh', you are 'Gentiles'. You are the people who the so-called 'circumcision' refer to as the so-called 'uncircumcision' – circumcision, of course, being something done by human hands to human flesh. [12]Well, once upon a time you were separated from the Messiah. You were detached from the community of Israel. You were foreigners to the covenants which contained the promise. There you were, in the world with no hope and no god!

[13]But now, in Messiah Jesus, you have been brought near in the Messiah's blood – yes, you, who used to be a long way away! [14]He is our peace, you see. He has made the two to be one. He has pulled down the barrier, the dividing wall, that turns us into enemies of each other. He has done this in his flesh, [15]by abolishing the law with its commands and instructions.

The point of doing all this was to create, in him, one new human being out of the two, so making peace. [16]God was reconciling both of us to himself in a single body, through the cross, by killing the enmity in him.

We lived for four years by the banks of the Ottawa river, north-west of Montreal. It is a great river, already over 400 miles long by the time it passed our village. By the time it reached us it was over a mile wide. Not far downstream, however, this great river flows into the St Lawrence, which makes even the Ottawa river look small. It carries the water from the Great Lakes, and not only water; ocean-going boats sail to and fro up its seaway. The two rivers have quite different characters. The Ottawa rises in the cold, northern reaches of Quebec and Ontario. The St Lawrence runs along the twisting border between Canada and the United States.

Once the two rivers have joined together, just upstream from Montreal, they are simply known as the St Lawrence. They do not become the St Lawrence/Ottawa river. The noble river from the north is subsumed into the larger one from the west. If someone were to paddle a canoe downstream along the Ottawa river, once it had joined the St Lawrence they wouldn't be able to say that they were still really on the Ottawa. They would have joined the mainstream.

The peculiar thing about what Paul says in this passage is that what must have looked to his readers to be the vastly greater and wider river has joined a far smaller one – but it's the smaller one that gives its name to the river that now continues with the two streams merged into one. The great, wide river is the worldwide company of **Gentiles**,

19

the non-Jewish nations stretching across the world and back in time, including the glories of classical Greece, Rome, Egypt, Mesopotamia, China and the rest of the many-splendoured globe. The smaller river is the single family of Abraham, Isaac and Jacob, described here as 'the community of Israel'. Somehow, in the strange mapping system that the one God has chosen to operate, Gentiles and Jews have become one in the confluence that is Jesus the **Messiah**. And, as the river continues on its way, it bears not only the name of Israel, but also the hope that flows from the **covenants** of promise made with the Israelite patriarchs.

Not only so. As well as the hope, they now have – God! Paul, quite remarkably, describes them in their former state as having no God: the word he uses in verse 12 is the word from which we get our word 'atheists'. This is ironic, because that's what Gentiles used to call Jews, and then came to call Christians as well, since neither Jews nor Christians had statues of their gods. Neither, so far as the Gentile eye could see, offered animal sacrifice, consulted oracles, or did any of the other things that pagans associated with worship of their gods. Paul, boldly standing on the same ground as Jewish writers of the same period, declares that the pagan gods are actually non-gods. Those who think they worship them are worshipping something that doesn't really exist.

At the same time, he's just as emphatic that those who define themselves by the state of their male members – in other words, Jews who regard their **circumcision** as the ultimate badge of covenant membership – are equally out of line. Don't worry, verse 11 implies, about the so-called 'circumcision' that likes to call you the 'uncircumcision'. Circumcision, after all, is something that human beings make with their hands – which is what Jewish writers used to say about pagan idols! Paul is claiming the high ground. Those who belong to the Messiah are the new people of God.

At this point the illustration of the rivers, like most illustrations, breaks down. It isn't just that one stream is merged without trace into the other. Nor is it just that the new river is simply a combination of the two. It is as though, from that point, the whole river takes on a new and different character. Perhaps we could still make it work if we suggested that from that point on the river was tidal, with salt water meeting it from the ocean.

Paul now shows that this coming together of Jew and Gentile in the one family is achieved – as is almost everything else in his theology – through the cross of Jesus the Messiah. This has brought the pagans close in, from being far away (verse 13). It has torn down the barrier that used to stand between the two families (verse 14). It has abolished the Jewish law, the **Torah** – not in the sense that God didn't give it in the first place, but in the sense that the Jewish law had, as one of its main first-century uses, the keeping apart of Jew and Gentile (verse 15). The hostility that had existed between the two groups has itself been killed on the cross (verse 16). Paul probably didn't have in mind the way in which Herod and Pilate became friends at the time of Jesus' crucifixion (Luke 23.12), but that little story makes the point well.

The point of it all, as he says in verse 15, was to create a single new humanity in place of the two. Today's church may no longer face the question of the integration of Jew and Gentile into a single family, though there are places where that is still a major issue. But we face, quite urgently, the question which Paul would insist on as a major priority. If our churches are still divided in any way along racial or cultural lines, he would say that our **gospel**, our very grasp of the meaning of Jesus' death, is called into question. How long will it be before those who claim to follow Jesus, not least those who claim also to love Paul's thinking, come to terms with the demands he actually makes?

EPHESIANS 2.17–22

Unveiling the New Temple

¹⁷So the Messiah came and gave the good news. Peace had come! Peace, that is, for those of you who were a long way away, and peace, too, for those who were close at hand. ¹⁸Through him, you see, we both have access to the father in the one spirit.

¹⁹This is the result. You are no longer foreigners or strangers. No: you are fellow-citizens with God's holy people. You are members of God's household. ²⁰You are built on the foundation of the apostles and prophets, with Messiah Jesus himself as the cornerstone. ²¹In him the whole building is fitted together, and grows into a holy temple in the Lord. ²²You, too, are being built up together, in him, into a place where God will live by the spirit.

One of the greatest worldwide problems of our time is the plight of refugees and asylum seekers. People in the West sometimes try to pretend that the world is now a civilized place where most people can go about their business in peace, and at least relative prosperity. But the evidence suggests that this is over-optimistic. More people than ever, it seems, are displaced from homes and homelands, and find themselves wandering the world in search of somewhere to live. The countries where they arrive are often overwhelmed, and find that their resources, and their patience, are under strain, despite feeling sympathetic to people who have often suffered a great deal.

What refugees want above all, assuming that they can never return to their original homes, is to be accepted into a new community where they can rebuild their lives and their families. And the ultimate sign of that acceptance is to receive citizenship in the country they have adopted as their own. Their new passport is often their proudest possession. At last they can hold their heads up and build a new sense of identity. Once they have done that, they may well abandon all thoughts of going back where they came from. They have arrived. They belong.

That is the position, Paul declares, in which **Gentile** Christians now find themselves. Once they were 'foreigners' and 'strangers' in relation to Israel, the family of the one true God. But now they are full members – not because they have accepted the Jewish **law** or **circumcision**, but simply because of what Jesus himself has accomplished.

What Jesus has done is to make, and declare, peace. Peace is one of the best-loved words in the world, especially if you're a refugee or an asylum seeker. Often it must seem as though the world has gone mad. Many people escape from a war with nothing except the clothes they stand up in, only to find that the country where they arrive regards them with suspicion, hostility or even hatred. It is a wonderful thing to discover that peace has been declared. It is even better to know that it affects everybody, including both those who have come from a long way off and those who live near at hand.

This is what the **gospel** message announces. Gentiles and Jews alike are now to be at home in the same family. This must have sounded as extraordinary and revolutionary to traditional Jews – and Paul himself had of course been a traditional Jew – as it was wonderful and exhilarating for Gentiles who had looked at Judaism from the outside and felt drawn to the God of whom the Jewish scriptures had spoken.

But if this is revolutionary, more is to follow. The closing verses of the chapter take one of the central symbols of Judaism and turn it inside out. The **Temple** in Jerusalem was not only the religious heart of the nation, and the place of pilgrimage of Jews throughout the world. It was also the political, social, musical and cultural heart of Jerusalem – as well as the place of celebration and feasting. The reason for all this was, of course, that Israel's God, YHWH, had promised to live there. It was, many believed, the place where earth and **heaven** met.

But now Paul is declaring that the living God is constructing a new Temple. It consists, not of stones, arches, pillars and altars, but of human beings. Some Jews had already explored the idea that a community, rather than a building, might be the place where God would really and truly take up his residence. But until Paul nobody had said anything quite like this.

What it means, of course, is that for Christians a church building is not a 'Temple' in the strict sense. It is the people themselves who are the 'place' where God is now deciding to live. One might almost say that God himself has, in a sense, become a stranger and asylum seeker within his own world, the more so since, as the early Christians knew, the Jerusalem Temple itself had been solemnly condemned by Jesus. The living God was now seeking to make his home in the hearts and lives, and particularly the communities, that had declared their loyalty to Jesus, and were determined to live by the gospel.

In particular, this meant that the new 'Temple' had to be constructed out of two sorts of material, that would fuse together into a single building. The foundation of the building consisted of the **apostles** and prophets: in other words, the people (such as Paul himself) through whom God had announced, and was announcing, the worldwide message of peace through King Jesus. Jesus himself was the 'stone' reserved for the place of highest honour, the one which held the rest of the building together. This idea links the present passage with several other New Testament references to Jesus as 'stone' (e.g. Matthew 21.42; Acts 4.11; Romans 9.33; and 1 Peter 2.4–8). Most of these passages look back to Psalm 118.22; the early Christians were constantly searching and pondering the ancient scriptures to understand what the events concerning Jesus really meant.

But the building itself has, as its peculiar glory, the way in which bricks from two quite different quarries are to be built into it side by side, joined together in a new kind of architectural beauty. Jewish believers and Gentile believers, in other words, are not simply fellow members of the Christian community. Together, and only together, they form the community in which the living God will be delighted to take up residence.

Paul's breathtaking vision of the new community created in Jesus the Messiah leaves us today with several challenges. Do Gentile Christians today think of themselves as having been brought into an essentially Jewish community? Is it always possible for Jewish and Gentile believers in Jesus to worship together, and if not why not? What other racial and cultural differences must we overcome today if the beautiful Temple Paul has in mind is to be built in the way that will honour the one God of all the world?

EPHESIANS 3.1–7

God's Secret Plan Unveiled at Last

[1]It's because of all this that I, Paul, the prisoner of Messiah Jesus on behalf of you Gentiles . . .

[2]I'm assuming, by the way, that you've heard about the plan of God's grace that was given to me to pass on to you? [3]You know – the

secret purpose that God revealed to me, as I wrote briefly just now? ⁴Anyway . . . When you read this you'll be able to understand the special insight I have into the Messiah's secret. ⁵This wasn't made known to human beings in previous generations, but now it's been revealed by the spirit to God's holy apostles and prophets. ⁶The secret is this: that, through the gospel, the Gentiles are to share Israel's inheritance. They are to become fellow members of the body, along with them, and fellow-sharers of the promise in Messiah Jesus.

⁷This is the gospel that I was appointed to serve, in line with the free gift of God's grace that was given to me. It was backed up with the power through which God accomplishes his work.

Naomi had started a small dressmaking business. She had always been skilful with her hands, and had a good eye for colour and pattern. Now she realized she could turn these abilities to good use, not only to make clothes for herself and her family but to earn some money to supplement the family income. The brightly coloured fabrics of her part of Africa were popular not only in the surrounding district but also, she'd heard, in foreign countries as well. Who could tell where it all might lead?

She employed two local women to help with the actual dressmaking, and a young man who would travel to the city to buy supplies and sell the finished products. Together they worked hard and had a measure of success. People liked what they did and they were reliable. Soon they had more orders than they could easily complete. Naomi hired two more helpers to make sure they didn't fall behind what the customers wanted.

The little group worked happily together, until one day one of the younger women said, 'You know, I wonder if we could make other things as well as dresses? Curtains? Covers for chairs? Things like that?'

The others agreed enthusiastically. They were good at dressmaking, but were ready for a new challenge.

Naomi smiled. At last the moment had come.

She went to her desk, to the drawer she had always kept locked. She took out a plain sealed envelope, which had a date written across the seal – the day on which she had started the business in the first place. She passed the envelope to the woman who had asked the question.

'Open it,' she said, 'and read it out.'

The young woman opened the envelope, and took out a single typed sheet. She read it out. It contained the plan for a larger business that would make the wonderful fabrics into all sorts of things that people might want in their homes.

'I've kept it a secret from you all this time', smiled Naomi. 'I knew if I told you from the start you'd say I was daydreaming, and then you'd have started daydreaming yourselves. We had to prove we could make dresses first. But now I've shared the secret with you. This is what I planned all along. Let's do it!'

And the young man, sitting in the corner and listening to it all, suddenly realized that his job was about to change drastically, and for ever.

Paul's picture of God in this passage is a bit like the picture of Naomi. And Paul sees himself as we may imagine that young man saw himself. Suddenly he has been let in on an extraordinary secret. What might have looked like a strange innovation is in fact what God had had in mind all along.

God, it seems, had drawn up the blueprint for his worldwide family right from the beginning. He had hinted that there were developments yet to come – perhaps most strongly in the prophets, particularly Isaiah – but most of his people had thought that their present calling, to be his holy people and keep his **law**, would remain central. Now, however, he is letting people in on the secret, which had lain hidden for ages and generations; and Paul himself is to be the one to take the news of it around the world.

The secret plan is that God always intended to bring **Gentiles**, the non-Jewish peoples of the world, into fellowship with himself, on equal terms with his ancient people the Jews. And the **good news** – the 'gospel' – is that God has now accomplished this through Jesus the Jewish **Messiah**, Jesus who is also the world's true Lord.

Paul uses eager, excited language in verse 6 to describe just how great are the privileges to which the Gentiles now attain. First, they are to share the inheritance. Fancy hearing the news that a family down the street has come into a large and wealthy inheritance – and then being told that you are to become full members of that family, with instant privileges identical to theirs! That's the situation that Christian Gentiles now find themselves in. God has promised his people Israel that they will inherit the world (see Romans 4.13); when God renews the whole creation, his people will be kings and lords over it. Now Gentiles are to share in this inheritance (Romans 5.17).

Second, they are to become fellow members of one body. Paul probably still has in mind the image of the church as the 'body of Christ' (1.23). Gentile Christians aren't simply to be second-class citizens. They are to be limbs and organs of the Messiah's body, just as Jewish Christians are.

Third, they are to have an equal share in the promises. All God's promises had been made to Abraham and his family; now that family is shown to be a worldwide company.

And Paul is the one chosen by God to pioneer it. In terms of Naomi and her dressmaking business, he wasn't expecting the localized and family-based company (Israel) to expand like this (to reach out to include non-Jews on equal terms). But if this was the secret plan all along, and if God's own energy was now being offered him to help bring it about, he would go with it gladly and celebrate the fact. Thus, in this circular to churches in the Ephesus area who didn't know him personally, he wants to make sure that they know where he fits in to the millennia-old purpose of the one true God. He may be in jail (verse 1), but his vision is as free as the wind and as wide as the horizon. And he wants everyone who reads this letter – then and now! – to share the vision and to join in the work.

EPHESIANS 3.8–13

Wisdom for the Rulers

[8]I am the very least of all God's people. However, he gave me this task as a gift: that I should be the one to tell the Gentiles the good news of the Messiah's wealth, wealth no one could begin to count. [9]My job is to make clear to everyone just what the secret plan is, the purpose that's been hidden from the very beginning of the world in God who created all things. [10]This is it: that God's wisdom, in all its rich variety, was to be made known to the rulers and authorities in the heavenly places – through the church!

[11]This was God's eternal purpose, and he's accomplished it in Messiah Jesus our Lord. [12]We have confidence, and access to God, in him, in full assurance, through his faithfulness. [13]So, I beg you: don't lose heart because of my sufferings on your behalf! That's your glory!

There was once a young prince whose distant uncle was king of a great empire. The prince was carefree and happy, neither very rich nor very poor. One day, a great disaster struck. The king, his uncle, was killed in an earthquake, and all the senior members of the royal family died with him. The prince was solemnly informed that he, now, was to be king.

The prince remembered the stories he had heard of young kings in days gone by. He knew at once what he needed: wisdom. Like King Solomon, David's son and heir, he needed to know instinctively the best way of resolving a difficult situation. He needed to be able to see to the heart of the deepest and most subtle issues. The big picture and the little details; the well-pondered great questions, and the sharp, incisive practical judgment. That's what wisdom was all about, and he determined to seek it and make it his own.

26

There is a book called 'The Wisdom of Solomon', probably written about the time of Jesus. It's in the 'apocrypha' (Jewish books which were valued by Jews of the time, and by the early church, but not considered part of the Old Testament). One of the main themes of this book is a message to pagan rulers: what you need is wisdom! And the place to get this wisdom, according to the book, is in respecting the one true God and the people who honour him – in other words, Israel's God, and the true Israelites.

This can, of course, be turned around as a message to Israel itself. Your task, this message says, is to worship and honour the living God, whatever the pagan nations may do to you. Eventually they will realize that true wisdom consists in respecting and honouring this God, and you are to be the sign to them that this is so.

There are several passages in Paul's writings where he seems to show knowledge of 'The Wisdom of Solomon', and this is one of them. The heart of the present passage is verse 10, which is one of the New Testament's most powerful statements of the reason for the church's existence: the rulers and authorities must be confronted with God's wisdom, in all its rich variety, and this is to happen through the church! Not, we should quickly add, through what the church *says*, though that is vital as well. Rather, through what the church *is*, namely, the community in which men, women and children of every race, colour, social and cultural background come together in glad worship of the one true God.

It is precisely this many-sided, many-coloured, many-splendoured identity of the church that makes the point. God's wisdom, Paul is saying, is like that too: like a many-faceted diamond which twinkles and sparkles with all the colours in the rainbow. The 'rulers and authorities', however – both the earthly authorities and their shadowy heavenly counterparts – always tend to create societies and social structures in their own flat, boring image, monochrome, uniform and one-dimensional. Worse: they tend to marginalize or kill people or groups who don't fit their narrow band of acceptability. The church is to be, by the very fact of its existence, a warning to them that their time is up, and an announcement to the world that there is a different way to be human.

This, then, is what Paul means by 'the king's wealth'. He is referring to the richness of this new life, the new way of being human that has now been unveiled in and through Jesus, together with the future hope that it contains. The phrase will sound strange to many, both Christian and non-Christian, who have forgotten, or perhaps never known, that what can appear from the outside as a tedious or humdrum religious existence – all that going to church, people say, all that saying of prayers and trying to be holy! – is in fact meant to be a delighted exploration of untold and inexhaustible riches. Being a Christian is meant to consist of going from room to room in the king's palace, relishing the beauty and splendour of it all.

Part of Paul's task is to help people see that they are called to share in this inheritance themselves. He was by now a past master at exploring the treasury of wisdom and insight, of spiritual joys and hopes, that are there in **Christ**. He regarded it as a major element in his own vocation that he should invite others to share it as well. The newly established churches around Asia Minor needed to find out for themselves what was rightfully theirs 'in the king'. If they did so, they would be well on the way to maturity, to being able to go forward – with or without an **apostle** to guide them.

Central among the treasures given in the **Messiah** is of course free and confident access to God himself (verse 12). The Messiah's faithfulness to God's saving purpose has opened the door of the heavenly throne room itself. That open door reveals not an angry or capricious god, one who might be favourable one day and scowling the next (the young Christians Paul is writing to knew plenty of gods like that already), but the loving father who welcomed them all as beloved children into his presence. Access to him is everything one could want.

All these rich benefits should mean that the church can look at Paul's imprisonment without worrying (verse 13). But why does Paul describe his sufferings as their 'glory'? The answer is surely that he is suffering precisely because he is pioneering a way of life that challenges the sovereignty of the rulers and authorities. The fact that he is in prison is a sign that the Christian way is indeed posing a decisive threat to the rule of evil in the world.

The question this passage poses for us, then, is twofold. Are we learning to explore the riches of Christ? Or are we content to stay in the outer hallways of the great palace? Have we imagined that the inner rooms are too boring to claim our attention?

And are our churches, in the sort of life they lead, posing the kind of challenge to the power of evil which provokes a reaction?

EPHESIANS 3.14–21

God's Love, God's Power – in Us

[14]Because of this, I am kneeling down before the father, [15]the one who gives the name of 'family' to every family that there is, in heaven and on earth. [16]My prayer is this: that he will lay out all the riches of his glory to give you strength and power, through his spirit, in your inner being; [17]that the Messiah may make his home in your hearts, through faith; that love may be your root, your firm foundation; [18]and that you may be strong enough (with all God's holy ones) to grasp the breadth

and length and height and depth, [19]and to know the Messiah's love – though actually it's so deep that nobody can really know it! So may God fill you with all his fullness.

[20]So: to the one who is capable of doing far, far more than we can ask or imagine, granted the power which is working in us – [21]to him be glory, in the church, and in Messiah Jesus, to all generations, and to the ages of ages! Amen!

Love and power, power and love: these are the themes of perhaps two-thirds of the novels, plays and poems ever written. The love of power has laid waste continents and empires. The power of love has driven weak people to do powerful things – and, not infrequently, powerful people to do foolish things. These are the forces which shape our lives, our homes, our countries, our politics, our world.

And these are the themes that run through the great prayer that Paul prays for the young Christians to whom he is writing. People sometimes say that in a letter like Ephesians the first half is 'doctrine' and the second half is 'ethics' – half of the letter on what to believe, half on how to behave. But in fact, as a glance back through the first three chapters will reveal, much of Ephesians 1—3 is not 'teaching' so much as prayer. The present paragraph isn't a sudden change of style or mood. It is simply going back, explicitly, to where the letter has been all along, praising God, and praying for the young church.

This doesn't mean, of course, that these chapters don't *contain* 'doctrine'. Indeed they do. Perhaps the best Christian doctrine is that which emerges from the life of prayer. Better that way round than an arid intellectual exploration coupled with some perfunctory acts of worship

There is nothing perfunctory about Paul's worship and prayer. One gets the sense, here and elsewhere, that his life revolved around it. This, we may suppose, is part of the secret of the extraordinary power that seemed to flow through his preaching, his pastoral work and his writing.

One of the great Christian leaders of the late twentieth century, Archbishop Desmond Tutu of Cape Town, used to spend several hours in prayer very early in the morning. Nor was prayer then forgotten for the rest of the day. A friend of mine who travelled around with him described how, wherever they went, whatever new thing they were doing, Desmond would pause and pray.

The Western church has perhaps allowed itself to be lulled into thinking that prayer and action are at opposite ends of the scale of Christian activity. On the contrary. Those who want their actions to be effective for God's **kingdom** – as Desmond Tutu's undoubtedly were – should redouble their time and effort in prayer. Prayer brings together love and power: the relation of love that grows up between God and the person who prays, and the flowing of power from God to, and especially *through*, that person.

That is what Paul's prayer here is all about. Essentially, it is a prayer that the young Christians may discover the heart of what it means to be a Christian. It means knowing God as the all-loving, all-powerful father; it means putting down roots into that love – or, changing the picture, having that love as the rock-solid foundation for every aspect of one's life. It means having that love turn into a well-directed and effective energy in one's personal life. And it means the deep and powerful knowing and loving into which the Christian is invited to enter; or – to put the same thing another way – the knowing and loving which should enter into the Christian. Paul, quite clearly, knows all this in his own experience. He longs that those who have come to put their **faith** in Jesus should know it too.

At the heart of all this is a phrase which has become popular in the language of Christian experience: 'that the king may make his home in your hearts, through faith'. People talk easily, perhaps too easily, about 'inviting Jesus into your heart', or 'having Jesus in your heart'. The danger here is that it's easy for people, particularly when they are soaked in the culture of Western-style individualism, to imagine that being a Christian consists simply in being able to feel, or believe, that Jesus has somehow taken up residence within. In fact, Paul speaks far more often of Christians being 'in Christ' than of Christ being 'in Christians'. It's important to see our individual experience within the larger picture of our membership in God's family in the **Messiah**, within the worldwide plan Paul has been talking of in these three chapters.

But of course, when that's been made clear, then it is also important that the living Lord, the king, should make his home within each Christian. That is what strengthens and renews us in our inner being (verse 16). That, as verse 17 implies, is what enables us to put down roots into God's love and to be built up as a secure, unmoveable house. That, as Paul says in the climax of the prayer in verses 18 and 19, will expand our mental and spiritual vision of the whole range of divine truth. Everything that might be offered in the fancy religions of Paul's day and ours (just this morning I came across a book offering new, secret knowledge which could apparently revolutionize my life, but which of course bypassed Jesus), all the ups and downs and to-ing and fro-ing, the breadth and length and depth and height, of knowledge whether human or divine – all is ours in the king and in his love. Having him, we are filled with all the fullness of God. The prayer comes back to where it stopped in chapter 1 verse 23.

Once all this is in place, the results should start to emerge. Verses 20 and 21 are often used as a benediction in church services, and it's easy to see why. As we draw to the end of a time of prayer, the overarching aim should be to give God the glory. But if it's the true God we've been worshipping, we should be filled with a sense of new possibilities: of new tasks and new energy to accomplish them.

Read verse 20 carefully. Then think of what God might do in you and through you – you as a community, you as an individual. Now reflect on the fact that God is perfectly capable of doubling that, trebling that, going so far beyond it that you would look back at the present moment and wonder how you could be so short-sighted.

But this isn't a magic trick. God's power is not ours to do what we like with. If you want to get on the map of verse 20, ask yourself whether you're on the map of the three chapters it's taken to get Paul to this point.

EPHESIANS 4.1–10

Live Up to Your Calling!

¹So, then, this is my appeal to you – yes, it's me, the prisoner in the Lord! You must live up to the calling you received. ²Bear with one another in love; be humble, meek and patient in every way with one another. ³Make every effort to guard the unity that the spirit gives, with your lives bound together in peace.

⁴There is one body and one spirit; you were, after all, called to one hope which goes with your call. ⁵There is one Lord, one faith, one baptism; ⁶one God and father of all, who is over all, through all and in all.

⁷But grace was given to each one of us, according to the measure the Messiah used when he was distributing gifts. ⁸That's why it says,

When he went up on high
he led bondage itself into bondage
and he gave gifts to people.

⁹When it says here that 'he went up', what this means is that he also came down into the lower place, that is, the earth. ¹⁰The one who came down is the one who also 'went up' – yes, above all the heavens! – so that he might fill all things.

If you buy a new car, what's the first thing you do?

Do you sit down for an hour and read through the manual, to make sure you know every little detail about it before you take to the road?

Or do you at once get behind the wheel and go for a drive, enjoying all the things the car can do and not worrying about the details, at least for the moment?

I suspect that most of us give the second answer. In the same way, it's notorious that when people buy a new computer they tend to operate it first and read the instruction manual afterwards.

The trouble is, of course, that things go wrong with machinery. They may go wrong even quicker if you don't read the instructions. But most people will at least keep the instruction book handy and refer to it from time to time to see how the machine was meant to behave, what the fundamental instructions were, and what needs to be done to ensure that it remains at maximum efficiency.

In this section, which opens the quite long second half of the letter, Paul takes his readers back to the fundamental instructions on living the Christian life. He reminds them how they began and what it was all about. There are three things which emerge as basic: the meaning of their call to follow the king; the grace which has equipped each of them to play their part in serving him; and the unity they already have, but which they must make every effort to guard. Of these, the first is the one which Paul stresses, and the one we are most likely to forget. This is the basic manual for living the Christian life, and we need to go back and read it regularly.

What then is this 'call' or 'calling' which he speaks of at the start of his appeal in verse 1, and returns to in connection with Christian hope in verse 4?

He isn't referring here to the specific 'calling' or 'vocation' that different Christians have – this one to be a teacher, that one to run a small business, someone else to be a nurse, and so on. He is referring to the even more basic 'calling' of the **gospel** itself, summoning people to believe in Jesus as the risen Lord and king and to give him complete and undivided allegiance for the rest of their lives.

A key part of this calling is the Christian hope, which works like this. Because King Jesus has conquered death itself, all who give him their faithful allegiance are assured that the same victory will be theirs as well. This is the 'calling' to which they must 'live up'. At every moment, in every decision, with every word and action, they are to be aware that the call to follow Jesus the **Messiah**, and give him their complete loyalty, takes precedence over everything else.

In particular, this must lead them back again and again to celebrate their unity, to maintain and guard it. They are, after all, members of the same body and sharers in the same **spirit**. They possess the same hope. Above all, they have the same Lord, the same **faith**, the same **baptism**, and the same God – the true God, the sovereign one, who stands over against all other gods and goddesses as the rising sun does to man-made candles and torches. This list of the things all Christians have in common looks as though Paul, or perhaps a colleague, may have written it earlier on as a reminder, a list that new converts could memorize. If this is so, then he is here quoting something they might already know.

Unity is of course what he had stressed in chapter 2, where the emphasis was on the astonishing coming-together of Jew and **Gentile** in God's new family in **Christ**. Here Paul seems to be looking wider, and urging them to mount guard over that unity as one would set a troop of soldiers to guard a city or treasury. There are all sorts of things which can attack and spoil that unity, and these must be resisted, whatever they are and wherever they occur.

It may be hard for Christians today to grasp just how central this was to Paul's vision of the church. We have grown accustomed to so many divisions within the worldwide church: Orthodox and Roman, Catholic and Protestant, the dozens of churches that began a distinct life after the sixteenth-century Reformation and the thousands that have sprung up in the nineteenth and twentieth centuries. Sometimes customs and practices have grown up in these churches which are so different that members of one have difficulty recognizing members of another as fellow Christians. Sometimes, indeed, the boundaries *are* blurred, and it may be possible for a church to wander off course so much that its claim to be loyal to Jesus Christ is seriously called into question.

But whatever position we take today, the one thing we can't do is to pretend that this isn't a central and vital issue. Unless we are working to maintain, defend and develop the unity we already enjoy, and to overcome, demolish and put behind us the disunity we still find ourselves in, we can scarcely claim to be following Paul's teaching.

The third thing he emphasizes here is the way in which the risen and ascended Lord Jesus gives a variety of gifts to the different members of his body. As in some other passages in his letters, Paul is about to give a list of the various gifts that Jesus has given to his church. But before he does so he slips into almost poetic and reflective mode, quoting a well-known psalm (68.18) and explaining it, to create a biblical setting for what is to come. The gifts that Jesus gives are part of the great story of what he has achieved. The problem for us, reading this, is that the psalm in question, which talks of 'going up on high' and so on, seems difficult to understand. What is it about?

A first-century Jew might have understood this verse from the psalm to be speaking of Moses. After the **Exodus**, when the Egyptians were defeated and the Israelites rescued from slavery, Moses went up Mount Sinai and came down with the stone tablets of the law, the **Torah**. In line with several early Christian writings, Paul sees the ascension of Jesus as being in a sense like that of Moses. After the 'new Exodus' which had been achieved in his death and **resurrection**, setting the human race

33

free from bondage to sin and death, Jesus 'went up' into the heavenly realm where he now reigns as Lord. Instead of coming down again with the law, as Moses had done, Jesus 'returned' in the person of the spirit, through whom different gifts are now showered on the church.

Why then does Paul say that the king 'went up' and 'came down' like this? Verse 9 is one of the most puzzling in the whole letter, but it is probably meant simply to stress that, in the gift of the spirit, it is Christ himself who is received (see 3.17; and, e.g., Romans 8.9–11). This is how King Jesus makes the church into his own 'fullness' (1.23), giving us his own presence by the spirit.

This is no doubt a deep mystery. It is one of the things which only a significant growth in knowledge, love and power, such as is spoken of in 3.14–19, will enable us to grasp. But at least the practical point is clear. What matters is that, even with all the different gifts that Jesus has lavished on the church, it is the same Jesus, the same Lord, who is personally present, by the spirit, in each of them. He lives within each member of his body. To keep that in mind is to go some way towards the other great goals of this passage. This is how to maintain unity. This is how, above all, we are to live up to the calling we received.

EPHESIANS 4.11–16

Grown-Up Christianity

[11]So these were the gifts that he gave. Some were to be apostles, others prophets, others evangelists, and others pastors and teachers. [12]Their job is to give God's people the equipment they need for their work of service, and so to build up the Messiah's body. [13]The purpose of this is that we should all reach unity in our belief and loyalty, and in knowing God's son. Then we shall reach the stature of the mature Man measured by the standards of the Messiah's fullness.

[14]As a result, we won't be babies any longer! We won't be thrown this way and that on a stormy sea, blown about by every gust of teaching, by human tricksters, by their cunning and deceitful scheming. [15]Instead, we must speak the truth in love, and so grow up in everything into him – that is, into the Messiah, who is the head. [16]He supplies the growth that the whole body needs, linked as it is and held together by every joint which supports it, with each member doing its own proper work. Then the body builds itself up in love.

'Don't be a baby.' The words were meant to hurt, and they did.

But they had the desired effect. The schoolboy had been whimpering about somebody being mean to him. He was hoping that the teacher would come to his rescue. But he suddenly realized how silly he was looking – and how much sillier he would look if the teacher did intervene and protect him. There's no point in behaving like a baby if you aren't one.

But think how cruel it would be if a real baby, only a few months old, were to be told, 'Don't be a baby.' Always supposing the child could understand, there would be a real injustice in the command. A baby can't help being a baby. It takes time to grow up.

That's what Paul wants these young Christians to do. He wants to be able to tell them not to be babies – and for that they will have to grow up. Some aspects of Christian maturity do take time, but there are many ways in which, once someone has come to believe in Jesus as the risen Lord and discovered his presence and power in their life, maturity can follow swiftly. Here Paul shows how it happens, what God has given to the church to make it happen, and why it matters. Let's start with the last of these.

It matters because without maturity Christians are very, very vulnerable to all kinds of trickery that may well take them a long way away from where they ought to be. In verse 14 Paul brings together three ideas: babies, a boat being tossed about on a stormy sea, and cunning tricksters gambling with loaded dice. It's a bit hard to picture them all together, but we can see what he's driving at – and if we know today's world we'll see that new Christians are every bit as vulnerable now as they were then.

The world is full of people who are out to make money out of you, to catch you while you're emotionally fragile or excitable, or perhaps to recruit you for their particular brand of teaching. Paul's world was full of such people, just as ours is, and we should be as anxious as he was that we ourselves, and any younger Christians in our pastoral care, should grow up at least to the point where they can recognize such trickery for what it is, and resist it. Otherwise the best picture to describe the church will be a small boat on the open sea, rudderless and helpless against wind and wave.

The object, instead, is stated in verse 13. We must grow up. We must become mature, as human beings and as Christians (one of the popular lies the tricksters put about is that these two are incompatible). Jesus the **Messiah** has shown what genuine humanity looks like. With that standard in mind, we are not to rest until we've attained it. In verse 15 he points to one of the results: that we will learn to speak the truth, not just about anything and everything (though that is important, too), but about matters of Christian teaching and doctrine. Faced with clever but off-beam teaching, young Christians must learn how to state the truth without lapsing into rudeness or sneering. The truth of the God of love can't be commended by loveless speech.

The main result, though, is that by this process of maturity we shall become truly what we already are in principle: members of the Messiah's body (verses 15–16). Paul has said this several times already in this letter, but here he develops it in two ways in particular.

First, he envisages this body as growing up 'into **Christ**, who is the head'. This seems an odd way to put it, since a human body doesn't grow *into* a head, but gets its **life** and direction *from* its head. It may be that, as with the babies in the boat, Paul is mixing two pictures together at this point; or it may be that he means to refer to the way in which the body takes orders from the head and must be brought into line with what the head intends.

In any case, second, he points out the mutual need and concern of the different members of the body. Every Christian, equipped by God to play his or her part within the whole community, has a role in enabling the body to function as the complex and interdependent entity that it is. And all, we note once more, must be done in love.

So what provision has God made for all this? Once we realize that the passage is all about the whole body of Christ, and each member of it, coming to maturity, we are in a better position to understand the list of ministries in verse 11. Sometimes when the church debates the nature of different offices and ministries, you get the impression that these things exist for their own sake, as though the main point of there being a church in the first place was that certain people would be 'special' within it. The opposite is the case. The main point of certain people having special roles is so that every single Christian, and the church as a whole, may be equipped for their work of service. Make no mistake. Verse 12 indicates clearly that the point of God calling people to be **apostles**, prophets, evangelists, pastors and teachers is so that *every* Christian can serve in the way they are called to do, for the building up of the whole body.

The list of offices in verse 11 is not exhaustive. Elsewhere Paul adds others. But these five were crucial to the establishment of the first generation of the church. Apostles were witnesses to the **resurrection**; since the resurrection is the foundation of the church, the testimony of those who had seen the risen Jesus was the first Christian preaching. Early Christian prophets spoke in the name of the Lord, guiding and directing the church especially in the time before the New Testament was written. Evangelists announced to the surprised world that the crucified Jesus was risen from the dead, and was both Israel's Messiah and the world's true Lord. Pastors looked after the young churches; teachers developed and trained their understanding. They did this not least by setting out the many ways in which believing allegiance to Jesus linked Christians into the whole story and life of Israel, building on the promises of the Old Testament.

Where does your church need to grow towards maturity? What gifts has God given to enable this to take place? What challenges, what cunning tricks and false teaching, do you need to watch out for, and how can you combat it?

EPHESIANS 4.17–24

Off with the Old, On with the New

[17]So this is what I want to say; I am bearing witness to it in the Lord. You must no longer behave like the Gentiles, foolish-minded as they are. [18]Their understanding is darkened; they are cut off from God's life because of their deep-seated ignorance, which springs from the fact that their hearts are hard. [19]They have lost all moral sensitivity, and have given themselves over to whatever takes their fancy. They go off greedily after every kind of uncleanness.

[20]But that's not how you learned the Messiah – [21]if indeed you did hear about him, and were taught in him, in accordance with the truth about Jesus himself. [22]That teaching stressed that you should take off your former lifestyle, the old humanity. That way of life is decaying, as a result of deceitful lusts. [23]Instead, you must be renewed in the spirit of your mind, [24]and you must put on the new humanity, which is being created the way God intended it, displaying justice and genuine holiness.

We couldn't understand why the agency was being so unhelpful.

We had answered the advertisement and were eager to rent the apartment that we had been offered. There were some minor problems, but nothing too difficult to sort out. But every time we telephoned we spoke to a different person, and they never seemed to understand what was happening. They gave different answers each time we asked the questions. They quoted us different rates. The worst thing was that they didn't really seem to care whether we rented the place or not.

When we finally visited the office it became clear. The secretaries and assistants we had been speaking to on the telephone were bright enough. They obviously would have liked to be helpful. But the manager – who had never talked to us himself – was impossible. He was inefficient, haphazard, and we suspected he had a drink problem. But he covered it all up by being a bully. He shouted at his employees and gave them different instructions every day. No wonder they hadn't been able to help us very much. Only by confronting him directly and making him face the issues could we begin to sort everything out.

When we begin to get to grips with the wrong way and the right way to live a truly human life, it's no good starting with the junior members of the establishment. People often suppose that Christian behaviour is simply a matter of getting your body to do certain things and not to do certain other things. That's like trying to do business with the assistants rather than with the incompetent manager. Paul makes it clear in this passage that you've got to go about it the other way round. And the incompetent manager isn't the human body. It's the human mind.

To be sure, Paul longs to see the young churches changing their behaviour. The pagan way of life all around them is deadly. But you can't alter behaviour without changing the mind; and the pagan, **Gentile** mind, he says, is foolish (verse 17), with darkened understanding and deep-seated ignorance (verse 18). This in turn springs from sheer hardheartedness. A heart and mind like this produce moral insensitivity, the inability even to notice that some things are right and others are wrong. Once that's in place, anything goes (verse 19). You won't understand where the behaviour comes from unless you understand the state of heart and mind. And you won't *change* the behaviour unless you change the heart and mind.

This isn't what many people today expect to hear. There is a persistent untruth which has made its way into the popular imagination in our day: that Christianity means closing off your mind, ceasing all serious thought, and living in a shallow fantasy world divorced from the solid truths of 'real life'. Of course there are some Christians who try to live like that; and of course there are many non-Christians who use their minds in rich and varied ways. We mustn't simply reverse the popular stereotype.

But the truth is that genuine Christianity opens the mind (as Paul has been saying throughout this letter, and in its companion piece, the letter to Colossae) so that it can grasp truth at deeper and deeper levels. This isn't a matter of university degrees and paper qualifications, helpful though they may be. It's a matter of the heart and mind being open to the ever wider range of insight and imagination that comes with 'learning the Messiah' (verse 20).

This is one of the few places where Paul refers to the basic Christian teaching which he assumes new converts receive. His letters don't usually repeat this teaching, except on very rare occasions when a point needs rubbing in (e.g. 1 Corinthians 11.23–26). As a result, we are in the position of someone watching the sequel to a movie without seeing the original one. We have to work out from the letters, which are all written to people who have already become Christians and received basic teaching, what the original preaching and teaching consisted of. And here we have a clear indication: it has to do with Jesus himself.

Well, of course, you may think. What else would it be about? But many people have questioned whether Paul and his churches really knew much about Jesus himself, other than the fact that he was crucified, then raised to life, and now exalted as Lord of the world. But here Paul seems to envisage that part of the basic Christian teaching which converts in Asia Minor had received would include teaching on behaviour which came from Jesus himself. And since we have in the **gospels** teaching of just this sort – teaching which stresses that the human heart and mind are the source of evil behaviour, so that the heart itself needs to be changed (e.g. Mark 7.14–23) – we would be right to assume that this is what he has in mind.

So what Paul is urging the young Christians is that they allow this teaching of Jesus to have its full effect in their lives. Now that they are 'in **Christ**', they have the responsibility, in the power of the **spirit**, to take off the old lifestyle, the old way of being human, like someone stripping off a shabby and worn suit of clothing. It may have become comfortable. You may be used to it, and even quite like it. Familiar old clothes are often like that, and brand new ones often feel a bit strange. But if you want to live as a new person in and for the king, the old suit of clothes has to come off, and the new one has to go on.

The point, then, is not to be deceived by what lust and greed whisper in your ear. It's the mind and heart that matter. If they learn to recognize the deceitful whisperings, to name them and reject them, the first vital step to the new way of life has been taken. 'Be renewed in the spirit of your mind' (verse 23): that's the secret. If the heart is right, it's time to get the mind right. Then you'll have the energy of willpower to bring the behaviour into line. Off with the old, on with the new!

EPHESIANS 4.25—5.2

The Kindness That Imitates God Himself

[25]Put away lies, then. 'Each of you, speak the truth with your neighbour,' because we are members of one another. [26]'Be angry, but don't sin'; don't let the sun go down on you while you're angry, [27]and don't leave any loophole for the devil. [28]The thief shouldn't steal any longer, but should rather get on with some honest manual work, so as to be able to share with people in need.

[29]Don't let any unwholesome words escape your lips. Instead, say whatever is good and will be useful in building people up, so that you will give grace to those who listen.

[30]And don't disappoint God's holy spirit – the spirit who put God's mark on you to identify you on the day of freedom. [31]All bitterness

and rage, all anger and yelling, and all blasphemy – put it all away from you, with all wickedness. [32]Instead, be kind to one another, cherish tender feelings for each other, forgive one another, just as God forgave you in the Messiah.

5[1]So you should be imitators of God, like dear children. [2]Conduct yourselves in love, just as the Messiah loved us, and gave himself for us, as a sweet-smelling offering and sacrifice to God.

The best-known literary figure in eighteenth-century England was Dr Samuel Johnson. A native of Lichfield in Staffordshire, he spent most of his adult life in London. He wrote many works, especially his famous *Dictionary* and his discussions of Shakespeare's plays. He became famous for his table talk and dry wit.

Johnson was a devout Christian, some of whose published prayers are still in regular use in the Church of England. Despite the tendency of many of his friends to turn their conversation into displays of verbal brilliance, or into gossip and slander, he retained a deep sense that there was more to life than that. He was without malice. On one occasion his companion Boswell asked him what the point was of sharing a meal with people if, as sometimes happened, nobody said anything worth remembering. Johnson replied that the point was 'to eat and drink together, and to promote kindness'.

Kindness is a virtue not often enough considered, but it remains central to what Christianity is all about. The reason for this is stated clearly at the end of this passage: kindness is one of the purest forms of the imitation of God. How would it be if God were the kind of god who was always making snide or bitter remarks at us? What would worship and prayer be like if we thought God had been talking about us behind our backs, putting us down to others? How would we feel if we thought we couldn't trust God to tell us the truth, if he was always losing his temper with us? Well: how do people feel about us if that's what we're like? Wouldn't it be better in every way to be like God?

Of course, there are plenty of religions, ancient and modern, where the gods do behave in that sort of way. But when we learn through looking at King Jesus who the true God is and what he's like, then we see the standard at which we are to aim. There are, alas, all too many Christians, and sometimes whole churches, that have allowed themselves to forget that kindness and mutual forgiveness are the very essence of Christian community. After all, if we are called to unity, as this letter stresses repeatedly, it is going to be far easier to obey the call if we are working hard at 'promoting kindness'.

This passage is chock-full of practical advice on how to do it, not least in giving warnings about how *not* to do it. As we saw in the previous passages, living as a Christian demands that we grow up in our thinking: you have to learn to identify your own moods and behaviour patterns, to see which ones are going in the right direction and which ones in the wrong direction. You have to learn consciously to choose to follow the first and reject the second.

It simply won't do to go with the flow of whatever you happen to feel at the time. Some people think that, by doing that, they are being 'free', or are 'being themselves'; but that's usually an excuse for selfish behaviour and the lazy thought which sanctions it. Rather, we should regard our moods, and the speech which flows from them, as we might a strong but wilful horse, which needs to be reminded frequently of the direction we're supposed to be going in.

Paul highlights the importance of speaking the truth. He quotes in verse 25 from an Old Testament passage (Zechariah 8.16) which predicts that God is going to renew his people and restore their fortunes. Speaking the truth to each other is one of the ways in which this will be noticed. If we belong to one another in the way the letter has so far indicated, telling lies is a form of corporate self-deceit, and so is self-defeating.

So, too, anger must be dealt with appropriately. Paul, again quoting the Old Testament (Psalm 4.4), doesn't say you shouldn't be angry; anger itself is a natural human emotion, and to pretend it isn't there is a form of lying. But he insists that you mustn't let it lead you into sin. You must learn to tame it, to deal with it before you lie down to sleep. Otherwise you are leaving an open door and inviting the **satan** to come in. Everything that follows from anger – the raised voices, the shocking words, the sour taste in the room – all these must be put away (verse 31). It makes sense, doesn't it; would you rather live day by day with these or without them? But recognizing this and taking steps to bring it about – that's what really matters.

Paul adds some comments in the more positive direction. They seem almost casual, throwaway remarks, but they are very revealing. It isn't just that stealing is wrong. Rather, people who are used to petty thievery should say to themselves that they have a duty to help those in need, and they should work to make it possible (verse 28). It isn't just that bitter or sour speech is to be avoided. Your tongue gives you the opportunity to bring God's grace to people, by what you say and how you say it, and it's a shame to pass up this chance (verse 29).

In particular, you should behave as those on whom God's **holy spirit** has placed God's mark. The word Paul uses could refer to the 'seal' or official stamp on a document or package, marking it out for a particular use or occasion. The mark indicates who it belongs to and what it's for. The presence of the holy spirit in the community, and in the heart of the individual Christian, declares that we belong to God, and that we are destined for full 'redemption', that is, the liberation which will come on the day when God sets the whole world free and gives us our **resurrection** bodies. That is central to the Christian hope, and possessing this hope gives particular shape to our present lives.

People who are enslaved to anger and malice may think they are 'free' to 'be themselves', but they are in bondage. If we are marked out by the spirit's personal presence living in us, think how sad it makes that spirit if we behave in ways which don't reflect the life and love of God.

EPHESIANS 5.3–10

Darkness and Light in Matters of Sex

³As for fornication, uncleanness of any kind, or greed: you shouldn't even mention them! You are, after all, God's holy people. ⁴Shameful, stupid or coarse conversations are quite out of place. Instead, there should be thanksgiving.

⁵You should know this, you see: no fornicator, nobody who practises uncleanness, no greedy person (in other words, an idolator), has any inheritance in the Messiah's kingdom, or in God's. ⁶Don't let anyone fool you with empty words. It's because of these things, you see, that God's wrath is coming on people who are disobedient.

⁷So don't share in their practices. ⁸After all, at one time you were darkness, but now, in the Lord, you are light! So behave as children of light. ⁹Light has its fruit, doesn't it, in everything that's good, and just, and true. ¹⁰Think through what's going to be pleasing to the Lord. Work it out.

The poster in the college gateway had one large word in the middle of it: SEX. Underneath, in small print, it said, 'Now you're interested, how about joining the College Rowing Club?' Whoever designed the poster wasn't suggesting that taking up rowing had anything to do with sex. They were simply exploiting the fact that in contemporary Western society people are so obsessed with sex that the very word attracts people's attention. Anything associated with it seems attractive as well. Advertisers use the word 'sexy' to describe cars, computers, carpets, almost anything.

The world of Paul's day wasn't much different, particularly in the cities where he spent most of his time. Casual sex and all kinds of curious practices associated with it seem to have flourished. The wall paintings discovered in a house in Pompeii (where the eruption of Mount Vesuvius buried the whole city alive in AD 79) give a fair indication of what went on. So do many of the pictures painted on ancient pottery. In that world, as in ours, many people saw no need for restraint. If it seemed fun at the time, why not go ahead?

Many, indeed, went a stage further. Some religions, particularly some of those with secret initiation ceremonies, included sexual practices among their rituals. At one end of the scale, this amounted to little more than prostitution with a vaguely religious flavour. At the other, it might be suggested that sexual experience was part of the very summit of the religious quest. Those who were 'enlightened' could do what they wanted with their bodies; it was only people who were still 'in the dark' who thought they had to practise restraint. There are some in our own world who make similar claims. Indeed, there are some who, after the barren years of Western secularism, claim to have discovered that sex has given them a profoundly religious experience. Since they wrongly identify 'religion' with 'Christianity', they expect Christians to support them.

In the middle of all this, it is no wonder that many Christians today are confused. We are surrounded by misleading teaching on the subject, inside the church as well as outside it.

Many people who were brought up in the middle of the twentieth century, or even later, experienced repressive teaching, born no doubt of embarrassment, in which parents or teachers told them that their bodies were evil and dangerous, and that sex was intrinsically dirty and wicked. They then spent years, including sometimes the early years of marriage, feeling guilty about a whole aspect of human experience created and hallowed by God.

But when such people realize how wrong this teaching was, they often draw the quite false conclusion that now anything goes. Because God made us as sexual beings, some propose, he wants us to experience and enjoy whatever our inclinations suggest. Comparatively few Christians would take this to extremes, but many say that intercourse outside marriage, occasional 'recreational' sexual experiences, and same-sex practices, are to be welcomed and even celebrated by Christians. Not to do so, we are told, is to be dualistic, to imply that the human body is evil.

Paul has a way of cutting to the heart of the issue. Don't be fooled, he says (verse 6). There are a lot of empty words out there – words, that is, which sound big and important, which echo and resonate in our culture, but which have nothing inside them, no life, no truth. Precisely because sex is a good and important part of God's creation of the animal kingdom, and of humans within it; precisely because it is the means of tenderness and intimacy between husband and wife, as well as the means of God-given procreation; precisely because it is the occasion for great blessing and emotional fulfilment; because of all these, people on the road to the genuinely human existence promised in **Christ** must avoid all cheap imitations.

Casual sex is a parody of the real thing – like drinking from a muddy stream instead of fresh, clear water, or like listening to a symphony on a damaged record or tape player when a world-class orchestra is playing in the theatre around the corner.

Many will claim, of course, that sex within marriage is what becomes humdrum and boring, and that experimenting elsewhere is new and exciting. All the evidence of the 'liberated' Western world suggests that these are indeed empty words. Those who relentlessly pursue new experiences regularly end up bitter and disappointed. The emotional electricity, or even the danger, of an illicit or casual relationship may be exciting, but the excitement is of the same sort as you'd get from a drug like cocaine or heroin. It promises the earth and ends up killing you – if not physically, then certainly emotionally.

Every time two people make love physically, their bodies are saying, 'We belong to each other, totally, completely and for ever.' If that isn't true, and if it isn't known by both to be true – if it's just an experiment, a nice idea at the time, a trial arrangement – their bodies are telling a lie. Sooner or later, the lie will come out.

'God's wrath', in fact, isn't just a punishment waiting for people at the end of the **present age**. It isn't an arbitrary thing whereby God makes up some rules to stop people enjoying themselves and then threatens to get cross with them if they go ahead anyway. God's wrath is built in to creation itself. There are certain ways of behaving which are so out of line with the way God made the world, and humans in particular, that they bring their own nemesis. Sexual misbehaviour certainly comes into this category.

Paul's remedy is clear-cut, and very challenging in the modern world where newspapers, radio and TV hurl suggestive images at us all the time. Don't even talk about it among yourselves, he says. Every time you mention the words, every time an off-colour story or joke passes your lips, you defile yourself, and shift your thinking and imagination towards the way that leads to darkness and death. Of course you must avoid fornication itself – the casual sex that demeans and cheapens not only the participants but also the gift of sex itself. But the best way of doing that is to work at taking it out of your mind altogether; and the path to that goal is to remove it from your speech.

Verse 5 seems at first sight puzzling. What is the difference between the **Messiah**'s **kingdom** and God's kingdom? The answer is found, I think, in 1 Corinthians 15.23–28. The Messiah is *already* installed as king of the world, Paul believes. When his work as king is complete, and all enemies, including sin and death, have been defeated, then God himself will be king in the way he always intended.

What Paul means, then, is that people who behave in these ways not only won't inherit the final kingdom; they have no place in the present one either. Notice that he labels sexual greed as a form of idolatry, the worship of false gods; presumably this includes the entire pornography industry.

In fact, the true religious experience, the experience of knowing the creator God in and through King Jesus, produces the true 'enlightenment' (verses 8–9). Those who have *become* light, having formerly been darkness, must behave as light-bearers in God's world. Once again (verse 10) this will mean learning to think straight. Don't go with the flow. Think out who God is; who you are; and learn to live in the light of God and his love.

EPHESIANS 5.11–20

Light and Darkness

[11]So, then, don't get involved in the works of darkness, which all come to nothing. Instead, expose them! [12]The things they do in secret, you see, are shameful even to talk about. [13]But everything becomes visible when it's exposed to the light, [14]since everything that is visible is light. That's why it says:

Wake up, you sleeper!
Rise up from the dead!
The Messiah will shine on you!

[15]So take special care how you conduct yourselves. Don't be unwise, but be wise. [16]Make use of any opportunity you have, because these are wicked times we live in. [17]So don't be foolish; rather, understand what the Lord's will is. [18]And don't get drunk with wine; that way lies dissipation. Rather, be filled with the spirit! [19]Speak to each other in psalms and hymns and spiritual songs, singing and chanting in your heart to the Lord, [20]always giving thanks for everything to God the father in the name of our Lord Jesus the Messiah.

When I was studying for my undergraduate degree, which was in Classics, I had an idea for a special project. Keen as I was on music, I wanted to find out what sort of music people played and sang in the first century. I became quite excited about the project, and approached my tutor for advice.

My tutor, though, was discouraging. Quite a lot of work had been done on the subject, and it showed that we didn't know, and probably couldn't know, very much about what ancient music actually sounded like. Hardly any musical scores exist from the ancient world (about fifty, and most of them are in fragments). It is very debatable how precisely they were played. The subject very quickly became extremely technical, it seemed, and I would probably need a degree in physics to take it forward any further! I remain fascinated by the question, but frustrated at the difficulty of getting any clear answers.

What is clear, though, is that one of the main places where music was regularly employed in the ancient world was in worship. Pagan worship, Jewish worship, and of course early Christian worship, all used music extensively. This passage and similar ones in the New Testament and elsewhere indicate that singing was then, as it has remained ever since, an important part of Christian worship and of building up the church in celebration and instruction.

A further question, though, comes at this point: what did they sing? We can take it for granted that they sang the psalms from the Old Testament, and quite possibly many other Jewish poems, known to us and unknown, which spoke of God's mighty acts of old and of the way in which they would reach their fulfilment in the coming of the **Messiah**. What the long Jewish tradition had sung looking forward, the Christians sang with joy as they looked back to the recent events concerning Jesus.

But what else did they sing? Paul here mentions three categories: psalms, hymns and spiritual songs. It isn't clear whether these were three quite different types, or whether they would overlap. It's possible that the 'hymns' were like the ancient psalms, only now freshly composed to celebrate the Messiah and the new **life** that could be had in him. It's possible that the 'spiritual songs' were lyrics and melodies, made up more or less on the spot by people freshly inspired by the **spirit**. But we don't know for sure.

Tantalizingly, though, Paul quotes in verse 14 from what is almost certainly one of these early Christian poems or hymns. It's a call to wake up, to rise up, to live in the light of King Jesus. It is this sort of thing – and no doubt a good deal more of it – that we should imagine being sung both in formal worship by the early Christians and, as Paul here envisages, as they go about their daily business and leisure.

Paul doesn't see these hymns and songs as simply decorative, a pleasant aural embroidery around Christian **faith** and practice. Singing, whether aloud or in your heart, was, he thought, an excellent way of actually practising the faith. If you don't want your garden to grow weeds, one of the best ways is to keep it well stocked with strong, sturdy flowers and shrubs. If you don't want your mind and heart to go wandering off into the realms of darkness, one of the best ways is to keep them well stocked with wise and thankful themes, so that words of comfort, guidance and good judgment come bubbling up unbidden from the memory and subconscious.

Hymns and psalms today can still provide exactly this kind of Christian nurture. They are not merely entertainment; they are instruction, consolation, warning and hope. After some rather feeble attempts at new Christian hymns and songs in the late twentieth century, it would be good to think that the twenty-first century might see a fresh awakening of creative talent in this area.

The singing that Paul has in mind is the ultimate antidote to living in the darkness of immorality that pervades the surrounding world. Yet again his emphasis is on the mind, and the need for wisdom. It is vital not to slide along through life in a general foolish haze, hoping things will work out all right but not being prepared to think them through, to figure out where this or that type of behaviour will really lead. That is the way of death, and you need to wake up and rise from the dead, relying on the Messiah, already risen, to shine his light on you. Then you'll be able to walk in the light, instead of going down the dark alleys (whether literal or metaphorical) that lead to sin and death.

In particular, Christians are to see every day, every hour, every minute, as an opportunity for serving the Lord, for understanding what his will is and getting on and doing it. Verse 16 can, of course, lead people to an obsessive lifestyle, calculating and counting every minute and giving oneself and everyone else no peace. If that's a particular danger for you, then take note and learn how to relax, how to rest, how to let go of your over-organized life and allow God to bathe you in his peace. I once met a man who said, aware of the irony, that he had made a careful list of the things he should do to help him conquer his bad habit of over-organized thinking.

Here as elsewhere, learning how to worship is an excellent way forward. Sometimes formal liturgy enables those who attend it to relax into the love of God in a way which the frenetic informal style, so popular in some quarters, never does. Beware of worship which simply reinforces the wrong kind of behaviour patterns.

But for many people the danger is on the other side: of not taking each day and hour as a gift from God, to be used for his glory, but instead letting them wash over and pass by, like water down a river, never used, never to return. For such people, verse 16 is another wake-up call: these are evil times we live in, and you as a child of light have a chance to do something about it. Take that chance with both hands.

Of course (verse 18), there's nothing like a few drinks to make opportunities slip by unobserved. Paul has nothing against wine; but against getting drunk he is adamant. That's no way for Christians to behave. If you want to celebrate – and why not? – then you know what to do. Let the spirit fill your hearts and lives, particularly your minds and imaginations. Use all the resources of the rich Christian tradition – its poems, its pictures, its liturgies, its hymns – to help you do so.

EPHESIANS 5.21–33

Wives and Husbands

[21]Be subject to one another out of reverence for the Messiah.
[22]Wives, be subject to your own husbands, as to the Lord. [23]The man, you see, is the head of the woman, just as the Messiah, too, is head of the church. He is himself the saviour of the body. [24]But, just as the church is subject to the Messiah, in the same way women should be subject in everything to their husbands.

[25]Husbands, love your wives, as the Messiah loved the church, and gave himself for it, [26]so that he could make it holy, cleansing it by washing it with water through the word. [27]He did this in order to present the church to himself in brilliant splendour, without a single spot or blemish or anything of the kind – that it might be holy and without blame. [28]That's how husbands ought to love their own wives, just as they love their own bodies.

Someone who loves his wife loves himself. [29]After all, nobody ever hates his own flesh: he feeds it and takes care of it, just as the Messiah does with the church, [30]because we are parts of his body. [31]'That's why a man leaves his father and mother and is joined to his wife, and the two become one flesh.'

[32]The hidden meaning in this saying is very deep; but I am reading it as referring to the Messiah and the church. [33]Anyway, each one of you must love your wife as you love yourself; and the wife must see that she respects her husband.

At the start of the twenty-first century, it has been remarked that it is harder than ever to be a boy.

Today, in the supposedly civilized and sophisticated countries of the world, there is growing up a whole generation of young men who feel themselves discriminated against simply for being male. They have energy and drive – often turning into aggression and violence – with nobody to help them direct or channel it. Often they grow up in broken homes where their natural father has gone for good and a succession of other men come and go. Few, if any, care much for them. Still less do they provide appropriate role models.

The teachers at the schools they are supposed to attend – though they often play truant–are mostly female. Often the message they pick up is:

it would be much better to be like girls, to think and feel like girls. Girls are better. Boys – and men – are part of the problem in the world. Only by radical change can they be part of the solution.

The results are well known. Many boys end up in gangs. They use drugs; they become violent. They end up in jail. Many die young.

Of course, there are many boys who don't go this route. Often, though, they are the fortunate ones, who come from good homes, or who have been able to develop their minds and bodies by good education. But the point to note, which influences the way we approach a passage like this in Paul, is that the Western world has for an entire generation now reversed what used to be the assumed stereotype. Since Aristotle at least, men have regarded women as an inferior species, and many women have agreed with the assessment. In the last few decades this has been reversed in popular consciousness. Now it's the men who have to apologize for being male. The word 'testosterone' – which refers to the hormone that produces and sustains secondary male characteristics – is used dismissively or abusively, to indicate that some young male is displaying an unfortunate tendency to be, well, male.

In this climate of thought, for Paul to tell wives to be subject to husbands looks to many like an unfortunate social or cultural gaffe. People who cheerfully ignore traditional morality, and believe in freedom of expression, suddenly become heavily moralistic and say that passages like this are wicked and shouldn't even be read out aloud. But – as so often when reading the Bible – there's a lot to be said for checking our natural, and (let's admit it) sometimes aggressive attitude to passages that strike us as objectionable, and for thinking through why we react like this, and whether we have really understood the passage or not.

The fascinating thing here is that Paul has a quite different way of going about addressing the problem of gender roles. He insists that the husband should take as his role model, not the typical bossy or bullying male of the modern, or indeed the ancient, stereotype, but Jesus himself. But, you say, Jesus wasn't married. No; but throughout this letter Paul has spoken of the church as the body of the **Messiah**, and now he produces a new twist from within this theme. The church is the *bride* of the Messiah, the wife of the king.

The church became the Messiah's bride, not by being dragged off unwillingly by force, but because he gave himself totally and utterly for her. There was nothing that love could do for the Messiah's people that he did not do. Although the crucifixion plays a central role in Paul's thought in almost every topic, nowhere else outside this passage is it so lyrically described as an act of complete, self-abandoning love.

Paul, of course, lived in a world where women were not only regarded as lesser beings but, as often as not, as impure. Their regular bodily functions were deemed to make them dangerous for a man who wanted to maintain his own purity. Paul sees the action of Jesus – and, by the parallel he has set up, the action of the husband – as taking the responsibility to bring the wife into full purity. Instead of rejecting the wife at times of technical 'impurity', the husband is to cherish and take care of her, to look after her and let her know at all times that she is loved and valued. If husbands – not least Christian husbands! – had even attempted to live up to this wonderful ideal, there would be a lot less grumbling about bossy or bullying men in the world today.

Paul assumes, as do most cultures, that there are significant differences between men and women, differences that go far beyond mere biological and reproductive function. Their relations and roles must therefore be mutually complementary, rather than identical. Equality in voting rights, and in employment opportunities and remuneration (which is still not a reality in many places), should not be taken to imply such identity. And, within marriage, the guideline is clear. The husband is to take the lead – though he is to do so fully mindful of the self-sacrificial model which the Messiah has provided. As soon as 'taking the lead' becomes bullying or arrogant, the whole thing collapses.

If this guideline still seems outrageous in today's culture, we should ask ourselves: do our modern societies, in which marriage is often a tragedy or a joke, really offer a better model of how to do it? Does the spectre of broken homes littering modern Western culture indicate that we've got it right and can tell the rest of human history how we finally resolved the battle of the sexes? Or does it indicate that we still need to do some rethinking somewhere?

Paul underlines the rule of life he has sketched with a quote from Genesis 2.24, the passage about the man leaving his father and mother and cleaving to his wife. That is full of psychological insight. Often what pulls a marriage off course is the failure of one or other partner to distance themselves emotionally from their parents and devote themselves totally to their spouse. This is worth pondering in itself.

But Paul takes it in a different direction as well. Back there in Genesis, even before human rebellion had tainted the world in general, and the relation between the sexes in particular, he sees a glimmer of God's ultimate intention in creation. The man – the Messiah – will leave the place where he was at home, and go in search of a bride. Read Philippians 2.6–11 or Colossians 1.15–20 in the light of this rich and fascinating suggestion. Contemplate the many-sided ways in which the truth about God himself, and the truth about how we live out our most precious relationships, intertwine and create a God-given beauty the world never dreams of.

EPHESIANS 6.1–9

Children, Parents, Slaves and Masters

¹Children, obey your parents in the Lord. This is right and proper. ²'Honour your father and your mother' – this is the first commandment that comes with a promise attached! – ³'so that things may go well with you and that you may live a long life on earth.'

⁴Fathers, don't make your children angry. Bring them up in the training and instruction of the Lord.

⁵Slaves, obey your human masters, with respect and devotion, with the same single-mindedness that you have towards the Messiah. ⁶You must get on with your work, not only when someone is watching you, as if you were just trying to please another human being, but as slaves of the Messiah. Do God's will from your heart. ⁷Get on with your tasks with a kind and ready spirit as if you were serving the master himself and not human beings. ⁸After all, you know that if anyone, slave or free, does something good, they will receive it back from the master.

⁹Masters, do the same to them! Give up using threats. You know, after all, that the master in heaven is their master and yours, and he is no respecter of persons.

My first experience of a building site was disillusioning.

I was part of the work crew building a factory. (I did the job for four weeks during a university holiday.) Right from the start it became clear that, with only one exception, the other men working there were committed to doing the smallest amount of work they could during the main working hours. They were being paid by the hour, not by the job, so why not? The only time they really made an effort was if the foreman came in sight. Then, suddenly, there would be lots of digging, laying bricks, sweeping up, looking busy. As he disappeared again, tools would go down, cigarette packets would come out, and another 'smoke break' (in addition to the official coffee breaks) would begin.

Once the working day was officially over, everything changed. The foreman would ask people to stay on and work overtime – which was necessary to keep up with schedules, because so little work had been accomplished during the day. Several people would stay behind, and suddenly the work couldn't get done fast enough. What would take three hours during the day would be finished in a single hour. So the practice was to leave after one hour, but to bribe the nightwatchman to punch the cards in the machine after three hours. That way it looked authentic, and the workers were paid for a longer period at a higher rate. It was standard practice, people said.

I have no idea how that shabby and dishonest practice in the Britain of the 1960s compares with working practices in other places and times. But I know it was exactly the sort of thing that Paul had in mind when he warned slaves not to do their work only when people were watching them. If he said that to slaves, whose only pay, usually, would be their food and lodging, how much more would he have said that to people who were being paid, and quite well at that?

Just this morning I read in a newspaper, in a list of things which the writer thought Bible-believing Christians were committed to believing, and which (he implied) no sensible person could hold to, not only the seven-day creation and Noah's Ark, not only the **resurrection**, but also 'the idea that slavery might be a good thing'. This passage does indeed raise this question in an acute form. Did Paul believe that slavery was a good thing? What do we make of it all today?

The answer is that Paul could no more envisage a world without slavery than we can envisage a world without electricity. Most of what the modern world takes for granted – television, computers and a million lesser inventions – are impossible without electricity. And yet for most of human history it was unknown. In the same way, the way Paul's world worked was through slaves taking a vital place in most households except the very poor.

Treatment of slaves, and its legal regulation, varied enormously in the ancient world, from country to country and owner to owner. Many slaves were valued, respected and trusted family members – and many were used and abused in every way imaginable by careless and inhumane masters and mistresses. But they were simply part of the way the world worked. In this area at least, Paul wasn't starting from scratch and attempting to design a new way for the world to run. Everyone would be liberated, from every form of slavery, in the **age to come**; but in a world where many Christians were slaves working for non-Christian masters it was worse than useless to suggest instant emancipation. Paul wisely chooses a different route.

The remarkable thing about this passage, both the commands to children and parents and those to slaves and masters, is that the children and slaves evidently have, in Paul's eyes, what we would call 'rights' as well as the parents and masters. When ancient philosophers drew up codes of behaviour, as they did from time to time, the weight was always the other way round. Slaves and children were to be obedient, and that was the end of it. Now Paul insists on a mutual responsibility: parents must behave appropriately towards children, which means not being harsh and provoking children so that they become bitter and want to rebel or run away. Masters must remember that they, too, have a Master – the Lord Jesus himself.

The final phrase says it all: there is no respect of persons before the **Messiah**. Paul comes back to this point frequently in his writings, whether he is referring to the equality of Jew and **Gentile** before the **gospel**, the equality of Christians from different backgrounds within the church, or, as here, the equality of masters and slaves. Underneath what we see as his 'ethics' there is a strong and firmly rooted moral point: that the one true God is a God of justice and judgment, and there is no pulling the wool over his eyes.

Throughout this passage and the previous one, Paul is rightly seen as supporting the solidity of family life, and of the extended household. Families, like the marriage relationship, have often been seen in our culture as oppressive and enslaving. We all know of homes where this seems to be the case. But we shouldn't make the mistake of thinking that because some families get it horribly wrong it isn't possible to get it right, at least some of the time. Just because the garden grows weeds, we shouldn't pave it over with concrete. Just because there are oppressive families, that's no reason to dismiss family life altogether.

On the contrary. The reason the family can become a place of fear and bondage is because it is designed as the place of love, security, affirmation and new energy. The worst is the corruption of the best. As with marriage, so with family life, and attitudes to work, both from employer and employee: are we so sure that we in the modern world have got it right that we are in a position to turn round and tell Paul he's got it wrong?

EPHESIANS 6.10-17

God's Complete Armour

¹⁰What else is there to say? Just this: be strong in the Lord, and in the strength of his power. ¹¹Put on God's complete armour. Then you'll be able to stand firm against the devil's trickery. ¹²The warfare we're engaged in, you see, isn't against flesh and blood. It's against the leaders, against the authorities, against the powers that rule the world in this dark age, against the wicked spiritual elements in the heavenly places.

¹³For this reason, you must take up God's complete armour. Then, when wickedness grabs its moment, you'll be able to withstand, to do what needs to be done, and still to be on your feet when it's all over. ¹⁴So stand firm! Put the belt of truth round your waist; put on justice as your breastplate; ¹⁵for shoes on your feet, ready for battle, take the good news of peace. ¹⁶With it all, take the shield of faith; if you've got that, you'll be able to quench all the flaming arrows of the evil one. ¹⁷Take the helmet of salvation, and the sword of the spirit, which is God's word.

For some reason, almost whenever I write about passages like this one, dealing with spiritual warfare, I run into problems. One time a workman outside the house drove a nail through a main electricity cable, and I lost half an hour's writing on the word processor. Sometimes domestic crises suddenly arise and distract me. Today the computer jammed completely just when I was about to begin writing. I have come to accept this as normal – and to be grateful that this is all that has happened. So far.

I don't claim that this of itself makes my work anything special. But I have noticed, over the years, that the topic of spiritual warfare is itself the subject of spiritual warfare. It is as though certain hidden forces would much rather we didn't talk about it, or that we swept it under the carpet. As C. S. Lewis says in the introduction to his famous *Screwtape Letters*, the general public prefers either to ignore the forces of evil altogether – to pretend they don't exist, and to use cartoon images of a 'devil' with horns and hoofs as an argument to that effect ('You can't believe in that nonsense, so you can't believe in a devil at all, can you?') – or to take an unhealthy interest in everything demonic, which can be just as bad in the long run. What we have in the present passage, and what I believe is required again and again as Christians face the daily and yearly battle for the **kingdom**, is a sober, realistic assessment both of the struggle we are engaged in and of the weapons at our disposal.

It is, of course, a surprise to many people that there is a 'struggle' at all. Yes, they think, we find it difficult from time to time to practise our Christianity. We find it hard to forgive people, to pray regularly, to resist temptation, to learn more about the faith. But as far as they're concerned that's the end of it. They have never thought that their small struggles might be part of a larger campaign. They are like soldiers fighting in a fog: never seeing, and actually not knowing about, the others not far away in the same line of battle, let alone the other theatres where the war is continuing.

In most major conflicts, of course, hardly any front-line soldiers know very much about the rest of the war. That's the job of the generals. But at least they know that *something* is going on, and that their bit is part of that larger whole. That's the perspective that every Christian needs to maintain as we hold our bit of the line against attack.

And holding out against attack is what this passage is mostly all about. The weapons Paul speaks of are mainly defensive, equipping us to withstand attack and still be standing up at the end of the day. The belt, the breastplate, the shoes, the shield and the helmet, are all to enable you to remain safe under attack. Only the sword has a potentially attacking capability. We'll come to that in a moment; but notice what the Christian's defensive armour consists of.

First, truth. The primary thing about the Christian **message** is that it is *true*; if it isn't, it's meaningless. It isn't true because it works; it works (if it does) because it's true. Never give up on the sheer truth of the **gospel**. It's like the belt which holds everything else together and in place.

Second, 'justice', or 'righteousness'. This isn't just 'virtue', important though that is. It's the fact that the one true God is the one true judge, and intends to put the whole world to rights. Indeed, the process already began when God vindicated Jesus, and vindicated ('justified') us in him. The fundamental justice and goodness of God, and the status that Christians have of already being 'in the right' before him, is like a breastplate, protecting us against frontal attack.

Third, the 'gospel of peace' – the message, that is, of peace with God and peace between different previously hostile groups, as in 2.11–22. The enemy will do all he can to knock you off your feet. Holding fast to this message of peace will make you ready, like good shoes or boots would do, to stay upright.

Fourth, the shield of **faith**. Belief in Jesus as the risen Lord, and utter loyalty to this Jesus, will protect you when the enemy hurls flaming arrows at you. The arrows may take the form of doubt or despair; of adverse circumstances; of sharp temptation that will burn you up if you let it catch light on you; of personal tragedy; or indeed the kind of triumph that tempts you to arrogance and pride. Believing loyalty will quench them all.

Fifth, the helmet of salvation. Knowing that you already belong to the family of the risen **Messiah**, and that you have therefore already been rescued from the ultimate enemy, enables you to face all secondary enemies. Wear this helmet always.

But this still leaves the one offensive weapon: the sword of the **spirit**, which is the **word** of God. The 'word' in question is clearly the same as in 5.26, that is, the word of the gospel through which God accomplishes his powerful, cleansing work in people's hearts and lives. (Though people often, and with good reason, refer to the whole Bible as 'the word of God', this can hardly be what Paul means here, granted that most of the New Testament had not been written at this stage.)

It seems that here, and in some of the previous phrases, Paul is referring to various Old Testament passages, including Isaiah 11.4–5; 49.2 and 52.7. Interestingly, if this is so, he is taking passages that appear to be about the Messiah, clothed with righteousness and faithfulness, striking the earth with his words, with a mouth like a sharp sword, coming to announce the gospel of peace. This, then, is what he means by being strong 'in the Lord': it is because all these things are true of

Jesus himself, and because we, his people, find ourselves 'in' him, that they can be true of us too.

What, then, is the battle? Who is fighting against us? And what are we to do about it?

Paul clearly supposes that the forces of evil that put Jesus on the cross have been seriously upset by the victory of the **resurrection**. They are now positively panic-stricken at the thought that the message of this Jesus is everywhere challenging their power and authority, and that communities loyal to Jesus as Lord and king are springing up, bringing together peoples and communities in a new unity, a new humanity, that shows evidence of the creator's sovereign power and hence of their own imminent destruction. They are therefore doing their best to oppose this gospel, to distract or depress the young Christians, to blow them off course by false teaching or temptations to anger or immorality (see 4.17—5.20, where these are the main themes).

Sometimes this attack will take the frontal form of actual authorities in towns and cities who try to prevent Christians from spreading the message. Sometimes it will take the more oblique form of persuading Christians to invest time and energy in irrelevant side issues, or to become fascinated by distorted teaching. Sometimes it will be simply the age-old temptations of money, sex and power. But in each case what individuals and the whole church must do is, first, to recognize that attacks are coming; second, to learn how to put on the complete armour which God offers; and, third, to stand firm and undismayed.

The final weapon, if it is to be classed as one, is prayer. For this, we must turn to the last section of the book.

EPHESIANS 6.18–24

Prayer and Peace

[18]Pray on every occasion in the spirit, with every type of prayer and intercession. You'll need to keep awake and alert for this, with all perseverance and intercession for all God's holy ones – [19]and also for me! Please pray that God will give me his words to speak when I open my mouth, so that I can make known, loud and clear, the secret truth of the gospel. [20]That, after all, is why I'm a chained-up ambassador! Pray that I may announce it boldly; that's what I'm duty-bound to do.

[21]It's important that you should know how things are with me, and what I'm up to; so our dear brother Tychicus will tell you about it. He is a loyal servant in the Lord. [22]I've sent him to you with this in mind, so that you may know how things are with us, and so that he may encourage your hearts.

²³Peace be to the whole family, and love with faith, from God the father and the Lord Jesus, the Messiah. ²⁴Grace be with all who love our Lord, Messiah Jesus, with a love that never dies!

Imagine an eagle with clipped wings. Imagine a great ocean-going liner stuck in the Sahara sands. Imagine a basketball player with his ankles tied together. Imagine a railway locomotive in a ploughed field.

Now imagine an ambassador wearing chains in prison. Paul knows it's a bizarre picture, and he puts it like that deliberately to highlight his special need for prayer. An ambassador ought to be free to come and go, to take the message of his king wherever it is needed. How can he do that if they've tied him up?

And yet the eagle is determined to fly, the liner to sail again come what may. He will go on announcing the **good news** of King Jesus even from a prison cell. Every preacher, everyone who has tried to talk to others about the **gospel**, will know how he feels as he asks for prayer in his task. How can you find the right words to say? How can you make it clear? How can you get your own mind sufficiently around the extraordinary saving plan of God and then describe it in such a way that other people will find it convincing and compelling?

That's the problem we all face; but for Paul it was worse, granted his situation. And he was determined to do it with full boldness: the word he uses in verse 20 could almost mean 'brazenly'. He is settled in his mind that he will go on talking about King Jesus, his victory over death, and his present and future **kingdom**, no matter what happens. But he knows that unless people are praying for him he won't be able to do it, and it wouldn't mean anything if he did.

So, having begun the letter with an extended prayer, and then an extensive report of his own prayers for the young Christians in the area, he now finishes it with the urgent request that they join him in this ministry. Verse 18 is sometimes taken as a continuation of the 'complete armour' of the previous passage, as though 'all prayer' is itself part of the armour. There is truth in this, though Paul does not mention here a specific weapon or article of clothing. The point of prayer is, rather, that it accomplishes things we couldn't do by our own effort, organization or skill.

Prayer remains mysterious at one level. Nobody quite knows 'how it works', and this not knowing seems to be part of the point. But it remains a deeply practical thing to do. One of the great Christian leaders of the twentieth century, Archbishop William Temple, declared that whatever else one might say about whether prayer worked, he had noticed that when he prayed, 'coincidences' happened; and when he stopped praying, the 'coincidences' stopped happening. That reminds me of the great golfer who, when someone accused him of being lucky, agreed, but commented that he'd noticed that the more he practised the luckier he got.

Of course, William Temple didn't believe that the things which happened in apparent answer to prayer really were coincidences. This was how God worked. Paul is convinced of the same thing. He knows that the prayers even of young and inexperienced Christians are every bit as powerful and valid in God's presence as those of a seasoned **apostle**. And he knows that their prayers for him are therefore just as important as his for them.

Prayer is hard work. It can't be reduced to a few moments of sleepy meditation at the end of the day, or a few snatched moments at the beginning. (We must of course add quickly that that would be better than nothing, but only in the same way that a piece of stale bread is better than no food at all, but nowhere near as good as a proper meal.) Paul insists that you'll need to stay awake and keep alert if you're to engage properly in prayer.

If you're going to take praying seriously, you will probably want to plan it out a bit. You may find it helpful to make a few lists of things and people to pray for, not in order to be legalistic or regimented about it but in order to be faithful both to God and to the people who depend upon you for support. Just as in most families there are lists of birthdays, anniversaries and the like, so there is no shame, and plenty of good sense, in keeping a notebook of the people you want to pray for regularly. Some people I know keep a two-sided notebook: the left-hand side to record the prayers they've prayed, the right-hand side to fill in the way in which the prayer was answered (including times when the answer was 'no'). It is remarkable how many small but significant miracles would otherwise be forgotten.

The comment about Tychicus in verses 21 and 22 is almost identical to the equivalent passage in Colossians (4.7–8). If, as may be the case, Ephesians was written around the same time, as a circular to churches throughout the Lycus valley area (including Laodicea and Hierapolis, and possibly other churches within reach of Ephesus), then it seems as though Tychicus was going on a round trip, perhaps beginning with Colossae and then going on to the others. The underlying purpose of mentioning him here, though, is not just to introduce him, but to make sure the readers know how important it is that they see their lives as bound up with Paul's (see 3.1–13). Their hearts are to be encouraged by news about him: his sufferings, after all, are their glory (3.13).

The closing greeting emphasizes peace, as so much of the letter has done. Peace with God, peace with one another across all traditional barriers: that is central to the message of Ephesians, central to the great vision of God's people that it offers, central to our lives and vocations as we today try to follow those who first heard this letter and tried to live by it.

Peace, here as elsewhere, is bound up closely with love and **faith**. It comes from the one true God, the father, and the Lord, King Jesus, and it comes as a sure blessing on those whose love for this same Jesus will outlast death itself. That, after all, is what being a Christian is all about: loving Jesus with an undying love, in response to his dying love for us.

PHILIPPIANS

PHILIPPIANS 1.1–11

Paul's Reasons for Thanks

¹From Paul and Timothy, slaves of Messiah Jesus, to all God's holy ones in Messiah Jesus who are in Philippi, together with the overseers and ministers: ²grace to you and peace, from God our father and Messiah Jesus the Lord.

³I thank my God every time I think of you! ⁴I always pray with joy, whenever I pray for you all, ⁵because of your partnership in the gospel from the first day until now. ⁶Of this I'm convinced: the one who began a good work in you will thoroughly complete it by the day of Messiah Jesus.

⁷It's right for me to think this way about all of you. You have me in your hearts, here in prison as I am, working to defend and bolster up the gospel. You are my partners in grace, all of you! ⁸Yes: God can bear witness how much I'm longing for all of you with the deep love of Messiah Jesus.

⁹And this is what I'm praying: that your love may overflow still more and more, in knowledge and in all astute wisdom. ¹⁰Then you will be able to tell the difference between good and evil, and be sincere and faultless on the day of the Messiah, ¹¹filled to overflowing with the fruit of right living, fruit that comes through Messiah Jesus to God's glory and praise.

There is a wonderful old prayer attributed to the sixteenth-century sailor Sir Francis Drake (1540–96). He prays that when God leads us to undertake any great piece of work, he will also remind us 'that it is not the beginning, but the continuing of the same, until it be thoroughly finished, that yieldeth the true glory'. Drake himself was certainly a 'finisher' as well as a 'beginner'. As well as being a legend in his own lifetime for his military exploits, he had sailed right round the world. Once you've set off on a journey like that, there's no point stopping halfway.

The confidence Paul has throughout this letter is that God himself is a 'finisher' as well as a 'beginner'. The particular work which he has begun, and will finish, is the work of grace, through the **gospel**, in the hearts and lives of the Philippian Christians. Verse 6 sums it up, as a kind of motto or theme for the letter: the God who began a good work in you will complete it by the day of King Jesus.

Philippi, in northern Greece, was the first place in Europe that heard the news that there was a new king, namely the crucified and risen Jesus of Nazareth. You can read the story of Paul's first visit there in Acts 16. This letter makes it clear that as Paul looked at all the churches he had founded, the people of Philippi were the ones who gave him most joy. To be sure, he loved them all; but this letter breathes a confident trust and enjoyment which we don't always find elsewhere. Now, in prison – almost certainly in Ephesus, since he speaks of coming to see them again (1.26), and in his other imprisonments he had no intention of returning to Greece – the Philippian church have sent him a gift of money. One of the reasons he's writing is to say a heartfelt 'Thank you'.

When people were put in prison in Paul's world, they were not normally given food by their captors; they had to rely on friends helping them. Since Paul probably couldn't carry on his tent-making business in prison, he was completely dependent on support like this. The fact that people from a different country would raise money, and send one of their number on the dangerous journey to carry it to an imprisoned friend, speaks volumes for the esteem and love in which they held him. People sometimes speak today as though Paul was an awkward, difficult, unpopular sort of person, but folk like that don't normally find this kind of support reaching them unbidden from friends far away.

In fact, this letter is all about 'partnership' – one of the big, important words in Paul's vocabulary. It's sometimes translated 'fellowship', but it clearly has a practical, even financial, implication which our word 'fellowship' doesn't always carry. In fact, though it develops particular Christian meanings, including the delighted sharing of worship, prayer and mutual support and friendship which is what 'fellowship' normally means today, in Paul's world it was the normal word for a business partnership, in which all those involved would share in doing the work on the one hand and in the financial responsibilities on the other. The Philippians, then, are 'partners in the gospel' (verse 5), 'partners in grace' (verse 7); they are in the gospel business, the grace business, along with Paul, and their gift proves it.

This gives Paul added confidence when he prays for them, as he does constantly. He knows that when the gospel message of King Jesus does its life-changing work in people's hearts this isn't just a flash-in-the-pan 'religious experience' that might then fade away with the passing of time. If there is genuine **faith** in the risen Jesus, genuine loyalty to him as king, this can only be because the living God has worked, through the gospel, within people's hearts; and what God begins, he always finishes. This, of course, doesn't mean there aren't problems along the way; several of Paul's other letters, particularly 1 Corinthians, grapple with these. But Paul remains confident in the grace of God. Having begun the round-the-world journey of the work of salvation, God is going to complete it.

In this confidence, Paul prays for them; as so often, the opening of the letter looks ahead to what will come later by means of telling the recipients the content of his prayer for them. It has three elements.

First (verse 9), he prays that their love will overflow in knowledge and wisdom. This is not, perhaps, how we often think of love. We think of it as having to do with emotion and affection, not with knowledge and wisdom. For Paul they are all bound up together: what we call the 'heart' and what we call the 'head' were not separated, as we have sometimes allowed them to be. If Christian love is to be the genuine article – true love for God, true love for one another – it is bound to work its way out in a knowledge and wisdom which is more than mere book-learning. This kind of knowledge is a deep insight into the way God's world truly is, a knowledge open to everyone who is prepared to give themselves wholeheartedly in love to God through King Jesus.

Second (verse 10), he prays that this wise love will result in moral discernment. They lived, as we do, in a world where several moral issues were blurred and distorted, and it was often hard to see what was the right thing to do. Paul longs to see them grow in telling the difference between good and evil when so often they appear, at first glance, as shades of grey. That way, he says, they will approach the coming Day of the Lord, the king's great day, with confidence, because God will be transforming their whole lives into a holiness that goes beyond even the ritual purity demanded of **priests** in the **Temple** (the words he uses for 'sincere' and 'faultless' seem to carry that implication). This letter has quite a lot to say about the coming Day; and the main thing to say is that Christians can look forward to it with confidence and joy.

Finally (verse 11), he prays that they may be filled to overflowing with the fruit of right living. The word for 'right living' is another of Paul's big words. It's often translated 'righteousness', though that's not always a helpful word. It sometimes means God's own faithfulness, and sometimes the status of 'membership in God's family', with all the privileges such as forgiveness of sins, which is God's gift to those who believe the gospel. Here it emphasizes more the behaviour which results from both God's faithfulness and the status of being forgiven family members. The important thing throughout is that at every stage of the process – when people first hear the gospel, when they believe it, when they begin to live by it, and when they make progress in faith and love – nothing is done to the glory of the people concerned, as though they were able arrogantly to advance their own cause. Everything is done, as he insists here, 'through King Jesus' and 'to the glory and praise of God'.

As usual, Paul's prayer for the church is a prayer that every church leader might wish to use for the people in their care. It's also a prayer that every Christian might use for himself or herself. And remember, as you use it: the reason you're praying it at all is that God has begun his good work in you all. And what God begins, he completes.

PHILIPPIANS 1.12–18a

The Messiah Is Proclaimed

¹²Now, my dear family, I want you to know that the things I've been through have actually helped the gospel on its way. ¹³You see, everybody in the Imperial Guard, and all the rest for that matter, have heard that I am here, chained up, because of the Messiah. ¹⁴My imprisonment has given new confidence to most of the Lord's family; they are now much more prepared to speak the word boldly and fearlessly.

¹⁵There are some, I should say, who are proclaiming the Messiah because of envy and rivalry; but there are others who are doing it out of good will. ¹⁶These last are acting from love, since they know that I'm in prison because of defending the gospel; ¹⁷but the others are announcing the Messiah out of selfishness and jealousy. They are not acting from pure motives. They imagine that they will make more trouble for me in my captivity.

¹⁸So what? Only this: the Messiah is being announced, whether people mean it or not! I'm happy to celebrate that!

One of the most dramatic stories anywhere in ancient literature is that of Joseph, the second youngest son of the patriarch Jacob. His father spoiled him rotten, and his older brothers were jealous. They wanted to kill him, then they decided to sell him into slavery. Joseph was taken to Egypt, where he became a trusted servant of his new master, until his wife falsely accused him of trying to molest her, and he was thrown into prison. After a long while, he was suddenly brought out to interpret the dreams of Pharaoh, king of Egypt – with such success that Pharaoh put him in charge of his major project to alleviate the coming famine. In that capacity, he found himself selling corn to his own brothers without their knowledge. Eventually, having tricked them to test their state of heart, he told them who he was. The story ends happily, with the whole family surviving the famine and settled in Egypt.

After their father Jacob dies, Joseph's brothers worry that he will now take revenge on them for what they'd done to him many years earlier. So they come and tell him that Jacob had told them to seek his forgiveness. Joseph's reply is one of the most memorable statements of **faith** anywhere in the Bible. 'Don't be afraid', he says. 'Don't suppose that I am in God's place. After all, you meant evil against me, but God meant it for good' (Genesis 50.20). And he forgives them and continues to look after them.

Paul seems to have something of the same robust confidence in God's overruling power, even when everything seems to be going wrong. Joseph said what he did with hindsight, though he had probably clung to God in hope all through the story. Paul is saying all this while his story is still going on. But he, of course, knows of a much more recent story in which another Jew, falsely accused by his own people, suffered the extreme penalty at the hands of wicked people, and still demonstrated, through the **resurrection**, that 'God meant it for good'. With this story of Jesus echoing and bringing into focus the mainline Jewish belief, that Israel's God YHWH would somehow, strangely, produce good out of evil, we perhaps shouldn't be surprised at the robust statement of this belief which Paul now produces.

He is faced with two problems, one on top of the other, and in both cases he declares that what looks like a major difficulty is being turned by God into an opportunity for the **gospel**. It isn't, of course, an opportunity for his own advancement; as we shall see, he doesn't much care what happens to him, if only the gospel itself can go forward.

The first problem is, of course, that he's in prison. For a travelling **apostle** to be put in prison must have seemed like a concert pianist having his hands tied behind his back. How can he possibly continue the work he's been called to do? But Paul, with his strong belief in the way God works through unlikely circumstances, is ready with the answer. The Imperial Guard (every major centre of Roman influence had an Imperial Guard, and Ephesus was on its way to becoming an important centre of the actual worship of the emperor) were all now aware that there was a man in their custody who was going around proclaiming a new and very subversive message.

The soldiers were used, of course, to the 'gospel' of Caesar – the supposed 'good news' that a new emperor had taken the throne, bringing (so he claimed) peace and justice to the world. Now here was someone out of the blue announcing that there was a different 'gospel': that Jesus of Nazareth had taken the throne of the world, and was summoning every man, woman and child to bow the knee to him. Having Paul in custody meant they couldn't ignore this new message. They were having their noses rubbed into it. And Paul can see that already the other Christians in Ephesus (the 'family', his brothers and sisters in the **Messiah**) are taking courage from his example. They can see the impact he's having even on hardened soldiers. Why shouldn't they seize the moment and speak about King Jesus to their friends and neighbours as well?

This brings him to the second problem. There are some people going around talking about King Jesus who, Paul knows, don't really mean it. They don't believe the message; they merely want to make more trouble for him in his imprisonment. Some people have thought that these people were a rival Christian group, opposed to Paul's specific view of the gospel. But I think it's more likely that they are ordinary pagans who have heard what all the fuss is about and are talking about it on the street.

'Have you heard?' they'll be saying to each other. 'They've caught that strange fellow who's been going around saying there's a new king – a new emperor! And you won't believe it – this new king turns out to be a Jew whom they crucified a few years ago, and this jailbird is saying he's alive again and he's the real Lord of the world!'

Talk like that would be guaranteed to make people feel that Paul was a dangerous lunatic who should be kept locked up. But Paul's reaction is to celebrate. That's fine by me, he says. As long as people are going around saying that Jesus is the world's true Lord, I shall be happy.

Paul is saying all this, obviously, to encourage the church in Philippi. But it ought also to be a great encouragement to us. How often are we tempted to feel discouraged because the plans we had were badly thwarted, or because malicious people were trying to make life difficult. We need to learn from Paul (and, long before, from Joseph) the art of seeing God's purposes working out through problems and difficulties. 'God meant it for good.' 'The king is being announced, and I'm going to celebrate!'

PHILIPPIANS 1.18b–26

To Live or to Die?

[18b]Yes, and I really am going to celebrate: [19]because I know that this will result in my rescue, through your prayer and the support of the spirit of Messiah Jesus. [20]I'm waiting eagerly and full of hope, because nothing is going to put me to shame. I am going to be bold and out-spoken, now as always, and the Messiah is going to gain a great reputation through my body, whether in life or in death.

[21]You see, for me to live means the Messiah; to die means to make a profit. [22]If it's to be living on in the flesh, that means fruitful work for me.

Actually, I don't know which I would choose. [23]I'm pulled both ways at once: I would really love to leave all this and be with the Messiah, because that would be far better. [24]But staying on here in the flesh is more vital for your sake. [25]Since I've become convinced of this, I know that I will remain here, and stay alongside all of you, to help you to advance and rejoice in your faith, [26]so that the pride you take in Messiah Jesus may overflow because of me, when I come to visit you once again.

One of the great questions that people have asked throughout human history, and still address particularly to religious leaders, is this: where do we go when we die? Until recently, most people in what used to be the Christian Western world would reply 'to **heaven**', with some also warning that there might be other destinations as well that ought to be avoided if possible. Now, however, with the decline of Christianity in the Western world, people are turning again to folk religion to find alternative beliefs. Some think we'll all be merged into one great sea of consciousness, or perhaps unconsciousness. Some say (and really seem to mean) that we'll all become stars in the sky.

Paul doesn't intend that this should be the main subject of his letter to the Philippian church, but in this passage and one or two later ones he says things which should form the heart of serious Christian thinking on this subject. Here he faces the question: will he survive his present imprisonment, and then be released so that he can visit them again, or will the powers of the world decide that he's better off dead?

The curious thing about the second alternative is that Paul actually agrees with them: he would indeed be better off dead. 'What I'd really love', he says, 'is to leave all this and go to be with the king.' This isn't a 'death-wish' in the sense of someone losing self-esteem, becoming terminally depressed, and longing to get out of this life as quickly as possible. Paul, as this letter shows, is full of life and energy and quite ready to get back to work the minute they let him out of prison. But Paul is also a man in love – with the king, the **Messiah**, the Jesus who, as he says in Galatians 2.20, 'loved me and gave himself for me'. And the central thing about dying, as far as he's concerned, is that it will mean going to be with this Jesus, his Lord, master and king.

Nowhere, in fact, in the New Testament do we find people talking about 'going to heaven when they die'. The closest we come is when Jesus says to the penitent brigand beside him on the cross that he'll be in paradise with him that very day (Luke 23.43). But in the Jewish thought of the time 'paradise' was not usually a final destination. It was thought of as a place of blissful rest where the dead would wait until the day of **resurrection**.

Paul seems to have a similar view. Immediately after death, he implies, the Christian goes to be with the Lord. This language ('being with the Lord', or 'with the king') is perhaps the best and safest Christian way of talking about life after death. But for Paul, as for most Jews, that wouldn't be the end of the story. As we shall see in chapter 3, the resurrection is still to come. The dead will no longer be disembodied, but will receive new bodies to live in the new world that God will then make (3.11, 21). We shall say more about this when we reach those passages.

Paul's aim at the moment, of course, is to convince the Philippian church that, whatever happens to him in his present imprisonment, it won't mean that everything's gone badly wrong. He knows that there's a reasonable chance that the authorities may suddenly decide it's time to execute him. Human life was cheap in the Roman world, and perceived troublemakers were dispatched very easily. He wants to put the Philippians in a frame of mind that if news of his death suddenly arrives they will know that he was himself both ready for it and quite happy about it.

At the same time, he knows in his bones that there is more work for him to do. The churches he has already founded need much more teaching and leading of the sort that at the moment only he can give; and there are more churches to be planted. After all, if God has called him to be the **apostle** to the **Gentiles**, there are plenty more parts of the Gentile world where the name of Jesus has still not been heard. He is quite confident, then, that God will in fact allow him to be released and resume his travelling ministry; and one of the first places he intends to visit when that happens is Philippi itself.

Alongside this passage, we should read 2 Corinthians 1.8–11. There, Paul describes what actually happened before he was released. It looks as though things came to a point where he not only thought he was going to be killed, but where his own spirits reached such a low ebb that he felt the potential death sentence going right down into his own heart and mind. In other words, we shouldn't assume that, just because the present passage strikes a cheerful, almost jaunty note, this was how Paul always felt. His *belief* never wavered, indeed it came through the terrible experience strengthened. But his *feelings* came and went. Learning to distinguish between the two, and to maintain belief and hope with or without the accompanying feelings, is itself part of Christian maturity.

Paul wants them to join in the celebration. But especially, when he comes to see them again, as he's convinced he will, he wants it to be an occasion for them to 'take pride in' King Jesus. Even though his death in custody would be acceptable to him, his release and resumption of work would serve as a sign, to the churches that had been praying for it, that Jesus really is sovereign over the affairs of empires. That, after all, is one of the main messages of the whole letter, and we need to remind ourselves of it as much today as the Philippian church did then.

PHILIPPIANS 1.27–30

The Gospel in Public

[27]The one thing I would stress is this: your public behaviour must match up to the gospel of the Messiah. That way, whether I do come and see you or whether I remain elsewhere, the news that I get about you will indicate that you are standing firm with a single spirit, struggling side by side with one united intent for the faith of the gospel,

²⁸and not letting your opponents intimidate you in any way. This is a sign from God: one that signifies their destruction, but your salvation.
²⁹Yes: God has granted you that, on behalf of the Messiah, you should not only believe in him, but also suffer for his sake. ³⁰You are engaged in the same struggle which you once watched me go through; and, as you now hear, I'm still going through it.

'Don't let him see you're afraid.'

My aunt hissed the words into my ear as the big dog came bounding up the street towards us. It seemed silly advice at the time. I *was* afraid. I was only seven years old and the previous year a small dog had bitten me, unprovoked. What might a big one do?

Swallowing my feelings, I walked on beside my aunt. The dog came to a stop, nosed all round us, and then set off back where he'd come from. He was only inquisitive. Had he known, however, that I was ready to run away, he'd have thought it was a game, and chased me . . .

'Don't let your opponents intimidate you', Paul tells the Philippians (verse 28). Now of course those who oppose the **gospel** are not simply like large dogs. Something much more subtle and dangerous is often going on. From the first-century Mediterranean world to the twenty-first century in China, in the Sudan, and in many other places, there have been plenty of people determined to stamp out this Christian nonsense and to use every trick in the book to do so. And in the post-Christian West, today, the forces of scepticism and cynicism within our culture are extremely powerful, not least in newspapers and on television. It's easy for Christians to feel intimidated; but Paul insists that we mustn't.

Why not? Don't they have the power to harm us? Well, yes and no. As Jesus said, they can kill the body but not the soul; and the living God is looking after you. More particularly, from Paul's point of view, the whole business of being a Christian is about living by the belief that Jesus is *already* the true Lord of the world. Most of the world doesn't know this yet, so the loyal Christian is inevitably out of step with people all around, and this will result in misunderstanding, hostility and even persecution.

That is why it's all the more important that Christian behaviour in the public sphere should be beyond reproach. The Philippians' public behaviour, as he says, must match up to the gospel. They must not acquire a reputation for being uncivil, boorish or rude. They must be known as honest, reliable, good neighbours, even if people are accusing or attacking them. They mustn't be intimidated into retreating into a private ghetto where they can ignore the rest of the world and nurture their own **faith** away from it.

At the same time, they must maintain their solid unity of **spirit** and intention, working together like members of the same sports team all equally intent on winning the game. That's what 'struggling side by side' really means. Appropriate public behaviour and united work for the gospel will together send a signal to opponents: we're not afraid. And that signal is itself part of the gospel message. It functions as a sign to the Christians that they already belong to the coming king, and to their opponents that a new world is beginning in which the threats of the old one don't work any more.

This is such an important point that it's worth spelling it out a bit. Paul's world was familiar with the situation where a great army might be taken over by a new general, who would demand different standards of behaviour and different practices in warfare. News of this would take time to work through the ranks, and many of the old soldiers would prefer to remain loyal to their former general. But those who knew that the new general had indeed taken over and would get his way in the end would be in the position of strength. The fact that they would hold their nerve, believing that the new regime was firmly in place, would itself be a sign to their doubting fellow soldiers that it was actually true.

This is more or less exactly what Paul believes about Jesus. He is the new king; most people don't yet realize it; but those who do must hold their nerve and remain loyal to him, because one day the whole world will acknowledge him as Lord. And that very loyalty itself, that holding of their nerve, will themselves be the sign that the **message** they are proclaiming is true.

So, too, will their suffering be – and suffering is bound to come, sooner or later, if they really are loyal to Jesus. The world, the opponents of the gospel, will turn on loyal Christians for being out of line, out of step. Try telling people with heavy investments in the Third World that one of the major gospel issues today is global debt, and watch the angry or scornful reaction you get. Try telling people who believe they have the right to inflict their military solutions on the rest of the world – or who make a lot of money from making and selling weapons – that the lordship of Jesus stands for a radically different way of resolving conflict. Try telling people whose lives revolve around sexual immorality that the Lord Jesus summons them to use their bodies in a way that honours the world's creator. Or, in Paul's case, try saying 'Jesus is Lord' under the very noses of people who are living by the 'gospel' that 'Caesar is lord' . . .

Which gospel issues does your community face right now? Where is it important for you and your church to hold your nerve and remain unafraid in the face of opposition?

PHILIPPIANS 2.1–4

Unity in Everything

¹So if our shared life in the Messiah brings you any comfort; if love still has the power to make you cheerful; if we really do have a partnership in the spirit; if your hearts are at all moved with affection and sympathy – ²then make my joy complete! Bring your thinking into line with one another.

Here's how to do it. Hold on to the same love; bring your innermost lives into harmony; fix your minds on the same object. ³Never act out of selfish ambition or vanity; instead, regard everybody else as your superior. ⁴Look after each other's best interests, not your own.

We sat and watched spellbound as the actors moved at what seemed like the speed of light. It was a complex and intricate play, with many layers and double or treble meanings. At times things were happening so fast, all around the stage, that it was more like a circus act than a play. Everybody had to know exactly where to be and what to do so that the next move would work all right, and the next, and the next. It was like watching a highly complex piece of machinery with all its cogs and wheels working together in perfect harmony.

That's a bit like what Paul is urging on the little church in Philippi. On stage, the actors were not out for their own individual glory at each other's expense; if one single actor had tried to steal the limelight from the others, the whole thing would have fallen apart. It only worked because everyone was working together with the same object. That's how the church should be too.

If you read these verses in any other way, they sound (quite frankly) almost laughably impossible. There's an old Jewish joke that says if you've got two rabbis you've probably got three opinions, and often the church seems like that as well. Not only are there big theological differences, smouldering resentments from historical events long ago, and radical variations in styles of worship. There are also personality cults, clashes over leadership style, arguments on issues of moral behaviour, cultural politics, and so on. How can we even begin to think that it might be possible to live the way Paul indicates here – thinking the same, loving each other completely, regarding everyone else (and their opinions!) as superior to you and your own?

The answer must be that everyone must be focused on something other than themselves; and that something is Jesus **Christ** himself, the king, the Lord, and the **good news** which has come to take the world over in his name. In the next passage, Paul will set this out gloriously in a poem which sums it all up. But in this passage he's coming at the issue of unity from every possible angle: the motivation for unity, the inner life of unity, and the practical application of unity. Let's take them in turn.

The motivation for unity is set out in verse 1. You should *want* to live this way, he says, because you know – all Christians should know – the comfort that comes from belonging to the king's family, from being (as he puts it in his rather technical way) 'in Christ', 'in the **Messiah**'. In addition to the comfort that comes from belonging to this family, there should be a growing sense of love within the family, a love that sustains and cheers you from day to day. Thirdly, as the **spirit** lives within Christians, directing and strengthening them, and as they see one another also being (so to speak) spirit-carriers, they can hardly help the sense that they should work together in a single direction. Finally, all this should produce the natural human emotions of affection and sympathy. If, with all this, you still don't want to work at living in unity with your fellow Christians, something is seriously wrong somewhere.

The inner life of unity, though, is what seems at first sight completely unattainable. At the centre of it all – the basic command that drives this passage – he tells them to 'bring your thinking into line with each other'. Of course, if that meant that person A changed his mind to agree with person B, just at the moment when person B was changing her mind to agree with person C, while at the same time person C was struggling to think in line with what person A had been thinking a moment ago, then the whole thing would become like a silly and pointless party game. That's not what Paul has in mind. Unity by itself can't be the final aim. After all, unity is possible among thieves, adulterers and many other types. Those who commit genocide need to do so with huge corporate single-mindedness, as the Nazis showed when killing millions of Jews, gypsies and others.

No: what matters is that Christians, like the actors all focusing single-mindedly on the play, should focus completely on the divine drama that has unfolded before their eyes in Jesus the king, and is continuing now into its final act with themselves as the characters. Bringing their thinking into line with each other wouldn't be any good if they were all thinking something that was *out* of line with the **gospel**. The love that they must have is the love that the gospel generates and sustains. Their inner lives, which are to be bonded together, must be the inner lives that reflect the gospel. The 'same object' which they must fix their minds on must be the facts about Jesus the Messiah, and the meaning which emerges from them. That is the clue.

In particular – and this challenge, as Paul will shortly demonstrate, emerges from the very heart of the gospel itself – they are to perform the extraordinary feat of looking at one another with the assumption that everybody else and their needs are more important than they themselves are (verses 3–4).

I remember once going to lunch with a friend who had invited about twenty or thirty people. Some of them were quite well-known public figures. As he said the grace at the start of the meal, he also said, very firmly, 'Remember: the most interesting person in the room is the one you're sitting next to!' Multiply that up a bit into a congregation, and you'll get somewhere near what Paul is saying.

All this, too, is of course impossible, unless you keep your eyes fixed the whole time on the person at the centre of it all. That's what Paul is now going to show us. But before we get there, we should perhaps pause. Reading these verses always makes me sorry; the church has so often got it so wrong. How, I wonder, can we move beyond frustration and penitence, and towards getting it right in future?

PHILIPPIANS 2.5–11

The Mind of the Messiah

⁵This is how you should think among yourselves – with the mind that you have because you belong to the Messiah, Jesus:

⁶Who, though in God's form, did not
regard his equality with God
as something he ought to exploit.

⁷Instead, he emptied himself,
and received the form of a slave,
being born in the likeness of humans.

And then, having human appearance,
⁸he humbled himself, and became
obedient even to death,
yes, even the death of the cross.

⁹And so God has greatly exalted him,
and to him in his favour has given
the name which is over all names:

¹⁰That now at the name of Jesus
every knee within heaven shall bow –
on earth, too, and under the earth;

¹¹And every tongue shall confess
that Jesus, Messiah, is Lord,
to the glory of God, the father.

When people in the ancient world thought of heroic leaders, rulers and kings they often thought of Alexander the Great (356–323 BC). At the age of 20 he succeeded his father Philip to the throne of Macedonia, quickly made himself master of all Greece, and then set about the task – to him, it seemed, quite small – of conquering the rest of the world. By the time he died at the age of 33 he had succeeded to such an extent that it made sense, within the thought of the time, for him to be regarded as divine. (He had himself suggested this.)

In Paul's world the closest equivalent to Alexander was the emperor Augustus, who had put an end to the long-running Roman civil war and had brought peace to the whole known world. It wasn't long before many grateful subjects came to regard him, too, as divine. The power of military might and the immense organizational skills required to hold the empire together made this, for them, the natural conclusion. Other rulers did their best to copy this model. This was what heroic leadership looked like in that world.

Only when we grasp this do we see just how deeply subversive, how utterly counter-cultural, was Paul's **gospel** message concerning Jesus of Nazareth, whose **resurrection** had declared him to be Israel's **Messiah** and the world's true Lord. He was the reality, and Alexander and Augustus were the caricature. This is what true global sovereignty looked like. Hadn't Jesus himself said something similar? 'World rulers lord it over their subjects, but it mustn't be like that with you; with you, the ruler must be the slave, because the **son of man** came to give his life a ransom for many' (Mark 10.42–45).

Now take this stark contrast between the pagan gods and heroes and Jesus of Nazareth, and think it through against the background of the Old Testament. Who was it who arrogantly grasped at the chance to be 'like God, knowing good and evil'? Why, Adam, of course, in Genesis 3. Of course! Alexander and Augustus were just doing what the human race has always done. But what's the solution? Well, in the Old Testament, God's people Israel are the servant-people, whose suffering obedience to God's saving plan will be the unexpected way of dealing with the world's sorry state. But Israel, too, is in slavery; Israel, too, has gone the way of Adam. In Paul's own day there were would-be rulers of Israel who seemed only too eager to go the Alexander/Augustus route. So what was to be done?

There are some things that can, perhaps, only be said in poetry, and perhaps this is one of them. The poem Paul now places here, at the heart of this letter, answers this question and many, many more – all in order to give the deep groundwork for the challenge to self-sacrificing unity within the church. People still debate whether Paul wrote the poem himself, or was quoting an even earlier Christian writer. What is quite clear is that here we have a very, very early statement of Christian **faith** in who Jesus was and what he accomplished, which subsequent theology has gazed at in awe for its remarkably full and rich statement of what was later seen as the classic doctrine of the incarnation of God in Jesus the Messiah.

Let's clear one misunderstanding out of the way in case it still confuses anybody. In verse 7 Paul says that Jesus 'emptied himself'. People have sometimes thought that this means that Jesus, having been divine up to that point, somehow stopped being divine when he became human, and then went back to being divine again. This is, in fact, completely untrue to what Paul has in mind. The point of verse 6 is that Jesus was indeed already equal with God; somehow Paul is saying that Jesus already existed even before he became a human being (verse 7). But the decision to become human, and to go all the way along the road of obedience, obedience to the divine plan of salvation, yes, all the way to the cross – this decision was not a decision to stop being divine. It was a decision about *what it really meant to be divine.*

Jesus retained his equality with God; the point of the cross, for Paul, is that 'God was in **Christ** reconciling the world to himself' (2 Corinthians 5.19). The point of verses 6 and 7 is that Jesus didn't regard this equality as something to take advantage of, something to exploit. Rather, the eternal **son of God**, the one who became human in and as Jesus of Nazareth, regarded his equality with God as committing him to the course he took: of becoming human, of becoming Israel's anointed representative, of dying under the weight of the world's evil. This is what it meant to be equal with God. As you look at the incarnate son of God dying on the cross, the most powerful thought you should think is: this is the true meaning of who God is. He is the God of self-giving love.

The poem turns on the 'and so' at the start of verse 9. This means, basically, 'therefore'. What's the connection? Why should the Jesus who did what verses 6–8 say he did be honoured in this way?

The answer is that in his incarnation and on the cross Jesus has done *what only God can do.* Here is the very heart of the Christian vision of God himself: that within the Jewish vision of one God, the creator and sustainer of the universe, we are to see different self-expressions – so different, yet so intimately related, that they can be called 'father' and 'son'.

Paul is quite clear that he's not moving away from Jewish monotheism. In verse 11 he quotes Isaiah 45.23, a fiercely monotheistic Old Testament passage ('To me and me alone, says YHWH, every knee shall bow and every tongue shall swear'). Here, then, is his point: the God who will not share his glory with anyone else has shared it – with Jesus. Jesus, therefore, must somehow be identified as one who from all eternity was 'equal with God'. And his progression through incarnation to death must be seen, not as something which required him as it were to stop being God for a while, but as the perfect self-expression of the true God.

Most people in Paul's world, besotted with an idea of the gods into which people like Alexander and Augustus could be fitted without much difficulty, were shocked beyond belief at the idea that the one true God might be known at last in the person of a crucified Jew. Many people in our world find it very difficult as well, and we might like to ask the reason why. Could it be that we, too, have allowed ourselves to slide into pagan views of what deity or divinity consist of – views that would then make it difficult to fit Jesus into them? If so, isn't it about time we did what the New Testament writers urge us to do, and what this wonderful passage poetically invites us to do: to start from Jesus himself and rethink our whole picture of God around him?

If and when we do that, we shall find of course that the picture is very challenging. This is a God who is known most clearly when he abandons his rights for the sake of the world. Yes, says Paul; and that's 'the mind of Christ', the pattern of thinking that belongs to you because you belong to the Messiah (verse 5). And if you are truly living in him and by his kind of **life**, the exhortations of verses 1–4 may suddenly make a lot more sense.

PHILIPPIANS 2.12–18

How Salvation Is Worked Out

[12]So, my dear people: you always did what I said, so please now carry on in the same way, not just as though I was there with you, but much more because I'm not! Your task now is to work at bringing about your own salvation; and naturally you'll be taking this with utter seriousness. [13]After all, God himself is the one who's at work among you, who provides both the will and the energy to enable you to do what pleases him.

[14]There must be no grumbling and disputing in anything you do. [15]That way, nobody will be able to fault you, and you'll be pure and spotless children of God in the midst of a twisted and depraved generation. You are to shine among them like lights in the world, [16]clinging on to the word of life. That's what I will be proud of on the day of the Messiah. It will prove that I didn't run a useless race, or work to no purpose.

[17]Yes: even if I am to be poured out like a drink-offering on the sacrifice and service of your faith, I shall celebrate, and celebrate jointly with you all. [18]In the same way, you should celebrate, yes, and celebrate with me.

It was an ugly city. The fine old buildings had been pulled down over the years, and they had been replaced by huge square concrete monstrosities. They were designed for function, not good looks – though by the time I went there they were getting tatty and ragged at the edges, and I wondered just how functional they were now. It was a depressing place.

But then, just a few years ago, an architect was appointed by the city council to design a new civic centre right in the heart of the city, in the middle of all that ugliness. They couldn't afford to pull everything down again, but they could just afford, they reckoned, to begin the process of making the city once more the beautiful place the old pictures showed it to have been.

The architect was not a young man, but he had cherished this sort of opportunity all his life. He went to work on the design, and some while later, when the preparations were complete, he saw the foundations laid. He was then taken ill, and unable to carry on his work on the project. But he still cared passionately about it and gave detailed instructions to his colleagues as to how it was all to proceed.

'After all,' he said to them, 'when people think of me, I want them to think of this beautiful building! You've got to make it so that it stands like a lighthouse in a dark storm, showing people that there is such a thing as beauty even if everything else around is ugliness. That will be my reward.'

Paul, in this passage, is like that architect. He is looking forward once more to the 'Day of the **Messiah**' – the day when God will bring the whole cosmos to justice and peace, through the return of Jesus as Lord (see 3.20–21). He doesn't know whether he will live to see that day. But he has designed a building that, if the builders keep working at it the way he's showed them, will stand out as the one thing of beauty in a world of ugliness, the sign of what God will eventually do to the whole city.

Look how he puts it in verse 15. You are, he says, to shine like lights in the world, in the middle of a twisted and depraved generation. You are to be the beacon of hope that they need, the sign of God's beauty in a world that had all but defaced it. In fact, when he speaks of them shining like lights he is quoting a passage from the book of Daniel (12.3), which speaks of 'the wise' – by which they meant Israelites skilled in knowing and applying God's **law**, not least in a time of persecution – shining in that way to the world around. And, what's more, the passage is very closely connected with Daniel's promise that God would raise the dead, another theme that will become very important in the next chapter of Philippians. In a sense, then, what Paul is saying is not just that the Philippians are to be a sign of light and beauty in a world of darkness and ugliness. They are to be a sign of God's new **life** in a world that only knows the way to death.

For Paul's part, he will be able to look on, even if from a distance, and know that his work has borne fruit. Like the architect of the one beautiful building, he will know that he has fulfilled his God-given vocation. He hasn't run the race on the wrong track, or spent all his energy on a building that was going to fall down the minute his back was turned. Even if he dies before all this comes about (verses 17–18), he will know that he can celebrate a job well done, and he wants them to celebrate with him.

Now we can return to the earlier verses in the section and see how they fit in. He is telling the Philippians that they must grow into maturity and take responsibility for themselves. He may be absent, but this simply means that they will have to think through with an independent though still obedient mind what the **gospel** means for them where they are.

Verse 12 is often misunderstood. People frequently suppose it means that Christians are responsible for doing things which will earn them their salvation, on the principle of 'the Lord helps those who help themselves' (which is not, of course, a text from the Bible!). But that's quite out of line with what Paul says anywhere else. Salvation – as he goes on to stress in the next verse – is God's work from start to finish. No: he wants the Philippians to work out for themselves what this business of being saved will mean in practice. The phrase 'your own salvation' isn't meant to contrast this work of theirs with any work of God in salvation. It is contrasting their own responsibility for their spiritual welfare with the responsibility that Paul would take if he was with them. He isn't there, and for all either of them know he may never be again. They therefore need to be obedient – to him, but much more to God – in Paul's absence even more than in his presence.

They need to do it all, finally, without grumbling or disputing. This is a reference to Israel in the wilderness, questioning God and Moses all the time. As often, Paul sees the church as the people of the new **Exodus**: brought out of the Egypt of sin and death through the Passover action of God in Jesus, and now on the way home to the real promised land. And this time they are going to get it right. That remains the challenge before the church today just as in the first century.

PHILIPPIANS 2.19–24

On Timothy

[19]I hope in the Lord Jesus to send Timothy to you soon, so that I in turn may be encouraged by getting news about you. [20]I have nobody else of his quality: he will care quite genuinely about how you are.

²¹Everybody else, you see, looks after their own interests, not those of Messiah Jesus. ²²But you know how Timothy has proved himself. Like a child with a father he has worked as a slave alongside me for the sake of the gospel. ²³So I'm hoping to send him just as soon as I see how it will turn out with me. ²⁴And I am confident in the Lord that I myself will come very soon as well.

When I taught in the university, one of my annual tasks was to interview candidates for admission the following year. The first time I did this, a young man came for interview who seemed quiet and subdued. He wasn't very sure of himself, and didn't always do well in answering questions. He seemed, though, to be intelligent, and my colleagues and I were puzzled about him. We went back and read again the letter of reference written about him by the headteacher of his school. 'Very bright . . . lively mind . . . extremely able and intelligent . . . should do very well indeed. . . .' With some hesitation, we decided to admit him to the college to start the following year.

When he arrived, it quickly became apparent that the headteacher had been absolutely right, and the impression made at interview had been very misleading. The young man took an excellent degree and went on to become a university teacher in his own right. It was only later we found out that the day before the interview a close family member had died, leaving him emotionally drained and devastated. He had not wanted to mention this in case it looked as though he was asking for special treatment. Fortunately, on this occasion at least, we trusted the reference we had received.

All that we know of Timothy, one of Paul's closest co-workers, suggests that he sometimes came across as somewhat nervous and unsure of himself. But Paul has complete faith in him as a man and as a Christian, and is writing this short reference for him because he intends to send him to Philippi once there is more news about his own situation. (Verse 23 looks like a cryptic reference to the possibility of a trial which might end with Paul's release – or perhaps with his condemnation.) The Philippians clearly know Timothy already, but Paul is eager to emphasize that he will care genuinely for them and be a true servant of the **gospel** in Paul's place. Epaphroditus, who we shall meet in the next paragraph, will take the present letter, but he lives in Philippi and will stay there. Timothy will visit them in order to bring news back to Paul of how things are with them.

The portrait of Timothy here, brief though it is, gives plenty of food for thought about the nature of Christian ministry, and of the training and (what we today might call) mentoring of younger workers by older ones. The key to it in this case is that Paul and Timothy have worked together like father and son – in a culture where, as in many parts of the world to this day, most sons follow their fathers into the family occupation, and learn how to do it by watching and copying. Something of that intimate bond has now happened with Paul and Timothy, and Paul trusts the younger man fully to act as he would himself.

It is interesting that he doesn't say 'Timothy is a wonderful teacher', or even 'Timothy is a very devout and holy man', but, 'Timothy will genuinely care about you'. The definition Paul seems to be adopting for a good pastor – and the implication is that he himself was like this – has more to do with sheer unselfish love than anything to do with the person themselves. Indeed, Paul contrasts Timothy favourably with others (whom he doesn't name; but it's a rather bleak picture of the other Christians working in Ephesus at the time): the others, he says, are all looking after their own interests, rather than those of Messiah Jesus; but Timothy is different.

Notice, particularly, how looking after Messiah Jesus' interests and 'he will care quite genuinely about how you are' are, for Paul, two ways of saying the same thing. For Paul, the communities that gave allegiance to Jesus as king and Lord were not as it were distantly related to their master. He and they were bound up together, he was present with them, his own **spirit** lived in them individually and corporately. Thus, to serve Jesus and to serve his people are one and the same. To care for the church is to care for the **Messiah**'s body. And doing this, clearly, is part of what Paul means by 'working as a slave alongside me for the gospel'.

Observe, finally, the way in which Paul is holding Timothy up as an example of the attitude he has urged the Philippians themselves to adopt in verse 1–4 – the attitude which was supremely shown by Jesus himself (verses 6–8). He has learned, through the gospel, the art of putting others before himself, and is thereby fit not only to speak the gospel but also to stand as a model of what it means.

As so often, we see here how the personal networks which Paul set up served not just to keep people in touch with each other (in a world, of course, long before telephones and radios); they served to maintain the unity of the church. Timothy's forthcoming visit to Philippi would be one more link binding the church there, in northern Greece, to the church in Ephesus and the surrounding area. In our own day, too, it is vital that churches in different parts of the world develop and maintain lively contacts with one another. Friendship in the gospel across barriers of race, geography, culture and class is an excellent way of helping today's church to be what Paul believed it should be: the single new humanity, the light in God's dark world.

PHILIPPIANS 2.25–30

On Epaphroditus

²⁵But I did think it was necessary to send Epaphroditus to you. He is my brother; he has worked alongside me and fought alongside me; and he's served as your agent in tending to my needs. ²⁶He was longing for you all, you see, and he was upset because you heard that he was sick. ²⁷And he really was sick, too; he nearly died. But God took pity on him – yes, and on me as well, so that I wouldn't have one sorrow piled on top of another.

²⁸This has made me all the more eager to send him, so that you'll see him again and be glad, and my own anxieties will be laid to rest. ²⁹So give him a wonderfully happy welcome in the Lord, and hold people like him in special respect. ³⁰He came close to death through risking his life for the Messiah's work, so that he could complete the service to me that you hadn't been able to perform.

When I was at school a first-year physics teacher once asked us the question in an examination: What are the advantages of having two eyes?

The correct answer, of course, was that with two eyes you can see things in three dimensions, and learn to judge distances, speeds and so on. One boy, however, wrote as his answer: 'Having two eyes means that you can see twice as far; and if one eye stops working you've always got the other one to fall back on!'

The teacher enjoyed this so much that he read it out to the class as a fine example of making up in ingenuity for what you lack in information. But of course the true answer remains important: with only one eye you don't get things in their proper perspective. You need two if you're to see them with all three dimensions.

The little paragraphs about Timothy and, now, Epaphroditus are enormously important in helping us to get Paul and his work – and his feelings and emotions – in true perspective. If all Paul's writing was solid, dense, abstract theology we would never have known what he was really like as a human being.

Indeed, we might have had the idea that Paul lived the kind of Christian life one imagines from some popular literature: a life without stress or strain, a life of pure unmitigated joy and gladness, cheerfully doing the work of the Lord and preaching the **gospel** without a care in the world. Worry? Why, wasn't that sinful? Human anxieties? Why couldn't he submit them to the Lord and forget about them? Doesn't he say, in chapter 4 of this very letter, that you should rejoice at all times, commit everything to God in prayer, and know his peace which passes understanding?

Yes, he does, and that is important. But the present passage enables us to take a two-eyed look at all of this; to see in three dimensions what this joy really is – and what it isn't. The passage gives us a window not only on Epaphroditus – his journeys, his mission and his nearly fatal illness – but also on Paul. He was truly glad to have Epaphroditus with him, and he was truly horrified at the thought that he might die. Verse 27 is most revealing: God took pity not only on Epaphroditus (in other words, he recovered from his illness), but also on Paul, so that he wouldn't have one sorrow piled on top of another.

'Well, Paul', we want to say. 'What was the sorrow you already had?' Presumably he would reply: 'Being in prison, and being unable to see my brothers and sisters in the Lord.'

'Why couldn't you let go of the sorrow and simply rejoice, as you're telling us to?' we might ask. 'And how can you say that if Epaphroditus had died you would have been overwhelmed with that as a second sorrow on top of your first one? Wouldn't you have wanted to rejoice that he'd gone to be with the Lord?'

Again he might reply: 'I do rejoice, and I am rejoicing. I know that God has won the victory over the powers of evil, and that he will one day fill the world with his love and justice, raising us to new **life** in his final **kingdom**. That sustains me, and I celebrate it day by day. But at the same time I love my friends, especially those who work and struggle alongside me in the prayer and witness of the gospel. We are bound together by ties of real human affection and love.' (Look back at 2.1 and think what that actually meant in terms of Paul's bonding with his 'family' in the **Messiah**.)

'I'm not a Stoic', he would say. 'I don't believe that our human emotions are silly surface noise and that we should get down beneath them to a calm, untroubled state. That's not what I mean by "joy". The joy I'm talking about goes hand in hand with hope; it doesn't mean that everything is already just as it should be, only that with Jesus now enthroned as Lord we know it will eventually get there. But if, while we're waiting for that day, we pretend we don't have human emotions – we pretend that we don't *need* human emotions! – then we are denying part of what God has given us.'

We should not imagine, then, that the call to rejoice, which does indeed sound through the second half of this letter, is a call to ignore or forget the multiple human dimensions of our daily lives. After all, part of Jesus' own path of humble obedience (2.6–8) was his weeping in agony both at his friend's graveside (John 11.35) and in Gethsemane (Hebrews 5.7). Would we dare rebuke Jesus himself for failing to have a pure, untroubled joy at those moments?

Paul's description of Epaphroditus, then, reminds us of the vital truth that we are all of us, whether first-century **apostles** or twenty-first-century converts, expected to be fully human beings, facing all that life throws at us and being honest about the results. Paul didn't need or want to hide from the young church, from his own converts. He was not afraid to admit to his own vulnerability; that, indeed, is part of the whole point of 2 Corinthians, written most likely not very long after this letter. He believed, after all, in the Jesus who 'was crucified in weakness, but lives by the power of God' (2 Corinthians 13.4).

As for Epaphroditus himself: he, like Timothy, has followed the path laid down in verses 1-11. He, too, has not sought his own well-being, but that of others. He, too, has been prepared to lay down his life for the gospel. He, too, is a visible reminder of Jesus the king, the Lord.

PHILIPPIANS 3.1-6
Warning: Don't Trust in the Flesh

¹So then, my dear family, it comes down to this: celebrate in the Lord! It's no trouble for me to write the same things to you, and it's safe for you.

²Watch out for the dogs! Watch out for the 'bad works' people! Watch out for the 'incision' party, that is, the mutilators! ³We are the 'circumcision', you see – we who worship God by the spirit, and boast in Messiah Jesus, and refuse to trust in the flesh.

⁴Mind you, I've got good reason to trust in the flesh. If anyone else thinks they have reason to trust in the flesh, I've got more. ⁵Circumcised? On the eighth day. Race? Israelite. Tribe? Benjamin. Descent? Hebrew through and through. Torah-observance? A Pharisee. ⁶Zealous? I persecuted the church! Official status under the law? Blameless.

If you saw a movie advertisement which highlighted the word FLESH, you would know what it meant. Pornography, no doubt. Graphic sexual scenes, quite likely. Or at least that's what they would want you to think, to try to lure you through the door.

If a Christian preacher warned you against 'sins of the flesh', you'd probably think he was talking about the same area. He or she might expand the subject a bit. After all, gluttony and drunkenness are also 'sins of the flesh' in that sense – things you do with your physical body which dishonour that body and disobey the loving will of your wise creator.

But when Paul warns the Philippians against the 'flesh', he means something much more subtle. Indeed, it's not always easy to know whether our word 'flesh' is the best English word to give the sense he has in mind. The trouble is that some of what he means is indeed directly connected with the straightforward 'sins of the flesh', and part of his point is that the more subtle thing he's talking about is in fact closely linked to them, despite what many people think.

The main thing Paul means by 'the flesh', here and often in Galatians and Romans, is the pride of *physical descent* cherished by the Jews. As this passage makes clear, he knew all about it from the inside. This had been his pride too. Ancestry and all that went with it was very important in the ancient world, as it is in many societies in our own day. Jews of the first century, who could trace their ancestry back for 2,000 years to the patriarchs Abraham, Isaac and Jacob, and who knew which of Jacob's twelve sons they were descended from – such people were understandably and justifiably proud. But their natural human pleasure at the thought of such a remarkable family history had become, from Paul's point of view, the dangerous boast that because of all this they were superior, automatically and for ever, to all those who didn't share it.

The connection of all this with what we think of as the 'sins of the flesh' is complicated. For a start, the badge of the male Jew was **circumcision** – the cutting off of the foreskin, traditionally performed on the eighth day after birth. Paul sees some of his contemporaries so obsessed with this, particularly with inflicting it on **Gentiles** to try to make them acceptable to God, that he likens them by implication to people who cannot stop thinking about sex. Their minds are focused on genitalia – hardly what God had in mind in the original command to circumcise baby boys. The fact that they could refer to themselves as 'the circumcision' makes this point well enough.

Beyond this, though, Paul was clear in his mind that if you emphasized the 'flesh', and your identity 'according to the flesh', as he himself had done in his pre-Christian days, then, instead of stressing something that actually made you different from the pagan world around, you were instead stressing that which you had in common with them. You were setting up your Judaism as just another ethnic, geographical, religious and cultural grouping, along with all the other ones in the world. You were falling into the trap the ancient Israelites had dug for themselves when they said they wanted to be 'like all the nations'. The point of Israel was that it should be distinctive, different, a light to the nations. To emphasize ethnicity meant being the same.

Finally, when Paul says 'flesh' he not only means physical identity, membership in a family, and the inclination towards sin. He is also drawing attention to the fact that this sort of identity won't last. It will decay and die. Our word 'corruptible' covers both senses. Flesh is 'corruptible' in the sense that, like a politician on the make, it can easily be lured into shady practices. Flesh is also 'corruptible' in that it gets sick, decays, falls apart and dies.

Paul's warning against the 'flesh' in this passage has a very specific target. In Galatia, just a few years before, the churches he founded had almost at once been infiltrated by Jewish Christians. Paul was himself, of course, a Jewish Christian, but these ones, unlike him, were insisting that Gentile converts to Christianity had only come halfway. They now needed to take on the Jewish **law** as well. Otherwise they remained Gentile outsiders, 'dogs' as some Jews referred to them. (Dogs in the ancient world were mostly wild and verminous, not often family pets.) They needed to perform the 'good works' of the **Torah**. They needed, above all, to become circumcised.

You can read Paul's sharp initial response in the letter to the Galatians. Here his tone is only sharp for a moment. This problem hasn't actually arisen yet in Philippi, but Paul is aware that it could at any moment. More important for him just now is to use this necessary warning as a bridge to the positive things he wants to say in this chapter, to which we'll come in the next section.

The warning begins with a three times repeated 'look out!' His descriptions of what to 'look out' for are heavily ironic. Watch out for the dogs, he says! But these are not, of course, literally dogs. Nor are they 'dogs' in the sense many Jews meant it, i.e., Gentiles. They are the 'dogs' who are insisting on ethnic purity for the people of God.

Likewise, 'the "bad works" people' is Paul's contemptuous name for the 'good works' people. They are the ones who are insisting that only keeping the law will do as the standard for membership in God's people.

Third, and most shocking, the 'mutilation' people are the people who think of themselves as 'the circumcision'. Paul is implying that by marking themselves out in this way they are really just like the sort of pagan cult that insists on making ritual incisions, gashes or wounds in one's body.

His counter-claim is equally strong. 'The circumcision – that's us!' In other words, if you want to know who really should have the title that belongs to God's **covenant** people – well, here they are. Jews and Gentiles alike who worship God in **spirit** (as opposed to emphasizing the flesh), who take their pride in King Jesus (as opposed to taking pride in family descent) and who refuse to trust in 'flesh' at all. These people – he means, obviously, Christians of whatever ethnic and cultural background – are the proper inheritors of the title 'the circumcision'. He's going to say more about all this later in the chapter. At the moment he's putting down a marker for where the argument is going.

Paul's own list of privileges would have sounded pretty impressive to any Jewish contemporary. He wasn't sniping at the Jews from the outside. He was certainly not, as some have tried to suggest, anti-Jewish. He simply believed that the God of Abraham, the God of Israel, had now acted to fulfil his promises in a radically unexpected way; and that those who wanted to continue loyal to this God had no choice but to follow where he was leading. What that means will shortly become clear.

The section, and the second half of the letter, is introduced by verse 1, which sometimes seems a little cut off from what follows it. The basic command to celebrate in the Lord Jesus, though, forms the framework for everything that's coming (see 4.4). To celebrate and rejoice because Jesus is Lord, and because we are his people, is the sure antidote to all false or rival beliefs.

PHILIPPIANS 3.7–11

Gaining the Messiah

[7]Does that sound as though my account was well in credit? Well, maybe; but whatever I had written in on the profit side, I calculated it instead as a loss – because of the Messiah. [8]Yes, I know that's weird, but there's more: I calculate everything as a loss, because knowing Messiah Jesus as my Lord is worth far more than everything else put together! In fact, because of the Messiah I've suffered the loss of everything, and I now calculate it as trash, so that my profit may be the Messiah, [9]and that I may be discovered in him, not having my own covenant status defined by Torah, but the status which comes through the Messiah's faithfulness: the covenant status from God which is given to faith. [10]This means knowing him, knowing the power of his resurrection, and knowing the partnership of his suffer-ings. It means sharing the form and pattern of his death, [11]so that somehow I may arrive at the final resurrection from the dead.

A story is told of the great nineteenth-century Anglican pastor, poet and theologian John Keble. As a young don in Oxford in the early years of the century, he held at one stage the office of college bursar. Few clergy then, or now for that matter, were trained in the art of balancing columns of figures; and in one particular year Keble's accounts were stubbornly out of balance by nearly two thousand pounds. Eventually the mystery was solved. Having written the date at the top of the page, he had added the number of the year – it must have been somewhere near 1820 – into one of the columns of figures.

There are many methods of creative accounting, but normally bal-ancing the books is a matter of putting together a certain number of items on the credit side, a large number of items on the debit side, and calculating them to see how close they come. That is the picture Paul is working with in verses 7 and 8, before he drops the metaphor and concentrates on the new ideas that have emerged from it.

Paul's accounts, though, balance in a very odd way. He has just declared that, in terms of his status as a member of God's people, Israel, he had nothing on the debit side at all! Every way you looked at it, he was in the clear (verses 5 and 6). Does that mean, though, that his account is in credit? Certainly not! He strikes a line through all the items that looked as if they formed a credit balance, and places the whole lot on the other side of the page instead. They are now part of the debit column, rather than the credit one.

What has caused this extraordinary piece of what we might call *destructive* accounting? Simply this: Paul has discovered something to put on the credit side in comparison with which everything else he can imagine can only be a debit. And the 'something' is in fact, of course, some*one*: it is Jesus, the **Messiah**, the king, the Jesus who was the subject of the poem in 2.6–11.

That poem, in fact, remains important in the present chapter of Philippians, because what Paul says about himself in this passage and the following ones is quite close to what he there said about Jesus. Jesus didn't regard the huge advantage he had – equality with God, no less – as something to exploit; rather, he interpreted it as the vocation to die on the cross, and that was why God exalted him. So, here, Paul doesn't regard the huge privileges he had, which he listed in verses 4 and 5, as something to take advantage of; rather, he discovered in Jesus that the true meaning of membership in God's people lay in suffering and death, with the hope of **resurrection** out beyond.

This, it seems, is what he means by having the Messiah as his 'profit'. Jesus, as Israel's Messiah, has at last done what Israel (for all her privileges) had not and could not. He has been, in himself, the light of the world, the means of salvation, the doorway to the **age to come**. Israel, meanwhile – including Paul himself before his conversion – had been struggling to be God's people according to the **Torah**, and the main result had been to set up that law as a barrier of privilege between Jew and **Gentile**. That's why Paul now sees, and says, that what he wants is none of those privileges, but rather to gain the Messiah, to know the Messiah, to be found 'in' the Messiah, to be defined by the Messiah's faithfulness, to know the power of his resurrection, which lies along the road of his suffering and death.

The passage is thus Jesus-centred, Messiah-focused, to a quite remarkable degree. For Paul, this is a matter of *status*: God regards all Christians as being 'in **Christ**'. It is also a matter of *personal knowledge*: not just 'knowing about' Jesus the Messiah, but knowing him in a personal relationship. It is, thirdly, a matter of *conformity of life*: he is committed to the patterns of behaviour that characterize the Messiah.

The first of these is particularly important, and is the theme of verse 9, which sums up a good deal that he says at more length in Romans and Galatians. Paul draws out the contrast, the same contrast he's been talking about throughout the passage, between those who are regarded as members of God's **covenant** people because they possess, and try to keep, the Jewish law, the Torah, and those who are regarded as members of God's covenant family because of what the Messiah has done. In 2.8 he described the Messiah's achievement as his 'obedience, even unto death'; here he describes it as his 'faithfulness'; but the two mean substantially the same thing. And the way we share in 'the Messiah's faithfulness' is by our '**faith**'. Our *belief* that the crucified and risen Jesus is the Messiah, the Lord of the world, and our *loyalty* to him, are the sign and badge that we have a credit balance consisting simply of him, over against all the debits we could ever have from anywhere else. This is Paul's famous doctrine of '**justification** by faith', which continues to be a comfort and a challenge to millions around the world.

'Justification' isn't just about how someone becomes a Christian. It is about the status that they possess, and continue to possess, as full members of God's people, no matter who their parents were or what their moral, cultural or religious background may have been. And, as verses 10 and 11 indicate, the faith which reaches out and embraces Jesus as Messiah embraces, in him, the way of suffering and death which marked him out. If you want to get to the resurrection of the dead, this is the only way to go.

Whatever that means for us today – and for some it will mean literal and physical persecution, while for others it may be more hidden and secret – we should never forget that with all this the account still stays in credit. Better to have the Messiah, and to follow him through the cross to the resurrection, than to have anything and anyone else in the world.

PHILIPPIANS 3.12–16

Chasing on to the Finish

[12]I'm not implying that I've already received 'resurrection', or that I've already become complete and mature! No; I'm hurrying on, eager to overtake it, because Messiah Jesus has overtaken me. [13]My dear family, I don't reckon that I have yet overtaken it. But this is my one aim: to forget everything that's behind, and to strain every nerve to go after what's ahead. [14]I mean to chase on towards the finishing post, where the prize waiting for me is the upward call of God in Messiah Jesus.

> [15]Those of us who are mature should think like this! If you think differently about it, God will reveal this to you as well. [16]Only let's be sure to keep in line with the position we have reached.

The athletics match had reached a critical stage. One of the final races was left to be run: the 440 yards (the old version of today's 400 metres). The athletes were bunched together as they came to the first bend, and one of them was pushed over and fell right off the track. Quick as a flash he was back on his feet, and, as though electrically charged by the incident, caught the other runners with a few paces to go and overtook them to win on the line. It was a famous victory, which features now in the movie *Chariots of Fire*.

What would you have done? Most of us, I suspect, would have accepted from the moment we fell over that we were out of the race, with no hope left. We might have been angry, but there would be nothing we could do about it. What had in fact just happened would keep us enslaved, with no hope of going on to what *might* have happened. With the athlete in question – the famous Eric Liddell – it was just the opposite. It was as though he had been reading this passage of Paul: forget what's behind, strain every nerve to go after what's ahead, and chase on towards the finishing post.

Paul, in other words, has swapped his bookkeeping metaphor for an athletic one. This is partly because he ended the previous paragraph with talk of the **resurrection** which lies still in the future, and towards which, therefore, all Christians are drawn like athletes sprinting towards the end of the race. As he stresses in verse 13, it's important to concentrate on the one aim in view: keeping on going forward towards that goal.

But it's also partly because, in using his own path of discipleship as an example for the Philippian church to follow, he wants to head off any idea that once you have become a mature Christian you have, as it were, 'arrived', in the sense that there is no more travelling to do. He is gently warning against any tendency to a super-spiritual view of Christianity which imagines that the full life of the **age to come** can be had in the present, without waiting for the resurrection itself.

Paul is quite clear about this. He hasn't 'arrived' in that sense, and nor has anyone else. True maturity, he insists, actually means knowing that you haven't arrived, and that you must still keep pressing on forwards towards the goal. The seasoned athlete knows that the race isn't won and lost until the end has been reached. To imagine that because you find yourself out in front of the pack you can slack off and take it easy, having 'arrived', would be disastrous. As he says in verse 16, it's important to maintain the position you've reached.

What then is the goal, the finishing line? Paul describes it in verse 14 with an interesting phrase: the prize that is waiting there, like a silver cup or medal for the winning athlete, is 'the upward call of God in King Jesus'. This has often been seen as simply 'heaven', the place 'up there' where Christians aim to go at the end.

But this can't be what Paul means. In verses 20 and 21, which we shall come to in the next section, he speaks not of our going up to heaven, but of the Lord, King Jesus himself, coming *from* heaven to earth, in order to transform the world and change our bodies so that they are like his own resurrected and glorified body. Living in 'heaven' isn't the goal we are aiming at; rather, it's living in God's new world with our new bodies. So the 'upward call' seems to be the resurrection **life** itself. Straining forward towards it, like an athlete aiming at the finishing line and the prize that waits beyond it, means living in the present in the light of that future. (This is very close, in fact, to what Paul says a bit more fully in Colossians 3.1–4.)

None of this means, though, that Paul sees the Christian life as a gloomy struggle. Look again at verse 12. He is eager to 'overtake it' because the **Messiah**, Jesus, has 'overtaken him'. It's difficult to find one English word here that really catches the double meaning he wants. When he's talking about what he, Paul, still has to do, the word means 'to catch up', or 'to grasp the prize', or 'to attain the goal'. When he's talking about what Jesus has done to and for him, the word means 'has laid hold of me', 'has grasped me and taken control of me'. But it's the same word, and that's the point. All Paul's efforts after holiness, after the work of the **gospel**, after the eventual goal of resurrection, are not a matter of his unaided effort to do something that will make God pleased with him. They all take place within the context of God's grace: King Jesus has grasped hold of him, and all that he now does is a matter of responding in love to that firm hand on the shoulder.

PHILIPPIANS 3.17—4.1

Citizens of Heaven

[17]So, my dear family, I want you, all together, to watch what I do and copy me. You've got us as a pattern of behaviour; pay careful attention to people who follow it.

[18]You see, there are several people who behave as enemies of the cross of the Messiah. I told you about them often enough, and now I'm weeping as I say it again. [19]They are on the road to destruction; their stomach is their god, and they find glory in their own shame. All they ever think about is what's on the earth.

²⁰We are citizens of heaven, you see, and we're eagerly waiting for the saviour, the Lord, Messiah Jesus, who is going to come from there. ²¹Our present body is a shabby old thing, but he's going to transform it so that it's just like his glorious body. And he's going to do this by the power which makes him able to bring everything into line under his authority.

¹Well then, my dear family – I miss you so much, you're my joy and crown! – this is how you must stand firm in the Lord, my beloved people.

The word 'colony' today is not exactly popular. It rings of the old days of imperialism, when several European countries were expanding their influence in Africa, Asia and Latin America, and were vying with each other to see who could grab the wealthiest areas. To have a 'colonial' attitude is supposed, today, to mean being patronizing, perhaps bullying, looking down on local people in far-off lands as being an inferior species, good only to help increase the profits for the mother country back home.

Of course, many colonists and colonial administrators in days gone by had the best of motives. They aimed to bring healthcare and the benefits of modern technology, not to mention cultural and even spiritual blessings, to those in desperate need of them. But often what the local people saw was their land being taken by force and their own ancient culture scorned and squashed. That's what many people today think of when they think of 'colonies'.

Philippi was a Roman colony, and it's likely that many of the local people in that area of northern Greece saw Rome and the colonial administration in much the way I have described. What had happened was this. In 42 BC, about a hundred years before Paul came to the area, Philippi was the setting for one of the great battles in the Roman civil war that had broken out after the death of Julius Caesar. The two victorious generals, Antony and Octavian (the future Emperor Augustus), had found themselves with a lot of soldiers in northern Greece with nothing more to do. They certainly didn't want to bring them all back to Rome, or even to Italy. It would be dangerous to have thousands of soldiers suddenly arriving in the capital. So they gave them land in and around Philippi, making it a colony of Rome.

Once the colony was established, other veterans from other battles joined them. By the time Paul went there, Philippi contained quite a number of families descended from those original Roman colonists, as well as several local people who had benefited from the Roman presence – and a good many who hadn't, and who resented the alien, Latin-speaking elite that had taken over their Greek town.

Philippi was on a main road which ran west to the narrowest part of the Adriatic Sea, where you could sail easily across to Italy and travel on to Rome. Close contact could be maintained with the mother city. The Philippian colonists were proud of being Romans, and would do their best to order their civic life so that it matched the way things were done in Rome. The most recent innovation down that line was, of course, the establishment of the imperial cult: Caesar, the emperor, was to be worshipped as saviour and Lord.

All of this is important if we are to understand the present passage, which is in many ways the climax of the letter.

'We are citizens of **heaven**', Paul declares in verse 20. At once many modern Christians misunderstand what he means. We naturally suppose he means 'and so we're waiting until we can go and live in heaven where we belong'. But that's not what he says, and it's certainly not what he means. If someone in Philippi said, 'We are citizens of Rome', they certainly wouldn't mean 'so we're looking forward to going to live there'. Being a colony works the other way round. The last thing the emperors wanted was a whole lot of colonists coming back to Rome. The capital was already overcrowded and underemployed. No: the task of the Roman citizen in a place like Philippi was to bring Roman culture and rule to northern Greece, to expand Roman influence there.

But supposing things got difficult for the Roman colonists in Philippi. Supposing there was a local rebellion, or an attack by the 'barbarian' tribes to the north. How would they cope? Their best hope would be that the emperor himself, who after all was called 'saviour', 'rescuer', would come from Rome to Philippi to change their present somewhat defenceless situation, defeat their enemies, and establish them as firmly and gloriously as Rome itself. The emperor, of course, was the ruler of the whole world, so he had the power to make all this happen under his authority.

That is the picture Paul has in mind in verses 20 and 21. The church is at present a colony of heaven, with the responsibility (as we say in the Lord's Prayer) for bringing the life and rule of heaven to bear on earth. We are not, of course, very good at doing this; we often find ourselves weak and helpless, and our physical bodies themselves are growing old and tired, decaying and ready to die. But our hope is that the true saviour, the true Lord, King Jesus himself will come from heaven and change all that. He is going to transform the entire world so that it is full of his glory, full of the life and power of heaven. And, as part of that, he is going to transform our bodies so that they are like his glorious body, the body which was itself transformed after his cruel death so that it became wonderfully alive again with a **life** that death and decay could never touch again.

Knowing this will enable Christians to 'stand firm in the Lord' (4.1); and now we can see more clearly what that means. It doesn't just mean remaining constant in **faith**. It means *giving allegiance to Jesus, rather than to Caesar, as the true Lord*. Paul has described the church, and its Lord, in such a way that the Philippians could hardly miss the allusion to Rome and Caesar. This is the greatest challenge of the letter: that the Christians in Philippi, whether or not they were themselves Roman citizens (some probably were, many probably weren't), would think out what it means to give their primary allegiance not to Rome but to heaven, not to Caesar but to Jesus – and to trust that Jesus would in due time bring the life and rule of heaven to bear on the whole world, themselves included.

This is the sense in which they must copy Paul (verse 17). He has described how he cast aside his Jewish privileges in order to gain King Jesus (verses 4–11). They couldn't copy him exactly; few if any of them were Jewish. They must think out, and so must we, what this allegiance to Jesus will mean in terms of the other claims to allegiance that press upon us.

As they, and we, engage in this, we must also heed the warning of verses 18–19. All around the church, then and now, are people whose behaviour is conditioned by the world of the senses. It's possible that Paul is hinting that even some Christians end up behaving like this, but the main thrust of the passage is to warn the church against pagan behaviour. The argument is quite like that of 1 Corinthians 6.12–20, particularly 6.14. The fact that God is going to give **resurrection** life to our bodies means that we shouldn't regard them at the moment as the most important thing. We shouldn't be determined by their various appetites, as though our stomachs were our gods. That way lies destruction; the present body, after all, will die, and if we worship it we are entering a **covenant** with death itself. The **Messiah**'s cross (verse 18) stands in front of that path, to turn us back and point us to life.

Take some time to reflect on the way in which your church faces challenges from the world all around. What would it mean for your community really to live as a colony of heaven?

PHILIPPIANS 4.2–9

Celebrate in the Lord!

[2] I have a special appeal which goes jointly to Euodia and Syntyche: please, please, come to a common mind in the Lord. [3] (And here's a request for you too, my loyal comrade: please help these women. They have struggled hard in the gospel alongside me, as have Clement and my other fellow-workers, whose names are in the book of life.)

⁴Celebrate joyfully in the Lord, all the time. I'll say it again: celebrate! ⁵Let everybody know how gentle and gracious you are. The Lord is near.

⁶Don't worry about anything. Rather, in every area of life let God know what you want, as you pray and make requests, and give thanks as well. ⁷And God's peace, which is greater than we can ever understand, will keep guard over your hearts and minds in Messiah Jesus.

⁸For the rest, my dear family, these are the things you should think through: whatever is true, whatever is holy, whatever is upright, whatever is pure, whatever is attractive, whatever has a good reputation; anything virtuous, anything praiseworthy. ⁹And these are the things you should do: what you learned, received, heard and saw in and through me. And the God of peace will be with you.

You never know when it's going to happen. Two people who one day are good friends, working alongside each other in the church or community, can suddenly get across each other. A sharp word from one, half-heard by the other; a bitter response, said hastily and without quite meaning it; then the slamming of doors, the face turned away in the street, the sense (on both sides) of hurt so great, and offence so deep, that nothing can mend it. I remember my grandfather, a pastor himself, telling me of such things. I in my turn have had to deal with a few such incidents, and I guess most pastors have done the same.

It is particularly sad and tragic when it occurs within a Christian community where the whole ethos ought to be one of mutual love, forgiveness and support; but the chances are that since each one will accuse the other of being the first to break this code, neither is prepared to back down. It then calls for a certain amount of what in international relations is called 'shuttle diplomacy' on the part of a pastor or wise friend before any progress is made.

But a word addressed in public to both parties might just break the deadlock (though you'd have to know what you were doing; it might make it worse). We assume from verse 2 that Paul knew what he was doing. Two women in Philippi, Euodia and Syntyche, have fallen out, and he's appealing publicly for them to come to agreement. The commands of 2.1–4 were not, then, simply addressed to the church in general, though that was true as well; they had a particular case in mind.

These things are better dealt with sooner rather than later. I was talking yesterday to a sensible lady, a mother and grandmother, who told me that her golden rule was never to let more than two days' ironing pile up. After that it would be too daunting to contemplate. In the same way, something that needs to be ironed out within the Christian community should be tackled as quickly as possible, before resentment solidifies and cannot be softened and melted. The present disagreement between Euodia and Syntyche must have been going on for some time, since Paul must have heard about it from Epaphroditus. Maybe, he thinks, only a word from the **apostle** himself will now produce some change.

Who, then, is the 'loyal comrade' to whom he appeals for help on the ground in this pastoral dilemma? We don't know. Perhaps it was Epaphroditus himself, who was going to take Paul's letter back to Philippi; this mention here would then give him the authority to act in Paul's name. Or perhaps it was one particular church leader who Paul knew very well and who the rest of the church would recognize when addressed like this.

After this brief aside for a particular problem, Paul turns to his real final command before he moves towards the end of the letter. Everything comes under the great heading in verse 4: celebrate in the Lord!

Often the word here is translated 'rejoice'. We normally understand that word today, I think, as meaning something that happens inside people, a sense of joy welling up and making them happy from within. All that is important, and is contained within Paul's command; but in his world and culture this rejoicing would have meant (what we would call) public celebration. The world all around, in Ephesus, Philippi, Corinth and elsewhere used to organize great festivals, games and shows to celebrate their gods and their cities, not least the new 'god', Caesar himself. Why shouldn't the followers of King Jesus celebrate exuberantly? It's only right; and celebrating Jesus as Lord encourages and strengthens loyalty and obedience to him.

At the same time, it's interesting that he at once says that the public image of the Christian church should be of a gentle, gracious community (verse 5). Exuberance must not turn into mere extrovert enthusiasm which squashes sensitive souls and offends those who are by nature quiet and reserved.

The three main things that will come into line if the celebration is both joyful and gentle are the prayer which overcomes anxiety (verses 6–7); the patterns of thought which celebrate God's goodness throughout creation (verse 8); and the style of life which embodies the **gospel** (verse 9).

Anxiety was a way of life for many in the ancient pagan world. With so many gods and goddesses, all of them potentially out to get you for some offence you mightn't even know about, you never knew whether something bad was waiting for you just round the corner. With the God who had now revealed himself in Jesus, there was no guarantee (as we've seen) against suffering, but there was the certainty that this God was ultimately in control and that he would always hear and answer prayers on any topic whatever. People sometimes say today that one shouldn't bother God about trivial requests (fine weather for the church picnic; a parking space in a busy street); but, though of course our intercessions should normally focus on serious and major matters, we note that Paul says we should ask God about *every* area of life. If it matters to you, it matters to God. Prayer like that will mean that God's peace – not a Stoic lack of concern, but a deep peace in the middle of life's problems and storms – will keep guard around your heart and mind, like a squadron of soldiers looking after a treasure chest.

The command in verse 8, to think about all the wonderful and lovely things listed here, runs directly opposite to the habits of mind instilled by the modern media. Read the newspapers: their stock-in-trade is anything that is untrue, unholy, unjust, impure, ugly, of ill repute, vicious and blameworthy. Is that a true representation of God's good and beautiful world? How are you going to celebrate the goodness of the creator if you feed your mind only on the places in the world which humans have made ugly? How are you going to take steps to fill your mind instead with all the things that God has given us to be legitimately pleased with, and to enjoy and celebrate?

Finally, reflect for a moment on Paul's command in verse 9. It is one of the most demanding ethical commands anywhere in the Bible – not so much for those who receive it, though no doubt it's that as well, but for the person who gives it. Which of us could say, after staying in a town for a few weeks, that the way to be a good Christian was to do exactly what we ourselves had done?

As so often, Paul weaves into apparently brief and unconnected strands of thought a theme which turns, teasingly, this way and that. Where does 'the peace of God' come from (verse 7)? Why, from 'the God of peace', of course (verse 9). Get to know the one and you'll have the other.

PHILIPPIANS 4.10-13

The Hidden Secret

[10]I've been having a great celebration in the Lord because your concern for me has once again burst into flower. (You were of course concerned for me before, but you didn't have an opportunity to show it.)

[11]I'm not talking about lacking anything. I've learnt to be content with what I have. [12]I know how to do without, and I know how to cope with plenty. In every possible situation I've learned the hidden secret of being full and hungry, of having plenty and going without, and it's this: [13]I have strength for everything in the one who gives me power.

It was very dark and gloomy that March. There was still snow in the air, and sometimes on the ground, until midway through the month. The sun seemed hardly to peer out from behind grey clouds, and a sharp north-easterly wind blew in off the sea, keeping the temperatures not far above freezing point.

Then, a few days before Easter, there was a sudden change. The wind shifted, the skies cleared, and suddenly there was a warmth in the air. But the best of it was what happened in the little garden right outside the kitchen window. The daffodils which had remained as bare green stalks up to that point suddenly burst into flower. They seemed to radiate colour and light in themselves, whether or not the sun was on them. At last the world seemed to have turned a corner. Spring – and Easter – were on the way.

That's the image Paul uses in verse 10. After what had seemed a long time, as he sat there in prison in Ephesus with only a few friends and colleagues looking after him, suddenly Epaphroditus had come to town looking for him. He brought news of the church in Philippi; they were facing suffering and various difficulties, but they were firmly loyal to Jesus, and still deeply grateful to Paul for all that he had given them in bringing the **gospel** to them. As a token of it, they were now sending him this gift of money – presumably a quite substantial gift, since it would hardly have been worth while sending a messenger with a small amount.

For Paul, Epaphroditus's arrival was like spring flowers suddenly bursting into bloom, telling him the Easter **message** once more. He is, of course, eager not to imply any criticism of the Philippians for not sending the message, and the money, sooner; this was the first chance they'd had. But in a world without electronic communication, there was simply no other means of knowing how the church was getting on, whether they were still kindly disposed towards him (or whether, having faced serious persecution, they were angry with him for getting them into such a mess).

Paul is quick to say, as well, that his deep gratitude for the money didn't mean he was the sort of person who would grumble or moan at God if he wasn't kept well supplied with creature comforts all the time. On the contrary: God has put him through a tough school in which he has learned one of the most important lessons of life: contentment (verse 11).

Many other philosophers of the time spoke of contentment. They usually, though, developed the idea in terms of self-sufficiency. You should find resources within yourself, they said, so that you could smile at the fluctuating fortunes which life threw at you. Paul has a different view: I am strong enough for anything, he says – *because of the one who gives me strength* (verse 13). He leaves it open as to whether 'the one' in question means God, or Jesus the **Messiah**, but it seems more likely to me that he means God himself – the God, of course, who we know in Jesus.

Paul often speaks of the energy or power which he found welling up within himself, and which, as he declared, all came from God. He tells the Corinthians that he worked harder than any of the other **apostles**, but insists that it wasn't him, it was God's grace at work in him. He tells the Colossians that he works hard 'with all the energy which he inspires within me'. There is no doubt that Paul would have struck many people as something of a human dynamo. He achieved more in a comparatively short time – his main public ministry, including the letters, probably lasted not much more than ten years at the most – than most people achieve in a long life. He suffered hardships and faced dangers that most people then, and most today, can't even imagine. But his testimony in the middle of it all rings down through history to our own day: 'I have strength for everything in the one who gives me power.'

As with the previous section about Epaphroditus (2.25–30), we gain here a window on Paul as a very human Christian, facing difficulties and troubles, and having to learn the hard way how to cope with them. No instant or easy solutions for him. No casual 'leave-it-all-to-God' approach, ignoring the real problems of Christian living and ministry. No: the steady schoolwork God had set him, of finding out the secret of having plenty or having nothing. And this is the secret, as with everything else for Paul: the God he knew in Jesus the Messiah enabled him to face everything with a strength that came from outside. That's a promise for anyone and everyone who is prepared to go to the same school and learn the same lesson.

PHILIPPIANS 4.14-23

Closing Thanks and Greetings

[14]But you did the right thing by entering into partnership with me in my suffering. [15]Indeed, as you people in Philippi know well, when the gospel was getting under way and I was moving on from Macedonia, there wasn't a single other church, except yourselves, that entered into a two-way partnership with me, giving and receiving. [16]Yes: when I was in Thessalonica you sent help to me, not just once but twice.

[17]I stress that it isn't the gift I'm interested in. My concern is that you should have a healthy profit balance showing up on your account. [18]For myself, I've received full payment, and I'm well stocked up. In fact, I'm full to overflowing, now that I have received from Epaphroditus what you sent. It's like a sacrifice with a beautiful smell, a wor-

thy offering, giving pleasure to God. [19]What's more, my God will meet all your needs, too, out of his store of glorious riches in Messiah Jesus. [20]Glory be to our God and father for ever and ever, Amen!

[21]Give my greetings to all God's people in Messiah Jesus. The family with me here send their greetings. [22]All God's people send you greetings, especially those from Caesar's household.

[23]The grace of the Lord Jesus, the Messiah, be with your spirit.

Sometimes when you get to the end of a novel or short story, there is a moment when something is revealed that makes sense of a mood, a motive, a feeling that has been in the narrative all along. At last we understand why that man was so sad when his dog died. At last we grasp the reason why the old woman had never trusted her sister. Or whatever it is.

Philippians ends like that: at last we understand the full extent of why Paul is so grateful for the partnership in the **gospel** which this church in particular has exercised. It isn't just that they have now sent him money, with Epaphroditus as their willing messenger. It is that this has continued a habit which goes back right to the beginning. This, we see, is why the whole letter has the warm tone, the sense of deep trust and affection, that we have sensed throughout.

When Paul says 'as the gospel was getting under way' (verse 15), he is clearly referring to his ministry in Greece. Sometimes he writes as though the move to Greece (described in Acts 16.9–12) marked a completely new beginning; although he had been preaching and planting churches in Asia Minor (modern Turkey) for some while, he seems to have had a sense that when he came in to Europe he really was in new territory, and that if the gospel took root here it would prove in a further sense just how powerful it was. These, after all, were the Macedonians and Greeks, who had given the world one of its greatest cultures to date! And the Philippian church was the first of those churches on Greek soil.

It was the first and only church, in fact, to continue supporting Paul financially after he'd left them and gone on. Thessalonica was the next main place he visited (Acts 17.1–9), and while he was there they sent him financial help. Only when he got down as far as Corinth did he set up shop and work to pay his own way (not without some continuing help from Philippi) – a fact which, ironically, the Corinthians seem to have held against him (2 Corinthians 11.7–11).

He continues here to show both his gratitude for the gift and his anxiety lest anyone should think he is really in this business for the money. This continued to be a problem in the early church. There were many wandering teachers and philosophers in the ancient world who would go from place to place selling their ideas, and many of them came to be regarded as crooks and cheats. Paul is concerned, quite naturally, not only not to be that sort but to be seen not to be that sort. He therefore has to devise ways of saying 'thank you', and showing his deep gratitude, while making it clear that what matters is the partnership that the gift expresses.

He therefore declares, using the bookkeeping metaphor once more, that what's actually happened through their giving to him is that their own 'account' – presumably in God's eyes – has received a healthy credit balance as a result. Paul was not worried about speaking in this way about Christians doing things which pleased God. He wasn't suggesting for a moment that they were thereby earning their salvation, that they were being 'justified by works'; rather, that God was delighted that their **faith**, hope and love were finding this practical expression.

To rub the point in, he uses in verse 18 a picture from the Old Testament laws about **sacrifices**. Again and again the biblical regulations for how to offer sacrifices in the **Temple** speak of those sacrifices in the language Paul uses here: 'a beautiful smell, a worthy offering, giving pleasure to God'. Paul would, of course, have agreed with the psalmist: God doesn't really smell the aroma that a burning sacrifice gives off, and he isn't impressed simply by people going through the motions of the Temple cult (see Psalm 50.7–15). What really gladdens God's heart is the generous **spirit** which proceeds from love and trust. And all this means that he can promise the Philippians what he himself has found to be true: those who trust God in this way can be certain that he will supply all their needs as well (verse 19).

The letter ends with greetings, grace and glory: greetings to and fro within the church; the grace of the Lord and king, Jesus himself, freely available to all his people; but, as always, glory to the one true God, the father, for ever and ever. Paul adds 'Amen', and his hope would be that we today would do so too.

COLOSSIANS

COLOSSIANS 1.1–8

Thanksgiving for the Gospel's Work

¹Paul, an apostle of Messiah Jesus by God's purpose, and Timothy my brother; ²to God's holy people in Colossae, the Messiah's faithful family; grace to you and peace, from God our father.

³We always thank God, the father of our Lord, Messiah Jesus, when we pray for you, ⁴because we've heard of your faith in Messiah Jesus and the love you have for all God's holy people, ⁵because of the hope which is kept safe for you in the heavenly places. You heard about this before in the word of truth, the gospel ⁶which has arrived on your doorstep – just as, in fact, it's producing fruit and growing in all the world, as it has been among you, from the day you heard it and came to know the grace of God in truth. ⁷That's how you learnt it from Epaphras our beloved fellow slave. He's a loyal and faithful servant of the Messiah on your behalf. ⁸He it was who gave us the news about your love in the spirit.

When Susan bought the house, there wasn't much growing in the garden. A few tatty little shrubs; a mouldy rosebush or two; a tree that had been bent sideways by a storm and left to grow crooked. It was a depressing sight.

A few days after she'd moved in, a friend came to visit, and brought some seeds for the garden. They were special, he said; not what you'd expect. Once you'd sown them and watered them, plants would grow vigorously, and would quickly cover a large area with beautiful flowers. But that wasn't all. Hidden under the leaves would be a delicious fruit. When that appeared, and ripened, then you'd know the plants had come to stay.

Within a week or two the garden was transformed, and Susan decided to get rid of the old plants and let the new ones flourish. They quickly filled the small space with colour and perfume. She telephoned her friend. What on earth was this new plant? It wasn't in any of the gardening books she'd ever seen. Ah, he said, it's new. It's transforming gardens everywhere. You're part of a whole new world.

Now I don't think there really is a plant like that (though I'm such a poor gardener that I can't be sure). I tell the story because it's a scene like that that Paul has in mind as he starts the short letter to the Christians in Colossae. At this stage, Paul is most likely in prison in Ephesus, on the seacoast of modern Turkey; he's writing to the new church in Colossae, about a hundred miles inland. It's probable that the short letter to Philemon was on its way to Colossae at the same time; the present letter includes a mention of Philemon's slave, Onesimus (4.9). Onesimus is going back to Colossae, and to Philemon's household, along with Tychicus, to whom Paul is entrusting the letter we are now reading.

The main thing Paul wants to say can be summed up quite simply in terms of the gardening illustration, which he himself uses in verse 6. He is delighted to hear that the wonderful new plant of the **gospel** has been planted in Colossae, and that it's bearing fruit and growing, as indeed it is doing in the rest of the world. Since Paul himself is responsible for bringing the plant to this part of the world, he wants them to know that he's thanking God that it's taking root with them, and he wants to tell them how to nurture it and help it to bear more fruit.

The fruit, in fact, has already begun to appear, and it's interesting to see that this is what Paul focuses on when he tells them how he heard about the new church coming into being. He doesn't say that he's heard about their new learning and wisdom; he does of course want them to grow in understanding and wisdom, but that's not the tell-tale first sign of life. He doesn't say that he's heard about their new-found holiness and obedience to a strict new moral code; he does indeed want them to live a new sort of life, but that will come in due time. He puts his finger instead on the key thing, the fruit that appears quietly but surely within a genuine Christian community soon after it's been planted. Epaphras, he says (a man from Colossae who has come back to Paul in Ephesus) has told us about 'your *love* in the **spirit**' (verse 8). That's the sign.

This love doesn't simply mean that they all (as we might say) have good feelings about each other. They may or they may not. What matters is that the behaviour which marks out so much of the world – lust, anger, lies and so on, which split up familes and communities – is being replaced by kindness, gentleness, forgiveness and an acceptance of one another as members of the same family, even where there were major differences of race, background and culture. This, as far as Paul is concerned, is the true sign of God at work, and he is thrilled and grateful to hear about it.

How has this come about? The seed which was planted in Colossae was what Paul describes as 'the **word** of truth of the gospel' (verse 5). When Paul thinks of someone – himself, or in this case Epaphras, or anyone else – talking to people about King Jesus, the **Messiah** of Israel who is now the Lord of the world, he doesn't think of them simply conveying information, as though one computer was talking to another. This word is powerful. When it is spoken, God himself works through it, spreading the plant of new life, colour, fragrance and fruit in every place. The word of the gospel is 'producing fruit and growing'. This phrase reminds us both of Jesus' parable of the sower (Mark 4.8) and, way back beyond that, of God's command in creation to 'be fruitful and multiply' (Genesis 1.28). As we shall see, the gospel doesn't just produce a new religious experience for those who might like such a thing. It brings about something much greater: nothing less than new creation.

If the key tell-tale sign of that new creation is the love that marks out the Christian community, Paul can also speak of the three main features of Christian living: **faith**, hope and love. As in the famous passage in 1 Corinthians 13, so here in verses 4–5 these three stand out. They are there in the individual Christian, and in the community, from beginning to end: the faith which reaches out to grasp what God offers in King Jesus; the love which binds the community together; the hope that looks eagerly forward to the time when God completes what he began in Jesus. Paul has heard that this is all there in Colossae, and verses 3–8 declare that he is repeatedly thanking the God who has done it all. The garden is in good shape, and he's delighted.

The first sentence of the letter (verses 1–2) is a reasonably standard letter-opening. But Paul, as usual, fills the regular form with new content. God and Jesus, God and Jesus: they are there in his thinking, his writing, his praying, and even in his formal letter-opening. He and Timothy are writing to Colossae because they are following God's will, living as servants of King Jesus. The Colossian church is part of the same family; and what Paul most longs for is that God's grace and peace should reach out and enfold the new Christians in the small inland town.

The opening of the letter serves equally well as an opening to everyone who reads it today. Our prayer should be that, through reading and praying our way through it, the same grace and peace will reach out and embrace us too.

COLOSSIANS 1.9–14

Prayer for Wisdom and Gratitude

[9]For this reason, from the day we heard it, we haven't stopped praying for you. We're asking God to fill you with the knowledge of what he wants in all wisdom and spiritual understanding. [10]This will mean that you'll be able to conduct yourselves in a manner worthy of the Lord, and so give him real delight, as you bear fruit in every good work and grow up in the knowledge of God. [11]I pray that you'll be given all possible strength, according to the power of his glory, so that you'll have complete patience and become truly steadfast and joyful.

[12]And I pray that you will learn to give thanks to the father, who has made you fit to share the inheritance of God's holy ones in the light. [13]He has delivered us from the power of darkness, and transferred us into the kingdom of his beloved son. [14]He is the one in whom we have redemption, the forgiveness of sins.

We watched, holding our breath, as the mother duck left the pond at the head of her brood.

There were seven ducklings in all: four black ones and three yellow ones. They were lively and squeaky, scuttling to and fro. For days they had swum about with their mother in the little pond. Now it was time for her to take them to the nearby lake.

This meant danger. To get there they had to cross a main road and make their way through a park where dogs, cats, larger birds and several other predators would be watching. Fortunately, in this city at least, local residents are prepared for this moment and make sure that traffic comes to a stop to let the little procession pass through. They reached their destination safely. But we were left marvelling at the mother's apparent calm confidence as she led her little family through potential hazards and on to the larger world where she would then bring them up to maturity.

Paul, in prison in Ephesus, must often have felt like a mother duck. Here was he in a little church, just starting up, full of energy and enthusiasm but hardly yet aware of the great dangers and problems that were to be faced. He can't even be with them in person to guide them and teach them. The mother duck has to rely on instinct – her own, and that of her recently born babies – to see them through. But ordinary human instinct alone won't get the young church through to maturity. Human instincts are important, but they remain earthbound. When people become Christians, God implants into them a new sense of his presence and love, his guiding and strengthening. This sense needs nurturing and developing. New Christians need to understand what's happening to them, and how they must co-operate with the divine **life** that's gently begun to work in them.

Paul, in prison, can help this process in two ways: by writing, as he is doing, but supremely by prayer. He may not be with the Colossians in person. But the God who is with them is also with him, and in the mystery (and hard work) of prayer he can help their progress towards Christian maturity. That is what he's been doing; so, it appears later, has Epaphras (4.12–13). And in this paragraph he tells them what they have been praying for as they think of Colossae. Whether you're a new Christian yourself, needing to grow in the faith, or a Christian leader, wanting to nurture those in your care, Paul's prayer for the new church in Colossae provides a wonderful pattern.

The foundation of what he prays for is that the new Christian instinct may become firmly implanted in them. Just as the mother duck wants her brood to be able to work out for themselves how to feed, to avoid danger and to live wisely in a threatening environment, so Paul longs to see young Christians coming to know for themselves what God's will is (verse 9). They need 'wisdom and spiritual understanding'; not just book-learning (though some of that may help) or human traditions (though they are often useful, too), but a deep inner sense of who they now are, of the newly created human life which they have received from God, and of what will nurture it or harm it. Christian teachers can talk till they're blue in the face, but unless their hearers have this inner sense of wisdom and understanding, this awareness of the true God loving them and shaping their lives in a new way, it won't produce genuine disciples.

With that in place, however, Paul's prayer passes to two other things: behaviour and bearing fruit (verse 10). The new instinct implanted in the Christian will lead him or her to a new lifestyle, which delights God not least because it reflects at last his glorious intention for his human creatures.

There are two lies which the world often tells about God's intention for human behaviour. First, people say that God doesn't want us to have a good time; second, they say that even if we try to live as he wants all we'll ever get is a grudging approval. People often imagine that God is eager to spot the slightest wrongdoing and tell us off for it. This verse shows how wrong both of these are. God's intention is for human life to flourish and bear fruit: what Paul said in verse 6 about the **gospel**, God's powerful **word**, he now says again about the people themselves in whose hearts and lives that word is doing its work. And when this happens God is personally delighted. Paul often declares that genuine Christian living gives God pleasure. It is we, with our little **faith**, who have imagined him to be grumpy and hard to please.

But if this is to happen, the new life that's been implanted in Christians has to show itself in the form of energy, power and strength to live in the new way. That, too, is promised, and that too is what Paul is praying for. God's power has already delivered us from the kingdom of darkness and transferred us into the **kingdom** of his son, Jesus. That same power is now available to continue the work of bringing our lives into conformity with the new world which opens up before us.

When Paul speaks of God rescuing people from one kingdom and giving them another one, and of 'redemption' and 'forgiveness' as the central themes of that rescue operation, he has the **Exodus** from Egypt in mind. What God has done in Jesus, and is now doing for them, is the new Exodus, the great moment of setting the slaves free. To become a Christian is to leave the 'Egypt' of sin and to travel gratefully towards the promised inheritance.

Why 'gratefully'? Because the climax of Paul's prayer is that the young Christians will learn the art of thanksgiving. He will, in fact, mention this over and over again; it's a central theme of the whole letter. What Paul most wants to see growing in the church, as a sign of healthy Christian life on the way to maturity, is gratitude to God for the extraordinary things he's done in Jesus, and the remarkable things he is continuing to do in the world and in their lives.

Spontaneous gratitude of this kind is a sign that they are coming to know and love the true God, as opposed to some imaginary one. Gods that people invent can't compare with the true one when it comes to overflowing generosity. Paul would say to us, as he said to the young Christians in Colossae, that a life lived in the presence of this God will be a life full of thanksgiving. Or have we forgotten who our God really is?

COLOSSIANS 1.15–20

In Praise of Jesus Christ

[15]He is the image of God, the invisible one,
   the firstborn of all creation.
[16]For in him all things were created,
   in the heavens and here on the earth.
Things we can see and things we cannot,
   – thrones and lordships and rulers and powers –
all things were created both through him and for him.

[17]And he is ahead, prior to all else
   and in him all things hold together;
[18]and he himself is supreme, the head
   over the body, the church.

He is the start of it all,
   firstborn from realms of the dead;
   so in all things he might be the chief.
[19]For in him all the Fullness was glad to dwell
   [20]and through him to reconcile all to himself,
   making peace through the blood of his cross,
through him – yes, things on the earth,
   and also the things in the heavens.

I flicked the switch to turn on the television. I didn't know what the programme would be; I was tired at the end of a long day and just wanted to relax for a few minutes.

The sound came on a little before the picture appeared. A voice said, simply, 'This is the head.'

At once – still before the picture appeared – I found myself wondering what sort of a 'head' this might be. Was the programme about archaeology, with people looking at a human skeleton? Or was it perhaps about a small animal or insect? Or was it about a school or college, introducing us now to its principal? Was it about a particular musical instrument (the scroll and peg-box of a violin is called the 'head')? Was the programme showing us some coins, and pointing to the side where the monarch's head appears? Was it about the source of a river? Or the top of a foaming pint of beer?

Actually, it was none of these. It was about a new type of tape recorder, where the 'head' is the device which converts electric signals into recorded form. And no doubt there would have been other meanings that could have appeared as well.

The poem we are now looking at – and I've laid it out like a poem so you can see how it 'works' – is based on the different meanings of the Hebrew word for 'head'. As in English, so in Hebrew, the relevant word can carry several different ideas, and Paul is cleverly exploring and exploiting some of them. Watch how it works.

Jesus **Christ**, he says, is the *firstborn*. That's the first meaning, which comes twice (in verses 15 and 18).

Jesus Christ is *supreme* (verse 17). I've translated it here as 'ahead' to hint at the same point.

Jesus Christ is the *head* of the body, which is the church (verse 18).

Jesus Christ is the *beginning* (also verse 18).

By now you'll probably have noticed something else about this poem. It has carefully balancing sections. The first section ('He is the image of God . . . the firstborn . . . for in him . . .') matches, and is balanced by, the third section ('He is the start of it all . . . firstborn . . . for in him . . .). The middle section, in between these, holds the two outer sections together, looking back to the first and on to the second.

Now all this is fascinating simply as an exercise in clever writing (and actually there's much, much more going on as well which we haven't got space here to explore). Part of growing up as a Christian is learning to take delight in the way in which God's truth, whether in physics or theology or whatever, has a poetic beauty about it. But of course Paul isn't writing this poem just to show off his clever intellectual fireworks, or to provide a sophisticated kind of literary entertainment. He's writing this (or, if the poem was originally written by someone else, quoting it) in order to tell the Colossians something they badly need to know. What is it?

What they need to know above all, if they are to grow as Christians, increasing in wisdom, power, patience and thanksgiving, is *the centrality and supremacy of Jesus Christ*. The more they get to know, and know about, Jesus Christ, the more they will understand who the true God is and what he's done; who they are as a result; and what it means to live in and for him. Much of the rest of the letter, in fact, is an exploration of the meaning of the poem. Look on to 2.3, for instance, where Paul declares that all the treasures of wisdom and knowledge are hidden in Christ himself.

It's worth, then, going quite slowly through the poem and pondering the depths of meaning that are to be found in it. Christianity isn't simply about a particular way of being religious. It isn't about a particular system for how to be saved here or hereafter. It isn't simply a different way of holiness. Christianity is about Jesus Christ; and this poem, one of the very earliest Christian poems ever written, is as good a place to start exploring it as any. This is what the Colossians needed to know, and we today need to rediscover it.

There are three things in particular which the poem points us to about Jesus Christ and about what God has done in and through him.

First, it's by looking at Jesus that we discover who God is. He is 'the image of God, the invisible one'. Nobody has ever seen God, but in Jesus he has come near to us and become one of us.

If there is somebody sitting in the next room, I can't see them because there's a wall in the way. But if there is a mirror out in the hallway, I may be able to look out of my door and see, in the mirror, the mirror-image of the person in the next room. In the same way, Jesus is the mirror-image of the God who is there but who we normally can't see. We may be aware of his presence; many people, many religions, many systems of philosophy have admitted there is 'something or somebody there'. But with Jesus we find ourselves looking at the true God himself.

The great thing about that is that the more we look at Jesus, the more we realize that the true God is the God of utter self-giving love. That's why this poem comes right after Paul's prayer that the Colossians will learn how to be grateful to God. When you realize that Jesus reveals who God is, gratitude is the first and most appropriate reaction.

Second, Jesus holds together the old world and the new, creation and new creation. The 'salvation' or 'redemption' on offer in Christianity is sometimes described as if it meant that the old world, the ordinary world of creation we all live in, was worthless – or, worse than worthless, was itself evil, perhaps the creation of an evil deity, a devil. Some people, recognizing that this won't do (creation is full of beauty, power and sweetness as well as pain, bitterness and evil), have tried to say that evil isn't really all that important; or perhaps, in some more extreme philosophies, that evil and pain don't really exist. Getting this balance right, it seems, is very difficult. But this poem does it brilliantly.

Jesus Christ, says the poem boldly, is the one through whom and for whom the whole creation was made in the first place. This isn't just a remarkable thing to say about an individual of recent history (which shows how very quickly the early Christians came to see Jesus as one who had been from all eternity the agent of the father in making the world). It is also a remarkable thing to say about the 'natural' world. It was his idea, his workmanship. It is beautiful, powerful and sweet because he made it like that. When the lavish and generous beauty of the world makes you catch your breath, remember that it is like that because of Jesus.

But it's also full of ugliness and evil, summed up in death itself. Yes, that's true too; but that wasn't the original intention, and the living God has now acted to heal the world of the wickedness and corruption which have so radically infected it. And he's done so through the same one through whom it was made in the first place. This is the point of the balance in the poem. The Jesus through whom the world was made in the first place is the same Jesus through whom the world has now been redeemed. He is the firstborn of all creation, *and* the firstborn from the dead.

Third, Jesus is therefore the blueprint for the genuine humanness which is on offer through the **gospel**. As the head of the body, the church; as the first to rise again from the dead; as the one through whose cruel death God has dealt with our sins and brought us peace and reconciliation; and, above all, as the one through whom the new creation has now begun; in all these ways, Jesus is himself the one 'in whom' we are called to discover what true humanness means in practice. We have so often settled for second best in our human lives. Jesus summons us to experience the genuine article.

There is much more that could be said about this wonderful poem. I hope what we've already said will encourage you to explore it further and meditate on it more deeply. But let me end with a pointer, which is in fact another key to the meaning of Colossians as a whole. In the Judaism of Paul's day, quite a lot that he has here said about Jesus had already been said about the rather shadowy figure of 'wisdom'. Part of Paul's point is precisely this: if it's wisdom you want, Jesus is where you have to look. What that meant for the Colossians we shall see as we go along. What it means for the twenty-first century is up to each of us to explore, with delight and – yes, once again – with gratitude.

COLOSSIANS 1.21–23

Reconciled and Firm in Faith

[21]So what about you? Well, there was a time when you were excluded! You were enemies in your thinking, and in wicked behaviour. [22]But now he has reconciled you in the body of his flesh, through death, in order to bring you into his presence holy, blameless and without any accusation.

²³This assumes, of course, that you keep firmly on in the faith – by which I mean, solid on your foundations, and not shifting from the hope of the gospel which you heard. This gospel, after all, has been announced in all creation under heaven! And this is the gospel of which I, Paul, became a servant.

People come from all over the world to see it, but I would have been just as happy to stay away.

On the edge of Minneapolis, in the United States, is a shopping centre so vast that there is room for an entire fun-fair in the middle of it. The centre is called 'The Mall of America'. People who like shopping love the Mall. You can spend all day – no, all *week* – there, and not visit the same shop twice. You can also, of course, spend all your money there, and many people do. But I'm not a great shopper. I went there to buy a pair of shoes and almost at once I got lost.

Fortunately, there were maps on nearly every corner. I spotted one and lurched towards it. It swam before my eyes. How could I make sense of it? Then, at last, I saw the little red blob which meant 'You Are Here'. At last I could get things in focus and find my way.

Paul is aware, I think, that the poem he's just set out in verses 15–20 is quite overpowering. Many ordinary Christians might read it, or hear it read out loud, and think, 'Well, that sounds impressive, but what's in it for me?' So at once he brings things into focus. This section might be headed 'You Are Here'. If the poem is like a map of the entire cosmos, the whole story of creation and redemption, the present verses indicate where the ordinary Christian is located on the map.

The first thing Paul says is: not too long ago, you weren't on the map at all! God's great purposes for the world were going ahead, and you were outside in the cold! You were 'excluded', he says, or 'estranged'. What does he mean?

Paul believes that the purposes of the creator God, to reconcile the whole creation to himself, had been entrusted to Israel, the promise-bearing people. But people living in Colossae, and most other places in the world, were outside Israel. They were **Gentiles**, worshipping idols rather than the one true God, ignorant both of God's saving purposes and of how they themselves could share in the benefits of those purposes.

Their lives reflected the gods they worshipped. Their thinking was distorted, getting muddled and into one misunderstanding after another. Their behaviour, in consequence, was out of line with the wonderful, enriching human existence that the living God designed for his image-bearing creatures. (Don't be fobbed off with the idea that 'sin' or 'wickedness' means 'having a good time when God wants you to have a rotten time'. That's a typical example of the muddled thinking that people get into when they ignore or forget the true God.)

But now the Colossians find themselves inside. They are on the map, part of the action. Indeed, the very words 'but now' – one of Paul's favourite phrases – say it all. Once you were ... outside, muddled, sinful; *but now* God has acted, and everything is different. And being brought 'inside', being put on the map, has as its chief delight and privilege the fact of being brought into the very presence of God himself.

At this point the picture of a shopping mall breaks down completely. What we should think about instead is a royal palace, or perhaps a temple, or a combination of the two. The Colossians – and all of us who have come into the family of God from outside – are like people who had been on the street outside the royal palace, and who have suddenly been told they are invited in to appear before the king. Or, if you prefer, they are like people who have been outside the **Temple**: they were impure, unfit to appear in the presence of the God who lived in the Temple. Now, suddenly, they have been told they are summoned in, indeed, welcomed in. How has this happened? How can they come in without something happening to them?

What has happened to make them ready for the presence of this king, this God, is the death of King Jesus. Paul doesn't here explain in detail how precisely Jesus' death achieves this, but he declares that through it we have – another of his big words – 'reconciliation'.

We know about 'reconciliation' as something precious and wonderful that can happen when two family members who squabbled years ago, and haven't spoken since, are brought together, putting the past behind them. Or perhaps it's something we long for when two segments of a community, a village, a country or a tribe are brought to accept and trust one another again after a time of warfare or feuding.

Well, it's like that between humans and God, only more so. It is as though all the enmity, all the hostility, that was keeping humans and God shut off from each other did its worst to Jesus on the cross. That's how Paul puts it in Ephesians 2.16, which is like this passage only a bit more fully spelt out. According to the poem of verses 15–20, Jesus was and is the place where true God and true humanity meet. Now we see the result; that in his death God and the human race were brought together, were reconciled. Now, astonishingly, we are free to approach the living and holy God without a stain on our character. That is the heart of Paul's **gospel**.

But the effects of the gospel don't happen automatically. Christians, who have come into this experience of being ushered into the presence of the holy God, can't simply sit back and do nothing. They must 'keep firmly on'; they must now take responsibility for their own growth to maturity in **faith**. Like a house being built up brick by brick, secure in the knowledge that the foundations have been properly laid, Christians must develop their life of faith, hope and love (see verses 4–5) on this foundation and not somewhere else. Becoming a Christian can't be a one-off experience which then remains just as a memory of a wonderful moment. It must be something which continues day by day.

Without that 'keeping firmly on', even the original experience may seem remote and strange. You may start to question whether it was 'real' or not in the first place. But if you 'continue' you will know it is, because as the building grows and takes shape it will show by its stability that the foundations are indeed there, and are solid.

The foundation is of course the gospel itself (see verses 5–6), the good news of King Jesus. And here Paul says an extraordinary thing about this gospel. It was announced, he says, not just to a few men, women and children in a few small parts of the Mediterranean world – but to 'every creature under **heaven**'. What can he mean?

He can only mean that when Jesus of Nazareth rose from the dead, as king and Lord of the world, a kind of spiritual shock wave ran right through the entire cosmos. This was a new kind of event. Nobody had ever gone down into death before and come up the other side. God's new creation had begun: Jesus is, as the poem had said (verse 18), the beginning, the firstborn from the dead, and now he is bringing to birth the reconciliation and renewal of all things in heaven and on earth. The gospel doesn't just make its way from one person to another. When somebody hears the **message** and believes it, what is happening is that the new creation, which has already come into existence and already claims the entire cosmos, is becoming real and actual in another specific instance.

This gives Paul, in turn, a map, on which he can see the words 'You Are Here'. His work is not the struggling attempt to persuade a few more people to believe an unlikely story, to have a new spiritual experience. He is the servant of the message – the message which declares that new creation has come into being and that you are invited to share in it. This gospel is for the individual – you, me, and every man, woman and child; not despite the fact that it's about the renewal of the whole world, but because of it.

COLOSSIANS 1.24–29

The Messiah, Living within You

²⁴Right now I'm having a celebration – a celebration of my sufferings, which are for your benefit! And I'm steadily completing, in my own flesh, what is presently lacking in the Messiah's afflictions on behalf of his body, which is the church. ²⁵I became the church's servant, according to the terms laid down by God when he gave me my commission on your behalf, the commission to fulfil God's word.

²⁶This word declares the mystery that was kept secret from past ages and generations, but now has been revealed to God's holy people. ²⁷God's intention was to make known to them just what rich glory this mystery contains, out there among the nations. And this is the key: the Messiah, living within you as the hope of glory!

²⁸He is the one we are proclaiming. We are instructing everybody and teaching everybody in every kind of wisdom, so that we can present everybody grown up, complete, in the Messiah. ²⁹That's what I am working for, struggling with all his energy which is powerfully at work within me.

If trees could talk, imagine the sort of conversation that might go on.

Here is an old, weathered and seasoned oak tree, talking to the small sapling that's just started to grow up nearby.

'Soon it will be autumn, and the winds will start to blow hard and cold. But you'll be safe. I'll take care of you. The wind can do its worst to me. I don't mind if I have to lose a few branches here and there in the process. What matters is that while you're young and weak I should take the full force of the wintry wind on myself, and let you grow in safety'

That's something like what Paul is saying to the young church in verse 24. Unless we think of it like that, it seems very puzzling: how can Paul's sufferings be for the benefit of the young church? It seems as though (to change the image) he is drawing the enemy fire; as long as he stays in prison, those who are opposed to the **gospel** imagine they have gunned it down. In concentrating on Paul, and giving him a bad time, they are not bothering about the young Christians who are growing up around him, in Ephesus itself and in the outlying towns and villages.

But Paul develops this already rather strange idea a stage further. He says that in his sufferings he is completing 'what remains of the king's afflictions'. Here the image of trees sheltering one another won't take us quite far enough. We need to examine the 'royal' theme, the idea of the king and his people.

Near the heart of Paul's vision of reality, we find a sense of identification between the king, Jesus the **Messiah**, and his people. This underlies the present passage, much of the rest of the letter, and a good deal in his other letters as well.

Most human illustrations break down at this point, but we can get some idea of what Paul means through pictures we are familiar with. When an ambassador goes to a foreign court to represent a king or president, it is as though the king or president had paid the visit in person. In some societies, if someone wrongs or harms a person, it is regarded as though they had committed the offence against the whole family. When the head of a large company or organization makes a public statement, we don't treat it as a mere private opinion, but as the view of the whole organization in question. None of these is exactly the same as what Paul has in mind, but they are signposts pointing in the right direction.

For Paul, part of the meaning of Jesus' messiahship is that the Messiah represents all his people, so that *what is true of him becomes true of them*. This is what he has in mind when he talks about people being 'in' the Messiah, 'in' the king. Though he never loses sight of Jesus of Nazareth as a specific individual, whose individual death and **resurrection** were the turning point of all history, the reason why they formed that turning point is precisely that, because he was and is Israel's Messiah, when he died and rose *his people died and rose with him*. This is central to what he will go on to say in chapters 2 and 3.

In our present passage, this identification of the Messiah and his people takes three forms, one in each paragraph.

First, in verses 24 and 25, Paul sees his own sufferings as part of what he calls 'the king's afflictions'. He is drawing on an ancient Jewish belief according to which a time of great suffering would form the dark valley through which Israel and the world must pass to reach the **age to come**. This suffering would be the prelude to the age of the Messiah, the age of the king. For Paul, the Messiah himself had already passed through the suffering, and had brought the age to come into being. But because this new age is still struggling in tension with the '**present age**', there is still suffering to be undergone. This is not to be seen as an *addition* to the king's own suffering; rather, it is to be seen as an *extension* of it. Paul is thus content to take his share of suffering, in prison for the sake of the gospel. It will help to complete the afflictions through which the new age will emerge in its full and final form. And at the moment – as with the old tree and the saplings – it will shelter the young church from the wintry winds of persecution. It will draw off the enemy fire.

This isn't just about passing through dark times and eventually hoping to come out somewhere. The hope Paul wants the Colossians to share is much more specific than that. God's secret plan for the rescue of the whole world – to bring the treasure of his new age to the entire creation – has now come to light in the news about the king. Paul is eager, now that the secret is out, to bring as many people as possible to share its benefits. If in his death and resurrection the king has already brought the new age into being, his own risen life is the source of the church's hope.

Every individual Christian, in fact, has this hope within his or her own self. The reason is simple: Jesus the Messiah, the king, lives by his **spirit** within each one. He has already entered into the new state of 'glory', God's full intention for his human creatures. Because his own life is given to all his people, they can be confident in their hope of sharing this glory as well.

That's why Paul can't stop talking about King Jesus. The church in Colossae has never met Paul, but he says in verses 28–29 that if they want to know what he spends most of his time doing, it is this: he announces Jesus as king and Lord. And he does it with the aim of bringing as many as possible to mature Christian living 'in the king', 'in **Christ**'.

It is possible to be 'in Christ' and be immature, not understanding fully what it means, not grasping the new possibilities and responsibilities set before us. The road to maturity is through teaching and instruction. What you need for that is teachers with boundless energy; and what you need for that is the life-giving power of the king himself, working within Paul then and Christian teachers ever since. Great demands will be made on them. But the energy which Jesus inspires within them is always more than equal to the task.

COLOSSIANS 2.1-7

God's Hidden Treasure – Messiah Jesus!

[1]You see, I'd like you to know just what a struggle I am having on behalf of yourselves, and the family in Laodicea, and all the people who don't know me by sight. [2]I want their hearts to be encouraged as they're brought together in love. I want them to experience all the wealth of definite understanding, and to come to the knowledge of God's mystery – the Messiah! [3]He is the place where you'll find all the hidden treasures of wisdom and knowledge.

[4]I'm saying this so that nobody will deceive you with plausible words. [5]Though I'm away from you in person, you see, I am present with you in the spirit, and I'm celebrating as I keep an eye on your good order, and the solidity of your faith in the Messiah.

[6]So, then, just as you received Messiah Jesus the Lord, you must continue your journey in him. [7]You must put down healthy roots in him, being built up brick by brick in him, and established strongly in the faith, just as you were taught, with overflowing thankfulness.

In many adventure stories such as Robert Louis Stevenson's famous *Treasure Island*, the plot hinges on the discovery of an ancient chart or map. The people who have found it realize that, if only they could understand and follow it, it would lead them to buried treasure that had been hidden for many years, perhaps centuries. They would be rich beyond their wildest imagination.

There are always problems. Some people think the map is imaginary, a fantasy. Others say the hero isn't reading it right, isn't understanding its secret codes. Inevitably, there are dangers to be faced, both in the journey to the far-off island and in the threat from other people who want to stop them getting there first. But we know how the story should end. We want the hero to surmount the dangers and difficulties, find the treasure and get it safe back home.

Towards the end of chapter 1 (verses 26–27) Paul speaks of God's secret plan, a plan that has lain hidden, like a map in a locked and dusty cupboard, for ages and generations. Now, quite suddenly, it has come to light in the events concerning Jesus, the **Messiah**. Paul is in possession of the map, and is inviting as many people as possible to come with him to find the treasure.

In the present passage he tells them plainly what the treasure is; what dangers they will face as they try to make it their own; and which route they must take to get to it. After what he's already said, we shouldn't be surprised that the theme all through is King Jesus, King Jesus, King Jesus. He is the secret plan; he is the treasure; he is the one 'in whom' they will be able to ward off danger; he is the one 'in whom' they must find their way to the goal. Let's look at each in turn.

First, Jesus the Messiah, the king, the '**Christ**', is the heart of God's secret plan. Nobody, no matter how learned or devout they had been before, could have guessed that, when the one true God unveiled his blueprint for bringing the whole world under his sovereign and saving rule, that blueprint would consist of a man suffering the cruel punishment that the Romans used for rebel slaves and revolutionary leaders – and then rising from the dead three days later. But once these astonishing events had unfolded, Paul and others came to see that this map did indeed make sense.

And the treasure that was hidden, to which the map would lead them, was again Jesus Christ himself. We can't stress often enough that Paul didn't see the human plight like so many do today, that people need to have some kind of spiritual experience and that Jesus the Messiah could supply it if they wanted. It was that King Jesus himself was the centre of the cosmos, the key to **life** and the universe, the image of the invisible God, the clue to genuinely human existence.

Christianity, says the old slogan, is Christ. Put him in the middle of your picture of the world, and the world will stop spinning in incomprehensible circles and begin to make sense. Find him, and you've got the treasure. It may take you a while to get it all out of the treasure chest and inspect it, but when you do you'll find – so Paul is saying in verse 3 – that all the wisdom and knowledge that ever there was finds its full meaning in him. He is, quite simply, what it's all about.

This is of course fighting talk for many people in today's world, who regard Jesus as a curiosity of history, to be safely left behind by people who want to 'get on' in our brave new culture. This was actually a threat in the first century as well, and Paul will have more to say about alternative views in the following sections. But already in verse 4 he indicates that people are quite likely to try to deceive the new Christians with arguments that sound plausible but are in fact designed to lead them astray. Just like the treasure seekers being lured off course by people who are out to stop them finding their goal, Paul knows that young Christians – and not-so-young ones – are liable to face the scorn and the sneering of the wider world.

It may be even harder to deal with the apparently friendly persuasion of people who take pity on them. Fancy being taken in (they will say) by something as peculiar as that! Whoever heard of a crucified Jew being the Lord of the world? After all (they would continue), we've already got gods in this town who protect us and guide us. There are plenty of well-known religions about if you want new spiritual experiences. And the Roman emperor himself – well, he's a god, isn't he? So surely you can't be serious?

And such talk would be backed up by the strongly implied hint and threat: people like us don't do this sort of thing. And people who do, despite this warning, may be making trouble for themselves . . .

Paul is anxious, since he can't be personally present with the little churches, that they should be able to line themselves up in battle array against any such attack. The 'good order' and 'solidity' he speaks of in verse 5 would probably sound like military formation and readiness to defend. They mustn't be caught off their guard.

In particular, they must go forward in the direction they've already begun. Being a Christian is like riding a bicycle; unless you go forward, you'll fall off. And going forward as a Christian means, once more, nothing more nor less than going forward 'in Christ', in the king. You need, Paul says, to be rooted in him, like a tree in good soil. You need to be built up in him, like a solid house going up brick by brick on firm foundations. That's how you were taught, and that's how you must do it. At every stage of Christian experience, what you most deeply need is not something other than the king himself. You always need more of him. He is what it's all about.

And – the same note again, as so often in Colossians – you must have thanksgiving overflowing in your lives. Then you'll know that you're on the right track. In addition, your lives will be attractive and delightful to people outside. They will look in puzzlement at these people living a whole new sort of life. That, too, is part of the point of it all. Isn't that how the **gospel** is likely to spread?

Verses 6 and 7 sum up the centre of what Paul wants to say. Everything that's come so far – in particular the wonderful poem of 1.15–20 – prepares for this. Everything that's going to come after this leads on from it. It might be a good idea, as you read and pray your way through this letter, to write out these two verses and pin them up somewhere where they can remind you not only of what Paul was talking about, but also of what he might want to say to you today.

COLOSSIANS 2.8-12

Beware of Deceivers

[8]Watch out that nobody uses philosophy and hollow trickery to take you captive! These are in line with human tradition, and with the 'elements of the world' – not with the Messiah. [9]In him, you see, all the full measure of divinity has taken up bodily residence. [10]What's more, you are fulfilled in him, since he's the head of all rule and authority.

[11]In him, indeed, you were circumcised with a special, new type of circumcision. It isn't something that human hands can do. It is the Messiah's version of circumcision, and it happens when you put off the 'body of flesh': [12]when you're buried with him in baptism, and indeed also raised with him, through faith in the power of the God who raised him from the dead.

One of the greatest philosophers of the seventeenth century was John Locke (1632–1704). He rejected several previous schemes of thought and sketched out a way of looking at the world which influenced the thought not only of his native England but also of Europe, and of America as well.

What isn't so well known is that Locke was actively involved in politics. He opposed the rule of the English kings Charles II and James II, at a time when revolutionaries went about at the risk of their lives. He made many enemies, though he managed to survive, and to see William of Orange come to the throne after James.

Now supposing – as may indeed have happened, but I am making it up for the sake of the point – that somebody who strongly opposed the teaching of John Locke had wanted to warn other people against him. In the style of the time, when pamphlets and tracts were circulated, often using colourful language and imagery, such a person might have said: 'Take care that nobody Locks you up with their philosophy or empty deceit!' In other words, it would have been easy for someone to make a pun on his name, to rub in the warning, which would really mean: Take care not to follow the teaching of Locke, or you'll find yourself as good as in prison!

Paul has done something rather like this in verse 8. Take care, he says, that nobody 'takes you captive'. But the word he uses for 'takes captive' (*sylagogon*) is very close to the word 'synagogue' – just as 'Lock' and 'Locke' are very close. (Unfortunately, there isn't a way of expressing this 'synagogue' pun in English.) And when we look at the warning he then gives, and see how it works out, there is every reason to suppose that, just as my imaginary seventeenth-century thinker would be warning people against John Locke, so Paul is warning the Colossians against being lured into the synagogue.

Why would he need to do that? Well, think of what had happened in Galatia. There, Jewish zealots had told the new converts that in becoming Christians they had only got half of what they needed. What they now ought to do, to complete the experience, was to be **circumcised** and to keep the **law** of Moses.

Paul spent the whole of the letter to the Galatians arguing that this was a complete misunderstanding, and that to go this route would land the young Christians in real trouble. They would be buying into a system which wouldn't do them any more good than the paganism they had just left behind. And now he's anxious – Colossae wasn't, after all, that far from Galatia – that similar people would come to the little church there, and perhaps in Laodicea and Hierapolis as well, with the same dangerous message. Most towns or districts had a synagogue, and at least a small Jewish community. Don't get drawn into it, he says. It'll be a form of captivity for you.

It will, in fact, drag you down to the level you were on before. Now that the **Messiah** has come, and has been marked out by God, through his death and **resurrection**, as Israel's king and the world's true Lord, a form of Judaism that refuses to acknowledge him is no better than yet another type of 'philosophy'. There were plenty of those around already. It's just empty deceit, built up out of mere human traditions. (Jesus himself made the same accusation against his contemporaries, in, for instance, Mark 7.) It builds up its case by means of 'the elements of the world' (see Galatians 4.1–11). And the main problem with it is that it's 'not in line with the king'. Whatever new idea someone comes up with, this is the acid test: does it have Jesus, the Messiah, the Lord, as its centre and focus? If not, beware.

Paul then explains more particularly why, if you've already got Jesus the Messiah as your Lord, you don't need to be 'completed' by any other system at all, and certainly not by a Judaism that refuses to acknowledge him. The two main things he says (the first in verses 11–12 and the second in verses 13–15), are that you certainly don't need to get circumcised, and that the **Torah**, the law of Moses, has no claim on you. These were the two very things the 'opponents' in Galatia had been insisting on! And now Paul is outflanking them.

But he begins with something even more important – one of the most important points in all of Christianity from that day to this. 'In him', he says (verse 9) – that is, of course, in Jesus, in the king – 'all the full measure of divinity has taken up bodily residence.' Here he's referring back, of course, to what he said in 1.19, towards the climax of the great poem; only now he spells it out slightly further, and applies it. What he means, simply, is that Jesus was and is not simply a fully human being (though he is); not simply a man remarkably 'full of God' (though he's that as well). He was and is the bodily form taken by God himself, God in all his fullness. He isn't a demigod, half divine and half human. He doesn't have a human body and a divine **spirit**, or mind. He can only be properly understood as the human being who *embodies*, or 'incarnates', the fullness of divinity.

This meant, of course, that all the pagan deities and divinities were at once upstaged. The pagan world sometimes spoke of demigods, or heroes who became divine around the time of their death. Jesus wasn't like that. He was the real thing. But it also meant that Paul was cutting the ground away from any potential attack from the Jewish side. Jews, including Paul himself, believed that God was one. Many, perhaps Paul himself in his pre-Christian days, would have said that therefore Jesus couldn't be divine; that the best that could be said of his followers, particularly the ex-pagan ones, was that they should now go on to discover the true God, the creator, the sovereign Lord of all. Not so, says Paul: if you want to find the true God, you need look no further than Jesus himself. Verse 9 is perhaps the sharpest and clearest statement in all his writings of his belief that Jesus quite literally embodies the one true God, God in all his fullness.

If you possess Jesus, therefore, you are already 'fulfilled' in him, and no rule or authority can go, as it were, over his head and impose itself on you. He *is* the head of them all. The church in our own day still needs to recapture that vision of the supremacy of King Jesus over all other authority.

And in particular – the point of immediate relevance to Paul's young churches, if Galatia is anything to go by – you don't need to get circumcised. Why not? Because *you already have been* – in the only sense that really matters. The true circumcision, Paul boldly declares, isn't what people do physically to a male body. It's what happens when you're 'buried with the king' in **baptism**, and also raised with him through God's power.

Paul will shortly explain more about what that means. For the moment, the main point is that instead of, as in circumcision, 'putting off' a small piece of physical flesh, baptism (the mode and sign of entry into the Christian community from the very earliest days to the present) is all about 'putting off' an entire way of life, an entire sphere of existence. It means dying to the old world and coming alive to God's new one. How can people who've already done that ever suppose they need to go back and do something extra, something trivial by comparison?

Few of us are likely to face, as the young Christians in Paul's world did, a pressure to convert to Judaism. What are the religious and philosophical attractions in your world that are most likely to draw new Christians away from the 'fulfilment' they already have in the king? What arguments do you think Paul would use to combat them?

COLOSSIANS 2.13–19

The Law and the Cross

¹³In the same way, though you were dead in legal offences, and in the uncircumcision of your flesh, God made you alive together with Jesus, forgiving us all our offences. ¹⁴He blotted out the handwriting that was against us, opposing us with its legal demands. He took it right out of the way, by nailing it to the cross. ¹⁵He stripped the rulers and authorities of their armour, and displayed them contemptuously to public view, celebrating his triumph over them in him.

¹⁶So don't let anyone pass judgment on you in a question of food or drink, or in the matter of festivals, new moons or sabbaths. ¹⁷These things are a shadow cast by the coming reality – and the body that casts the shadow belongs to the Messiah. ¹⁸Don't let anyone rule you out of order by trying to force you into a kind of fake humility, or into worshipping angels. Such people will go on and on about visions they've had; they get puffed up without good reason by merely human thinking, ¹⁹and they don't keep hold of the Head. It's from him that the whole body grows with the growth God gives it, as it's nourished and held together by its various ligaments and joints.

The crowd was already angry, and it got angrier as we watched. They had come together to protest about the shooting down of a Korean jumbo jet over the south-west Pacific. Most of them had lost relatives or friends in the disaster. And, whether rightly or wrongly, they were blaming the Soviet Union for it.

First they simply chanted and waved banners. But then someone spotted, in the forecourt of a garage, a Soviet car. Suddenly it became the symbol of all that they were angry about. They set upon it with crowbars and hammers, and smashed it to pieces. Then, just as they were finishing, someone produced from somewhere a Soviet flag, with its hammer and sickle. With glee they tore it to pieces and set fire to it. They celebrated over it triumphantly.

These were not mere empty gestures. They were powerful symbols of what the crowd most wanted to say. This was not the only time in recent history that we have seen such demonstrations.

The ancient world didn't have cars. Instead of flags they often had 'standards' – military emblems stuck on poles. But they knew how to celebrate triumphs over hated enemies, and how to do so with maximum symbolic impact. In a world without electronic or printed media, victorious armies and generals would demonstrate to the folks back home what a splendid victory they had won, by bringing back the 'spoils of war'. This would consist of all the booty they'd captured; a long and bedraggled line of prisoners; and, if possible, right at the end of the line, the king of the nation they'd just defeated. Then, as the climax of the party, the king would be ceremonially executed. Just like burning a flag, only more so.

When the Romans crucified Jesus of Nazareth, under the sign that said he was 'King of the Jews', that's more or less what they thought they were doing. They hadn't thought he was worth taking back to Rome. He hadn't, after all, been leading an army, or a serious military revolt. But every crucifixion of a rebel 'king', even a strange one like Jesus, was another symbolic triumph for Rome, and hence, in Jewish eyes, for the power of paganism as a whole. Anyone looking at the cross of Jesus with a normal understanding of the first-century world would think: the rulers and authorities stripped him naked and celebrated a public triumph over him. That's what they normally did to such people.

Now blink, rub your eyes, and read verse 15 again. On the cross, Paul declares, *God* was stripping the armour off *the rulers and authorities*! Yes: *he* was holding *them* up to public contempt! God was celebrating *his* triumph over the principalities and powers, the very powers that thought it was the other way round. Paul never gets tired of relishing the glorious paradox of the cross: God's weakness overcoming human strength, God's folly overcoming human wisdom (as he says in 1 Corinthians 1).

But here the sharp edge of what he's saying is that all the authorities and rulers that might try to take over your **life** are included in the ones shamed by the triumph of God in the cross of Jesus. In particular, the 'handwriting that stood over against us' has nothing more to say. This refers to the Jewish **law**, the law of Moses, which prevented **Gentiles** from getting in to God's people, and condemned Jews for breaking its commands. When Jesus was nailed to the cross, Paul declares, this written code was nailed there with him. Now it has nothing more to say to those who belong to Jesus. 'There is therefore no condemnation', as Paul says in Romans 8, 'for those who belong to King Jesus.' He's forgiven you all the sins and offences that might have counted against you. In dying with him you have come out from under them all, and from all the condemnation they might have pulled down on your head.

The immediate result of this is that when people try to entice you into particular styles of piety and devotion other than single-minded devotion to Jesus, you need take no notice. Once again, the things he mentions are typical of the way Jews, not least out in the Gentile world, tried to order their life of worship: festivals, new moons and sabbaths. They're irrelevant, Paul declares. They are like the shadows cast by a solid object, and the solid object is what matters, not the shadows. The solid object, the 'substance', is of course the **Messiah** himself, the king. The celebrations of the Jewish law look forward to him. Now that he's here they simply aren't needed any more.

Nor is there any need for elaborate and complex systems of prayer and meditation. Of course, there are all sorts of techniques which may help us to be attentive and obedient to God, to listen to his voice and seek his help in bringing our rebellious lives under his authority. There's nothing wrong with finding out what methods of prayer suit you best. But what Paul is talking about here is a system imposed by a certain sort of teacher, who goes on and on about visions he or she has had, living in a fantasy world in which only that one type of spiritual experience really 'counts'. Such people – and they're as frequent in the modern world as in the ancient – may then try to disqualify, or rule out of order, others who haven't had their type of experience, or who don't see why they should dance attendance on that type of teaching.

Paul's answer is quite simple, and by now we ought to know what it is before he says it. All you need is **Christ**, the king. Hold fast to him and you'll have all you need. He is the head of the 'body', as Paul said already in 1.18. The body gets its life from the head, through what it thinks, sees, smells, hears, eats and drinks. In the same way, the body which is the church is nourished and sustained, in all its joints, muscles and ligaments, not by embracing this or that new teaching, but by holding fast to the Head.

Can you sense the sigh of relief the Colossians may have experienced on being reassured that they were already complete in Christ and didn't need anything else, just more of what they already had? Have you ever come under pressure to 'add' to your Christian experience? Do you know the same sigh of relief yourself?

COLOSSIANS 2.20—3.4

Dying and Rising with Christ

[20]If you died with the Messiah, coming out from the rule of the 'worldly elements', what's the point of laying down laws as though your life was still merely worldly? [21]'Don't handle! Don't taste! Don't touch!' [22]Rules like that all have to do with things that disappear as you use them. They are the sort of regulations and teachings that mere humans invent. [23]They may give an appearance of wisdom, since they promote a do-it-yourself religion, a kind of humility, and severe treatment of the body. But they are of no use when it comes to dealing with physical self-indulgence.

[31]So if you were raised to life with the Messiah, search for the things that are above, where the Messiah is seated at God's right hand! [2]Think about the things that are above, not the things that belong on the earth. [3]Don't you see: you died, and your life has been hidden with the Messiah, in God! [4]When the Messiah is revealed (and he is your life, remember), then you too will be revealed with him in glory.

'I'll just be two minutes,' I said, leaving my friends on the street corner while I went to fetch the car. It was raining, and we'd just come out of the theatre.

But I wasn't two minutes. I took more like ten. They were starting to worry that I'd had an accident. I hadn't. I had driven out of the car park and tried to turn into the street where they were waiting for me. But I wasn't allowed to turn that way. There was a one-way system. I was forced to set off in exactly the opposite direction and to go a long, long way round through narrow, twisting and winding streets before I could find my way back. What looks like the shortest way is often impossible. Sometimes the correct way is what seems the hardest.

Paul is continuing to warn the Colossians about the dangers of being drawn into Judaism, as the Galatians had been. But in this passage he's doing something else as well: he is showing them the way to a genuine, full-blooded holiness. It isn't what might seem the shortest, most obvious way; but it's the way that will bring them where they need to be.

One of the principal appeals of Judaism in the pagan world of the first century was its high moral code. It made heavy demands, and often when people are sick and tired of the murky and immoral world of paganism they are glad to embrace a way of life which offers clear, bright, clean lines. Serious-minded people in a place like Colossae, people who had begun to realize that their pagan gods weren't doing them any good, might well feel that the regulations of the **Torah** itself, and of the numerous explanatory additions that first-century teachers expounded, were going to be a great help to them in finding a new way of life that would leave the messy world of paganism behind once and for all. 'Don't handle this, don't taste that, don't touch this'; the very detail of the regulations, and the severe self-discipline needed to keep them, would make them feel they really must be making advances in their moral and spiritual lives.

Well, says Paul, it may feel like that, but it's an illusion. Go that way, and the street will soon come to a dead end. These are simply regulations that function at a worldly level. You will merely be giving up a worldly self-indulgence of a sensual kind for a worldly self-indulgence of a spiritual kind. A religion that focuses purely on the details of things you're allowed, or not allowed, to touch or eat – he obviously has the Jewish food regulations in mind – is dealing with perishables; and if you want to do business with God you have to get beyond that. In short, when Judaism sets itself against its own **Messiah**, it may well have the appearance of wisdom in the kind of religion it comes up with, but it won't actually attain the goal. It won't succeed in making you genuinely holy, through and through.

For that, you need to go what seems like a much harder and longer route, but it's the one that will get you there in the end. You need to die and be raised. You need, that is, to come out altogether from the 'worldly' sphere presided over by the 'elements of the world', the shadowy powers that operate within the present creation, doomed as it is to decay and perish. You need to belong instead to God's new world, the new creation that is being brought in to replace the old. The truly human life you seek – the life of a genuine, glad holiness that runs right through the personality – is to be found in that new world.

And the **good news** is that, if you belong to the Messiah, you already do belong to that new world. One of the main things Paul longs for new Christians to realize is *what is already true of them 'in Christ'*. Because the Messiah and his people are so closely bound up with one another, he lays it down as a basic principle: what is true of him is true of them. It may not feel like it. Learning to *believe* what doesn't at the moment *feel* true is an essential part of being a Christian, just as learning that I had to drive off in the opposite direction was an essential part of getting where I wanted to be. This is what the life of **faith** is all about.

And the key things that are true of the Messiah, which are already true of those 'in him' whether they feel it or not, are of course the two Paul highlights here: he died, and he was raised from the dead. The two paragraphs of this little section (which together look back to 2.12) make this quite clear. You died with the Messiah; so you don't belong in the old world any more, and regulations that are relevant there aren't relevant for you. You were raised with the Messiah; so you possess a true life in God's new world, the 'upper' or 'heavenly' world. That's where the real 'you' is now to be found.

This isn't a 'super-spiritual' world in the sense of a world which leaves the created order behind for ever. One day God will flood the present creation with the new life which is currently hidden in the heavenly realm. One day Jesus the Messiah, who cannot at the moment be seen within the old world, will appear again – when God transforms the whole cosmos so that what is at present unseen will become visible, and earth and **heaven** be joined for ever in the fulfilled new creation. And when that happens, all those who are 'in Christ', whose present true life is 'hidden with the king, in God', will appear as well, as the glorious renewed human beings they already really are.

Once you realize that, there appears before you the new way towards a genuine, fulfilling holiness. 'If you were raised to life with the king, search for the things that are above!' Learn to think about the things that are above, not the things that belong to the present world of change and decay. In fact, learning to *think*, rather than merely going with the flow of the world on the one hand, or blindly obeying what look like stringent regulations on the other, is part of the key to it all. One aspect of Christian maturity, and certainly one of the road signs on the surprising route to Christian holiness, is that the mind must grasp the truth: 'you died, and your life has been hidden with the Messiah, in God!' Once the mind has grasped it, the heart and will may start to come on board. And once that happens the way lies open to joyful Christian holiness. Don't settle for short cuts.

COLOSSIANS 3.5–11

Old Clothes, New Clothes

⁵So, then, you must kill off the parts of you that belong on the earth: illicit sexual behaviour, uncleanness, passion, evil desire and greed (which is a form of idolatry). ⁶It's because of these things that God's wrath comes on the children of disobedience. ⁷You too used to behave like that, once, when your life consisted of that sort of thing.

⁸But now you must put away the lot of them: anger, rage, wickedness, blasphemy, dirty talk coming out of your mouth. ⁹Don't tell lies

to each other! You have stripped off the old human nature, complete with its patterns of behaviour, [10]and you have put on the new one – which is being renewed in the image of the creator, bringing you into possession of new knowledge. [11]In this new humanity there is no question of 'Greek and Jew', or 'circumcised and uncircumcised', of 'barbarian, Scythian', or 'slave and free'. The Messiah is everything and in everything!

My daughter and I still laugh about her seventh birthday.

It was a Sunday in February. The church we attended, in Canada where we lived then, held a cross-country ski day each year. People came to the morning service, stayed for soup in the church hall, and then set off in groups along different trails, graded according to whether they were fast, medium or slow. We joined the slow group, and very soon found ourselves in a very slow group consisting of just the two of us. She fell down in the soft snow about every thirty strides, and she loved every minute of it as I picked her up again and again, and we carried on.

Eventually, tired but happy, we arrived back at the church much later than we had intended. There was an anxious message from my wife: where were we? The birthday party was due to begin in 20 minutes. We hurried home. Then came the key moment: getting a 7-year-old out of a full skiing suit, and getting her into the full outfit appropriate for a birthday party. Both elements of the process – putting off the old, and putting on the new – were complicated, but finally we managed it and the party went ahead.

Paul sees clearly that if the Christian party in Colossae is to go ahead the young church needs to know very clearly what's involved in putting off the old suit of clothes and putting on the new one. Verses 9 and 10 are the keys to this passage, and this is the image he uses there. In the early church it was frequently the case that a candidate for **baptism** would take off the old suit of clothes they were wearing and then, after coming up from immersion, would be given a new set of clothes to wear. They would be coloured white to signify the purity of the new **life** they were now entering. This may well be in Paul's mind here.

The point is, of course, that there are certain patterns of behaviour which are the common coin of the world that remains ignorant of the God revealed in Jesus. These must be taken off, like a suit of clothes that's inappropriate for the new occasion – like a ski suit at a birthday party, in fact. And the new clothes – the new patterns of behaviour – must be put on in their place. Paul will have more to say about the new clothes in the next passage. Here most of his attention is focused on the old ones that are to be got rid of.

There are two main areas of behaviour which he lists as typical of the old lifestyle that is now to be abandoned. They have to do with sex on the one hand and speech on the other – two central areas of human life, both involving great potential for good and also for evil. In both cases Paul offers a list which includes most of the problem areas. These are practices which are abuses, rather than proper uses, of these two gifts of God. The way to deal with such practices, he says, is quite clear. There is to be no gentle, half-hearted approach to such things, no toying with them as continuing possibilities. They are like vermin that mustn't be allowed into the house in case they poison the food or the water supply. They are not to be pitied. They are to be killed off, put to death.

The catalogue of sexual misbehaviour includes both actions and thoughts. 'Illicit sexual behaviour' is a wide term which includes sexual intercourse outside marriage, whether or not it involves prostitution (as in the ancient world it often might). The other terms are probably not intended each to denote something completely different, but are overlapping ways of referring to sexual lust of all sorts and its gratification outside the God-given context of marriage.

We should note particularly that Paul labels greed (here presumably meaning sexual greed) as a form of idolatry. Sexual fantasies, in other words, are off limits for the Christian, not simply because of the actions they may produce, but because they are in themselves a way of worshipping a false god, the pagan divinity of erotic love. Like all pagan worship, this consists of giving one's allegiance to something in the transient world of present experience, rather than to the living God, the creator. The inevitable result is death.

Paul is just as concerned with sins of speech as he is with sexual sin. (It would be good if today's church could get this balance right.) Both alike inflict serious damage on the one who commits them, those who are immediately affected by them, and the wider community. Again, the list in verse 8 consists of overlapping words for angry and hurtful speech; and in verse 9 he highlights one danger in particular, the telling of lies. The Christian **gospel** is about truth, and there is no place for untruths in the Christian community.

Paul is, of course, concerned for the individual behaviour of every single Christian. But, even greater than this, he is concerned for the well-being of the community as a whole. Sexual misbehaviour can tear a community apart (people often pretend that it's a purely private matter, but it seldom if ever really is); so can malicious and abusive speaking. And the point of the new clothes which the Christian must put on is that the new life is about unity, about the whole community coming together in love. Old divisions must be done away, whether social, cultural, geographical or whatever (verse 11; the 'Scythians' were regarded in Paul's world as the people furthest away from what they regarded as civilization). Jesus the king is present and active in everyone, and indeed in everything. Nothing lies outside the sphere of his sovereign rule.

The key to the new life which Christians are called to live is found in verse 10. The new self 'is being renewed in the image of the creator', and one of the results is new *knowledge*. How does this relate to the instructions Paul is giving them here?

The answer is clear. Paul expects the Christian, as part of his or her renewal in the image of God – in other words, part of their discovery in practice of what it means to be a genuine human being – to be able to see clearly, and understand, the deeper issues involved behind apparently casual sexual behaviour and apparently casual talk. As so often in Colossians, it seems that, contrary to what a lot of people today imagine, being a Christian means learning to think harder, not to leave your brain behind in the quest for new experiences. Thinking straight and knowing the truth are part of what it means to be a truly human being, the sort of human being the gospel is meant to create.

COLOSSIANS 3.12–17

Love, Peace and Thanksgiving

> [12]These are the clothes you must put on, then, since God has chosen you, made you holy, and lavished his love upon you. You must be tender-hearted, kind, humble, meek, and ready to put up with anything. [13]You must bear with one another and, if anyone has a complaint against someone else, you must forgive each other. Just as the master forgave you, you must do the same. [14]On top of all this you must put on love, which ties everything together and makes it complete. [15]Let the Messiah's peace be the deciding factor in your hearts; that's what you were called to, within the one body. And be thankful.
>
> [16]Let the Messiah's word dwell richly among you, as you teach and exhort one another in all wisdom, singing psalms, hymns and spiritual songs to God with grateful hearts. [17]And whatever you do, in word or action, do everything in the name of the master, Jesus, giving thanks through him to God the father.

Here's the acid test for whether Paul is talking sense or not. Read again through the list of sexual and speech-related misbehaviour in verses 5–9. Then read through verses 12–17. Ask yourself this: supposing there was a town in which everybody behaved in the way described in verses 5–9. And supposing, a few miles down the road, there was a town where everybody behaved in the way described in verses 12–17. Which town would you rather live in?

There will always be some cynics who say they would prefer the first. People are free there, they'll say. People are having a good time. All right, they may lose friends now and then. Some people who can't look after themselves may get hurt. But they'll be doing their own thing, living cheerful and robust lives. Whereas the other lot (the same people will say) look like a bunch of wimps. Goody-goodies who can't stand up for themselves. Always saying 'sorry' and singing hymns. This reaction is, I think, quite common in today's world.

But a moment's thought will show how shallow such an approach would be. The practices Paul outlines in the earlier section result in communities – families, villages, whole towns – tearing themselves apart. Unbridled sexual licence and untamed angry speech result in the breakdown of relationships at every level. Some people may fool themselves that they're having a good time in that atmosphere. But again and again, in moments of truth, they will admit that they are lost, confused, lonely and bitter.

Nor are the people Paul is describing in this section a bunch of weak-willed, wimpish people without much to say for themselves. Anyone who thinks that simply doesn't know what they're talking about. Have you ever seriously tried to forgive someone who has wronged you? Have you ever seriously tried to be compassionate and patient? Have you ever tried to let **Christ**'s peace, Christ's word, Christ's name be the reality around which you order your life? If you have, you'll know it's not easy. It takes serious prayer and real moral effort. And people who engage in that effort tend to be people who are also capable of taking difficult decisions and engaging in challenging activities in other spheres as well. Christian behaviour, in other words, makes you more human, not less. Self-indulgence and habitual anger and lying may seem like fun for a while, but they destroy you sooner or later – often sooner.

Of course, there is a question of balance. Some churches are very concerned to stamp out sexual sin, but seem to ignore the positive things that Paul insists should be put in its place (kindness, humility, and the rest). Notice how sexual sin, which often disguises itself as 'love', is a caricature of what real love looks like, as sketched in these verses. A church with no (obvious) sexual sin but which is full of malicious gossip has only swapped one evil for another. Equally, a church where everyone is very caring and supportive but where immorality flourishes unchecked (perhaps precisely because people are afraid to confront it in case they're told they are being 'unloving') is allowing noxious weeds to grow all around the flowers in the garden. You can't select some parts of the picture and leave others. For any of the parts to make sense, they all need to be in place.

Once again, Paul's list of behaviour patterns forms an overlapping sequence. But that doesn't mean, in this case, that we can just glance at them and think, 'Oh yes – he's just saying we should be nice to each other.' (Though of course we should.) Being 'nice' is only the start. It's worth taking a moment and thinking about each word here, asking yourself (or, if you're reading this with a group, asking each other) what sort of actions and words will make each one come true in your life, in the life of your church, in the life of your village or town. Think about them: tender-hearted; kind; humble; meek; ready to put up with anything (the word Paul uses here literally means 'large-hearted').

Remember that with most of these words there are people, like the ones we mentioned before, who will mock the very idea of behaving like this. Remind yourself that to be tender-hearted doesn't mean being sentimental. That being kind doesn't mean being a soft touch. That humility isn't the same thing as low self-esteem. That meekness is not weakness, but is what you get when a powerful wild horse has been tamed (all the same power, but now under control). That large-heartedness doesn't mean letting everyone do what they want with you. Don't let people scoff at the central virtues that make the Christian life what it's supposed to be. Why do you think people do that? Are they, perhaps, threatened by such a dazzling and demanding way of life?

In particular, notice how Paul draws the picture together, again and again, with reference to the Lord, the king, to Jesus himself. Jesus forgave you, so you must forgive; that's what gives you the energy to use love as the belt, or perhaps the outer garment, which holds together and in place all the new clothes that you must put on (verse 14). King Jesus is to be the decider in all your deliberations, and his desire for peace among his people is the key factor (verse 15). His **word** is to be alive within the Christian community; there is always more about the **gospel**, and also about the written gospels, to explore and discover, and different gifts are needed in the community to draw out the meaning and apply it to the church's life (verse 16). And, finally, whatever you do or say must be able to stand having these words written above it: 'In the name of the Lord Jesus'. Settle that in your hearts and minds and a great deal else will fall into place.

COLOSSIANS 3.18—4.1

The Christian Household

[18]Now a word for wives: you should be subject to your husbands. This is appropriate in the Lord. [19]And for husbands: you should treat your wives with love, and not be bitter with them. [20]And for children: obey

your parents in everything; this pleases the Lord. [21]And for fathers: don't provoke your children to anger, otherwise they might lose heart.

[22]A word, too, for slaves: obey your earthly masters in everything. Don't do it simply out of show, to curry favour with human beings, but wholeheartedly, because you fear the Master. [23]Whatever you do, give it your very best, as if you were working for the Master and not for human beings. [24]After all, you know that you're going to receive the true inheritance from the Master as your reward! It is the Master, the Messiah, that you are serving. [25]Anyone who does wrong will be paid back for wrongdoing, and there will be no favourites.

[1]Here's a word, too, for masters: do what is just and fair for your slaves. Remember that you too have a Master – in heaven.

There was once a country ruled by a strict and severe president. He made laws about everything and enforced them rigidly. He laid down what time people were to get up and go to bed. He told them what food they should eat and how to cook it. He made regulations about who could own a car and where and when they could drive it. Nothing was left to chance. The country was tidy, but utterly repressed.

One day, quite suddenly, the president was taken ill and died. His successor declared that things were now going to be very different. All the old restrictions were to be abolished. People were to be free to do as they wished. There was great celebration, and everyone was thrilled to think of all the new possibilities that would open out in front of them.

The next day two cars were coming towards each other down the main street of the capital city. Both drivers were enjoying their new-found freedom; neither had been allowed, up to this point, to drive in this part of town. Neither driver was looking where he was going. The next minute, they had crashed headlong into each other. Fortunately, they weren't going very fast, and both men, though shaken, were unhurt. They stood there, angry and puzzled. Their conversation became a defining moment in the new life of the country.

'Why were you driving on that side of the road?'

'Why shouldn't I drive where I like?'

'But people drive on the right-hand side of the road!'

'Who says?'

'Well, that's the law, isn't it? That's the custom. That's what we do!'

'Not any more, we don't. The president's dead! All his old laws have been torn up. We're free now! We don't have to do what anybody tells us!'

By the time the police arrived, most observers were aware of one thing in particular: you can tear up the old rules if you like, as many as you want, but you'll still need a Highway Code. There have to be ground rules for how and where you drive a car. And – this is the underlying point – if you have a Highway Code you are not *less* free to drive a car. You are *more* free – considerably more free – than if you don't.

The modern Western world in the second half of the twentieth century has given a fair imitation of the repressed country after the death of the old president. New freedoms have burst upon us. The old rule books – the codes and conventions by which people used to order their lives – have gone. We can do what we like. This has been particularly so in the area of relations between the sexes in general, and assumptions about marriage in particular. Millions of people have claimed their 'freedom' to go about things in quite a different way from how their parents did. Any attempt to question this freedom provokes the instant response that surely nobody wants to go back to the days of the old president.

And yet. You would have to bury your head in the sand, stop up your ears and lose all contact with the real world if you wanted to ignore what has happened as a result. The one thing we can certainly say about the parts of the world that have claimed this 'freedom' is that relationships between the sexes, and especially within marriage, are more confused and destructive than ever. All too often 'freedom' has meant the same thing as the freedom of the drivers to drive all over the road without looking. Short-term freedom, maybe, leading to long-term captivity – slavery to chaos, injury and death. Nobody who drifts into a sexual relationship, let alone a marriage relationship, remains 'free' thereafter. We are formed by the relationships in which we live, whether they are wholesome and life-giving or ugly and destructive. How long does it have to be before someone comes to the conclusion that we need a new Highway Code for family relationships?

Of course, many will scream blue murder at the very suggestion. 'Freedom of choice' is one of the idols of our time, and the suggestion of regulating or curtailing it is unthinkable for many people. What they fail to realize is that every exercise of this supposed free choice severely limits all subsequent freedoms. One short 'free' drive down the wrong side of the road could stop you ever being free to drive anywhere again.

What Paul is offering in this passage is a very brief Highway Code for household relationships. It is remarkable for several reasons. Perhaps the first is that he doesn't just tell wives, children and slaves how to behave (as many pagan moralists of his day would have done). Their duties are balanced by the corresponding duties of husbands, parents and masters. This is every bit as revolutionary as what people today often wish he had said – for instance, that all slaves should be freed at once (which was unthinkable in his day, where slaves did much of the work done today by gas, electricity and the internal combustion engine). Rather than dreaming of impossible freedoms, he prefers to offer practical guidelines.

His command to wives has come in for particular criticism. In many translations, the key word comes out as 'submit', and this conjures up in many people's imaginations the image of a downtrodden woman, the victim of her husband's every whim, unable to be herself, to think her own thoughts, to make a grown-up contribution to the relationship. The fact that there are still one or two places in the world where women are treated like that is enough to make some people suggest that this is what Paul intended.

Nothing could be further from the truth, as his parallel command to husbands indicates. Indeed, Paul's own fellow-workers included women, and married couples, where it appears that the women were, in our phrase, 'people in their own right' rather than shadowy figures screened from view by a bossy husband. At the same time, Paul is quite clear that, in the mutuality of respect and love that makes a marriage what it should be, the roles are reciprocal, not identical. It would take a longer section than this one to explore why that is so, or how the differences on either side of the reciprocal relationship should best be worked out in different circumstances or with different people. But these are only, after all, brief guidelines. Paul must have intended his audience to work out the details for themselves, and it's no bad thing if we do so as well.

Of course, there are plenty of places in the world – including some of the places where Christianity is growing fastest – which don't have the problems that the modern West has run into. Readers in such places will perhaps forgive me for addressing in such detail the situation where I find myself. And they will perhaps be alerted to other dangers which we in the West don't face. If we don't allow scripture to challenge us at places where our culture is doing its best to squeeze us into a different pattern, what use is it?

COLOSSIANS 4.2–9

The Fellowship of Prayer

²Devote yourselves to prayer; keep alert in it, with thanksgiving. ³While you're about it, pray for us, too, that God will open in front of us a door for the word, so that we may speak of the mystery of the Messiah – which is why I'm here in chains. ⁴Pray that I may speak clearly about it. That's what I am duty-bound to do.

⁵Behave wisely towards outsiders; buy up every opportunity. ⁶When you speak, make sure it's always full of grace, and well flavoured with

salt! That way you'll know how to give each person an appropriate answer.

⁷Our dear brother Tychicus will tell you all my news. He is a faithful servant, indeed a fellow slave in the Lord. ⁸This is why I'm sending him to you – to let you know how things are with us, and to encourage your hearts. ⁹I'm also sending Onesimus, who is a dear and faithful brother. He is one of your own number. They will tell you everything that's going on here.

The best teachers make sure they get their pupils to take on some responsibility of their own.

It's a lesson some never learn, in school, in church, or in the home. Most people, from quite small children upwards, are ready to rise to the occasion if asked to do something on their own account. Parents, clergy and teachers often hold back from making the request; maybe, they think, they're not ready for it yet; maybe they'll think I'm imposing on them. It's not usually the case. As long as the request is made in the right way, people are glad to be valued sufficiently to be entrusted with responsibility.

We shouldn't miss this flavour in what looks like a routine request for prayer. The Colossians are new Christians. They are taking their early steps in the **faith**. They have many problems to face, many challenges to rise to, many dangers to avoid. Paul is the great **apostle** who has already been half way round the northern Mediterranean, has preached the **gospel** and planted churches, has been beaten and stoned and imprisoned for the gospel, has been the hero and the villain by turns in a dozen major cities. How can *he* possibly ask *them* for help?

But that's exactly what he does. Having begun the letter by telling them that he is thanking God for them, and praying for them, he now draws towards a close by asking them to do the same for him. No matter how senior or respected anyone is in the service of the gospel, they still need the prayers of the most apparently junior, humble and insignificant Christian. (I am speaking, of course, in thoroughly worldly terms; in truth, no Christian is more or less senior or junior, significant or insignificant, than any other, in God's eyes.)

Paul's request for prayer indicates well enough the way in which he continued to see his vocation, in prison though he was. As he thanked God in 1.5 that the **word** had done its work in their community, so he asks them to pray that the same will be true as he carries on his own speaking and writing. He can talk all he likes, but unless God opens the door for the word to go through – the door, we assume, that lets the word into the hearts and lives of individuals and into the places where wider community issues are thrashed out – he will simply be making a useless noise. Paul was under no illusions. You can never take it for granted. The door doesn't open automatically.

What opens the door, again and again, is prayer. I have often found, preaching as a guest in a strange church, that I can sense as soon as I stand up whether the congregation have been praying that I will speak God's word to them, and that they will hear it. I can often sense when they haven't been doing so, as well. Of course, this doesn't absolve the preacher from his or her own prayer, preparation and care in delivery. But there is a strange web of interlocking causes that works when people pray and when the word is announced, and the newest and least experienced Christian is summoned to play his or her part within it. Indeed, they may be expected to take a lead in praying for God's word to be made clear, since that is what they themselves will most need if they are to grow and become strong in faith.

If Paul's job is to make the 'mystery of the king' clear, it is the Colossians' job as well (verses 5–6). They too must learn to speak with grace and 'salt' – presumably meaning that whatever else they do they mustn't be boring! And they must use every opportunity to do so, becoming skilled in the art of real listening to the questions and comments made by puzzled onlookers and being sure they answer the person appropriately, rather than just parroting stock responses. Here as elsewhere Paul longs for them to become mature Christians, able to think for themselves and to speak with the quiet confidence that comes from having thought things through.

To ask the Colossian church to pray for him is to bind them to him with ties of mutual obligation. They have never seen him face to face; but once you have prayed for someone, and once you realize they are praying for you as well, a bond grows up which creates a relationship of love and trust ahead of any personal contact. This bond is further increased by the mention of Tychicus and Onesimus. Paul speaks glowingly of them, not least of Onesimus, the runaway slave now returning to Philemon. They have the task of telling the Colossian church everything that is happening in Ephesus. They will bring news of how Paul is, and of his hopes to visit them before too long.

Paul is just as concerned to maintain his personal relationships with the churches as he is to expound high-flying theology. In fact, of course, the most high-flying things he says in Colossians already point him in this direction. The 'mystery of the king', of which he has spoken so much, is all about the way in which Jesus himself was and is both the full revelation of the one true God and the truly human being. For Paul the thinker to become, and remain, Paul the pastor and Paul the friend in **Christ** – the friend, moreover, who now comes to them with a request for help – should not surprise us. The question is, can we in our day hold together the thinking and writing of great thoughts and the challenge of pastoral care, prayer and concern? If not, perhaps there is something wrong with our great thoughts.

COLOSSIANS 4.10-18

Greetings from Others

[10]Aristarchus (who's in jail with me here) sends you greetings. So does Mark, Barnabas's nephew. You've received instructions about him; if he comes to you, do make him welcome. [11]Jesus Justus sends greetings as well. These three are the only fellow Jews I have among my colleagues working for God's kingdom, and they have been an encouragement to me.

[12]Epaphras, one of your own folk and also one of Messiah Jesus' slaves, sends you greetings. He's always struggling in prayer on your behalf, praying that you will stand firm and mature, and have your minds fully settled on everything that God wants you to do. [13]I can bear him witness that he's gone to a lot of trouble on your behalf, and also on behalf of the family in Laodicea and in Hierapolis. [14]Luke, the beloved doctor, sends greetings; so too does Demas.

[15]Pass my greetings on to the family in Laodicea, and to Nympha and the church in her house. [16]When this letter has been read to you, make sure it's read in Laodicea as well; and you, too, should read the letter that will come on to you from Laodicea. [17]And say to Archippus: 'Take care to complete the commission that you have received in the Lord.'

[18]I'm signing off in my own hand: PAUL.

Remember the chains I'm wearing.

Grace be with you.

As a typical young man growing up in England after the Second World War, I was never taught to sew. I can hardly manage to replace a button on a shirt, let alone do anything more complicated with needle and thread.

But I have sometimes been fascinated by the way in which a small thread, which in itself is not very strong, and can be snapped with one sharp tug, will hold two pieces of cloth together very firmly, and withstand all kinds of pressure, once there are enough stitches in a line, and close enough together. Individually they are weak; together they are strong.

What Paul is doing in these closing greetings is stitching his own little group in Ephesus, in the prison itself and among the friends who visit him there, on to the little group of Christians in Colossae.

Aristarchus, Mark, Jesus Justus, Epaphras, Luke and Demas: six friends with their own stories and journeys, their own joys and sorrows, all supporting Paul. (Mark's earlier story can be found in Acts 13.1–13, where he's called, confusingly, by his other name, 'John'.) Nympha and Archippus: two leaders, we may suppose, in the little church in Colossae, which may after all have numbered no more than a dozen or so, quite possibly in only two or three households. There is no mention of Philemon, as we might have imagined; presumably the fact that he's getting a letter all to himself at the same time made it more tactful for Paul not to single him out here as well. Anyway, Archippus appears to be part of Philemon's household, according to verse 2 of Philemon's own letter from Paul. And then there are Tychicus and Onesimus, travelling the hundred miles or so inland not only to deliver the letter but to provide the first-hand human contact, the major thread that will then bind the two groups together.

Paul's own vulnerability emerges in his remarks about Aristarchus, Mark and Jesus Justus. Paul had been violently opposed by his fellow Jews wherever he had gone – not that he would have been surprised, because that had been his own reaction to the **gospel** before his conversion. Many, even among the Jews who believed in Jesus as **Messiah**, held radically different interpretations of the gospel from his, so that often he felt isolated. These three colleagues, he says here, are his only fellow-workers who are also Jewish. It is a comfort to him. Paul was not, as people often make out, an arrogant man, cocksure in his own rightness. He was deeply human, and this mention of one comfort of this sort reminds us just how many conflicting emotions he must have had to cope with, living the life he did and facing new challenges and dangers every day.

Although Epaphras is staying with Paul, he is another vital thread in all this. His home is in Colossae, but he must have originally heard the gospel from Paul while on a visit to Ephesus, and he in turn became (as we saw in 1.7–8) the evangelist responsible for announcing the **message** to his own people. Now, Paul declares, he has spent the time while he's away from them hard at work on their behalf in prayer. And he, like Paul, is praying for their growth to Christian maturity.

Paul also intends that the other churches in the locality of Colossae should be in touch with them, and should share in fellowship. To that end he has also written a letter to the church in Laodicea, just a few miles away from Colossae. When the two letters have been read, he wants them to swap them over and read each other's. Clearly both letters are not just specific to one location; they are, as we might say, 'circulars'. Interestingly, the letter we call Ephesians (another of the 'prison letters' in the book you are now reading), seems most probably to have been a circular. Since it is similar to Colossians in several ways, it is possible that it was in fact the original 'letter to Laodicea', a copy of which was also kept by the church in Ephesus itself.

But the point Paul is making throughout is the thousand ways in which Christians belong to one another in a fellowship of mutual love, prayer, instruction and service. It is undesirable, and ultimately impossible, for any individual Christian or church to 'go it alone' and imagine they have nothing to gain or learn from other Christians and churches. The greetings at the close of Paul's letters – there are more here than in some, perhaps precisely because he didn't know the Colossians personally and wanted to be sure to bind them to him in love and fellowship – serve as constant reminders to us of what the gospel is all about. Three things stand out: the gospel is not about abstract ideas but about people; in Jesus the word became flesh; and the God who is the main subject of the gospel is known supremely as the God of love.

PHILEMON

Greetings

¹Paul, a prisoner of Messiah Jesus, and Timothy our brother: to our beloved Philemon, our colleague and partner, ²to Apphia our sister, and to Archippus our comrade-in-arms, and to God's people who meet in their house. ³May grace and peace be upon you, from God our father and Messiah Jesus the Lord.

⁴I always thank my God when your name comes up in my prayers, ⁵because I've heard of your love and faithful loyalty towards the Lord Jesus and to all God's people. ⁶My prayer is this: that the partnership which goes with your faith may have its powerful effect, in realizing every good thing that is at work in us to lead us into the Messiah. ⁷You see, my dear brother, your love gives me so much joy and comfort! You have refreshed the hearts of God's people.

Jonathan knew it was going to be a difficult meeting. He had woken up very early that morning and gone through it again and again in his mind. He was quite clear about what needed to be done, but he was equally clear that the others wouldn't see it like that. As chairman of the board he could, of course, put pressure on them to come into line with his plan whether they wanted to or not. But he knew perfectly well that forcing them like that would store up trouble for later. They would be secretly keen to see the plan fail and then say 'I told you so'.

He knew, in addition, that they would have perfectly good reason, in law and company practice, to refuse his proposal. He was wanting, after all, to sign a major contract with a company that had let them down badly in the past. Normally they wouldn't touch them again; indeed, some members of the board still thought they should sue them for what had happened last time. But Jonathan knew, for reasons he couldn't easily explain to them, that the chief executive of that company had undergone a huge change in his personal life and was eager to show that this time he could be trusted. And Jonathan was keen to give him that chance.

He opened the meeting with quite shameless praise for his fellow directors. They had been with him throughout the recent difficulties. They were all in the business together, and had learned to trust one another through thick and thin. He was enormously grateful for their loyalty and personal support. What they had achieved was quite remarkable, and the whole company was grateful to them. And he knew that in the decisions that lay on the table today he could count on them to continue with that loyalty and support, so that the company could go forward and become the even better outfit that it had the potential to be.

Some of Jonathan's colleagues saw at once what was coming, but he was obviously sincere and they could hardly object to being praised. Some basked quietly in the glow, unaware of where it was all leading. And some were wondering if they were going to have to resign.

I suspect that those conflicting thoughts were rather like what Philemon felt when he got this letter from his senior partner. 'Partnership' is the key to the whole letter, and Paul plays on it for all it's worth. Actually, the word he uses for 'partnership' is often translated 'fellowship', but that word could lead us away from the key thing Paul is emphasizing. It could then make us ignore the fact that, as well as warm Christian affection, there is something akin to a business partnership that is linking Paul, Philemon and the others. They are in this together. They share a joint project, and if it's to go forward they must be prepared to stand loyally side by side.

Philemon lived in Colossae, roughly a hundred miles inland from Ephesus; the letter to the Colossians was being sent there at the same time (see Colossians 4.9). He had become a Christian, it seems, through hearing Paul preach, presumably when Philemon was visiting Ephesus. Paul at this stage hadn't been to Colossae itself, but had remained working in Ephesus.

Paul had been thrilled with the way Philemon, a man of some means and influence, had responded to the **gospel**. It had gripped his heart and made him a man of love and generosity. He and his wife, Apphia, and their son, Archippus, had joined Paul in the work of the gospel. They had gone home to Colossae and made their home a place of love and hospitality, where the handful of Christians in the area had begun to meet.

And now Paul had a problem. It seems a simple one to us, but we don't live in his world. Like every person of any substance in that world, Philemon owned slaves. To them, this was as natural as owning a car or a television is for people in the Western world today. Indeed, most people would wonder how you could get on without them. To us, of course, slavery is now abhorrent. To them (as we saw when looking at Ephesians 6 and Colossians 3) it was like electricity, gas or cars. You couldn't imagine society without it. Suggesting you should get rid of it altogether was about as realistic as suggesting today that we should abandon all electric appliances and petrol-fired transport, including cars and planes.

But one of Philemon's slaves had run away. That, in his world, was a capital offence, and many owners would take that severe vengeance. Worse, the slave had probably helped himself to some money as he did so. And he had gone, as a runaway would, to the nearest large city, in this case Ephesus. There, perhaps when the money ran out, he had met . . . Paul. And that's where his story really took off.

The slave's name was Onesimus. (It's a Greek name, so you pronounce the 'e' separately: 'Own–ee–si–mus'.) The name, ironically enough, means 'useful', which was precisely what he hadn't been to Philemon; perhaps Philemon had crossly told him he wasn't worth the cost of his own food. But anyway, Onesimus had now come under Paul's influence; perhaps he had sought him out, having heard the family speak so warmly of him. And he had become a Christian. So eagerly had he embraced the **faith**, and so grateful was he to Paul for telling him about Jesus, that he had started to look after Paul in prison, to attend to his needs with a devotion he'd never shown to his real master. He and Paul had become friends, brothers in the Lord Jesus, close partners in the gospel.

But Paul couldn't shield Onesimus from what had to happen next. Nor could he shield Philemon from it. He was going to make huge demands on them both, and, like the chairman of a company, he was going to come up with a proposal that his partners would instinctively resist, and perhaps even resent. He was going to send Onesimus back to Philemon and ask Philemon to accept him back again without penalty – and perhaps even hint that Onesimus should be set free.

Everything in that society was against it. You can imagine the feelings on both sides. If everybody did that, the world would grind to a halt! Philemon will be the laughing stock of all his friends! If runwaway slaves get rewarded with freedom, then they'll all want to do it! Yes, Paul knew all the arguments. And he outflanked them – with the gospel message of Jesus, King Jesus, the Lord before whom he, Philemon, Onesimus and all others were themselves slaves, household servants.

The reason for it all, and the method by which it had to happen, were contained in the gospel itself. The gospel, after all, isn't simply a message about how people 'get saved' in a purely spiritual way. It's about the lordship of Jesus the king over the real world, over people's real lives, over the difficult decisions that real people face.

The key sentence in this passage, in the middle of all the fine things Paul says about Philemon, is verse 6. This is what he's praying for (often when he tells people what he's praying for when he thinks of them this gives us the clue to the inner meaning of the letter): he's praying that the partnership which he and Philemon share in the gospel will be productive, will have the effect it's meant to. Each element of this matters, so we need to take his rather dense statement and lay out its bits side by side.

The partnership in question is the partnership Paul and Philemon have in the gospel. That is, they are as it were in business together, and must be loyal colleagues. It is the partnership *that goes with your faith*: that is, when people believe the gospel, they are brought into that partnership with all others who believe it. They are members of the board in this business.

This partnership *must have its powerful effect*. When two or three work together in the service of the gospel new things happen, things previously thought impossible. This is what all the partners want; when Paul puts it like this, Philemon will be agreeing with him. Whether he will still agree when he sees what Paul has in mind is another matter.

The effect will be *in realizing every good thing that is at work in us*. 'Realizing' means not only 'recognizing and knowing' but also 'putting into practice'. The gospel itself is at work in Christians by the power of God's **spirit**. As it does its work, it produces new things, good things, new ways of living for individuals, households and communities.

These new things that are at work in us *lead us into the king*. This is perhaps the hardest idea to grasp, but it's central to what Paul intends. The king, the **Messiah**, is of course Jesus himself. But when people believe in Jesus and join his family through **baptism**, they become 'part' of him; and the sign of that is that they grow together in love, cutting right across all traditional barriers that separate one human being from another. That's what he means in Ephesians 4.12–13 when he speaks of building 'up the Messiah's body' and of growing together into 'the stature of the mature Man measured by the standards of the Messiah's fullness'. If the king is to be complete, Christians of all sorts must come together 'into' him. And the key is the phrase 'of all sorts'. Jews and Greeks together. Men and women together. And – Philemon, are you listening? – slaves and free together.

The opening statement has been made. Paul has laid the foundation. How would you build on it when facing tricky situations in your own community?

PHILEMON 8–14

Paul's Appeal

[8]Because of all this I could be very bold in the Messiah, and order you to do the right thing. [9]But, because of love, I'd much rather appeal to you – yes, it's me, Paul, speaking, an old man as I am and now a prisoner of Messiah Jesus! [10]I am appealing to you about my child, the one I have fathered here in prison: Onesimus, 'Mr Useful'. [11]There was a time when he was use*less* to you; but now he's very useful, to you and to me.

[12]I'm sending him to you for your decision – yes, sending the man himself; and this means sending my own heart. [13]I would have liked to keep him here with me, so that he could have been your representative in serving me in the chains of the gospel. [14]But I didn't want to do

anything without you knowing about it. That way, when you did the splendid thing that the situation requires, it wouldn't be under compulsion, but of your own free will.

There was once a leading bishop in the Church of England who took a strong line on several of the major issues facing the church and the society of his day. Many times he went to see the Archbishop of Canterbury to put pressure on him to steer the church in a particular direction. But the archbishop had a wider picture of the church than the bishop's rather narrow focus; and he also had a wonderfully persuasive manner. Even this bishop, a great thinker and speaker, found himself wooed and won over, again and again, by the archbishop's gracious approach. As he talked about it afterwards he would say, 'When I go to see the archbishop, I say to myself, "Now, you must be very careful not to give in on this one." And when I come out, I say to myself, "Well, you know you never meant to give in on that one!"'

Persuasion, particularly the persuasion that comes genuinely 'in the Lord', is a remarkable thing. Of course, it can be misrepresented: as manipulation, as bullying, as 'unfair pressure'. All those things do exist, and they're ugly. Often people who don't like the eventual decision are tempted to say that the persuasion that they received comes into one of those categories.

But there is a subtle and delicate interplay between explaining something in genuine love, with a true vision of the **gospel**, and someone else making up their mind in the light of it. That's how love works, after all. Supposing Jack loves Jill, but because he respects Jill's freedom to make up her own mind, he never speaks of his love or does anything to show it – does that actually create a context where Jill might be free to love Jack in return? We must beware of setting up a false idol of 'freedom' which would leave us each 'free' within our own little boxes, sealed off from all love, all persuasion, all human interchange, in case our 'freedom' might be compromised. Of course, it's always open to anyone to accuse someone of being 'manipulative', and people have sometimes wondered whether Paul was guilty of that. But to avoid all attempt to persuade, to encourage, to show people things in a new light, because you're frightened of that accusation, would leave us all free – but only 'free' to be hermits, bereft of all human contact.

Paul, in fact, knows the dangers of trying to force someone to do something. His style throughout this letter is one of gentle, almost playful, Christian persuasion. He knows Philemon well enough to adopt the right tone. What he's going to ask is very, very difficult, but he is reasonably sure that Philemon will take the point and act on it. But, just to be sure, he takes it step by step.

First, he builds a secure foundation: the relationship which he and Philemon have. Then he names the person at the centre of the problem. Then, quickly, he makes it clear that when Philemon is confronted with Onesimus himself, he is actually looking at . . . Paul! This is the heart of his strategy in this delicate and highly skilful piece of writing. Would that all Christian persuaders could learn from it.

The relationship between Paul and Philemon is itself that of father and son, or preacher and convert. As becomes clear later in the letter (verse 19), Philemon had come to **faith** through Paul's preaching. Paul is conscious, as well, that he himself has been given a strange authority by God, to be the church-planting evangelist through whom communities loyal to Jesus will spring up around major parts of the Greek and Roman world. Within the Christian fellowship, this gives him a status and position that would enable him, if the worst came to the worst, to give commands. But that's not the best way to do things except in an emergency. Much better that Philemon is helped to think through the issues and come to the right decision for himself.

Paul's appeal, then, is one of love. He appeals to Philemon's love, and sympathy and affection, by describing himself as an old man and in prison. Paul probably wasn't what we would call very old; quite possibly only in his forties or early fifties. But in a world where life expectancy was much lower than today he would be seen as a senior figure, with a natural claim on Philemon's respect.

And the claim now extends: because, having established that he and Philemon are bonded together with several strands of love, partnership, affection and respect, he is now going to show that he and Onesimus have established a similar bond. Onesimus is his 'child'; he has become a Christian through Paul's teaching and love. (Paul quite often refers to such people as his 'children': e.g. 1 Corinthians 4.14; Galatians 4.19.) And, like a fond parent sending a son or daughter off into the wider world for the first time, when Paul sends Onesimus to Colossae, he is sending his very heart. We humans are strange creatures. We really do feel as though part of our own deepest self is bound up in this person or that. Bereavement of all kinds happens to us on a regular basis, every time we are separated from someone we love.

But the point is now clear. When, to his surprise, Philemon discovers that Onesimus, his own runaway slave, has returned, Paul doesn't want him just to see Onesimus standing there. He wants him to see Paul himself. That is the foundation for the appeal Paul will make as the letter reaches its climax in the next section.

What we are watching here, of course, is a living example of the Christian practice of reconciliation. There are lots of heavy theological words ending in '-ation', and it's easy for us to hear them and not really take in what beautiful things they are. We are often like someone seeing the outside cover of a music tape or CD, being vaguely interested in it, but never listening to the music inside. If we listen, however, to the music of the word 'reconciliation', we will realize that it's the music that will heal the world.

This letter shows how costly it is, but also how explosive. Where in your world does reconciliation need to happen today? What social barriers stand in its way? How can people who believe in Jesus make it happen?

PHILEMON 15-25

Paul's Perspective

[15]Look at it like this. Maybe this is the reason he was separated from you for a while, so that you could have him back for ever – [16]no longer as a slave, but much more than a slave, as a beloved brother, beloved especially to me, but how much more to you, both as part of your household and in the Lord. [17]So, anyway, if you reckon me a partner in your work, receive him as though he was me. [18]And if he's wronged you in any way, or owes you anything, put that down on my account. [19]This is me, Paul, writing with my own hand: I'll pay you back (and far be it from me to remind you that you owe me your own very self!). [20]Yes, my brother, I want some benefit from you in the Lord! Refresh my heart in the Messiah.

[21]As I write this I'm confident that you'll do what I say. In fact, I know you'll do more than I say. [22]But, at the same time, get a guest room ready for me. I'm hoping, you see, that through your prayers I will be granted to you.

[23]Epaphras, my fellow prisoner in Messiah Jesus, sends you greetings. [24]So do Mark, Aristarchus, Demas and Luke, my colleagues here.

[25]The grace of the Lord, Messiah Jesus, be with your spirit.

'I have sometimes been told', said my friend, 'that God is an artist, and that we are his paintings.'

'Yes,' I said, 'and actually I think Paul says something like that, in Ephesians 2.10: "We are his handiwork."'

'Well,' my friend replied, 'that's as it may be; but I sometimes think that, in my life at least, God is the kind of artist who hurls a paint-pot at the canvas from the other side of the room, and then stands back and says to himself, "Now, that's very interesting; what shall we do next?"'

We can't very often look at the details of our lives and see exactly where they fit into the larger plan of God. If we try, we'll either become grandiose, imagining that we are the centre of God's universe, or depressed, wondering whether there is any pattern or meaning to it at all. From time to time, though, if we watch in **faith** and trust, we can glimpse something of what God is about, of what the divine painter has in mind. When we glimpse it, we are wise to go with it.

But it must always have a 'perhaps' or a 'maybe' attached to it. Never trust someone who tells you that they are 100 per cent certain that God wants you to do this or that particular thing. (Of course, this doesn't apply to issues of belief and behaviour in general; you can be 100 per cent certain that God wants you to believe in Jesus and his **resurrection**, to say your prayers, to be honest in your dealings, faithful to your marriage partner, generous to those in need and so on. There's no doubt about any of that. What I'm talking about is God's particular will in specific situations where you face a tricky decision.)

Paul is virtually certain of what Philemon must now do. But he is still restrained enough to insert the all-important 'maybe' in front of what is perhaps (there it is again!) the most important sentence in the letter. Supposing, he says – just supposing God had a purpose not just for you at this moment, but even in the fact that Onesimus ran away in the first place? That's an extraordinary thought, and he tactfully doesn't refer to the running away itself, merely to Onesimus being 'separated from you'. God moves in a mysterious way; as Jesus says about the **spirit**, it's like the wind: you hear the sound of it, but can't tell where it's coming from or going to (John 3.8). So, now, maybe God has been secretly at work, even through what seemed like sad, unfortunate or even wicked human actions (and they may have been all of that as well), in order to bring about a situation which would shine his light not only in Colossae but around the world ever afterwards.

Does this seem peculiar? Can God work through things which are themselves wicked or unhappy? Most certainly. The greatest act of rescuing love God ever did, and did moreover in person, was the death of Jesus on the cross. For his followers, this was the greatest tragedy of their lives. For his enemies, it was an act of folly, wickedness and shame. Somehow, throughout the New Testament, all this is put together so that the cross of Jesus becomes the point at which God, in sovereign love, takes up the pain and sin of the world and deals with it in himself.

That, in fact, is precisely what Paul has in mind in this passage. He doesn't mention the cross here; rather, he *applies* it. On the cross, Jesus hung with arms outstretched between **heaven** and earth, making a bridge upwards and downwards between God and the human race, and from side to side between all the warring factions of earth. And Paul has grasped the truth that so many have missed: *his achievement of reconciliation is put into effect when his people follow the same pattern*. When people allow the cross to shape their own lives, the love of

God is set free to change and heal in ways we cannot at the moment even imagine.

See what Paul has done. He has established that he and Philemon are partners in the **gospel**; that is, they share a common life, common goals, a common way of life. Now he has established that he and Onesimus, too, are bonded together in Christian love. So what is the result if it is the case (as it almost certainly is) that Philemon has every legal right to be angry with Onesimus, to punish him, perhaps even to kill him? Paul will stand in between them.

What will this achieve? He will represent them to one another. He will substitute for Onesimus. He will pay Philemon what Onesimus owes – reminding Philemon, precisely by telling him he's not going to remind him, that he, too, owes him his very life! He will stand in the place of risk and pain, with arms outstretched towards the slave and the owner; he will stand at one of the pressure points of the human race from that day until very recently; he will close the gap not just between Philemon and Onesimus but between the two sides of the great divide that ran through, and in some places still runs through, the life of the world. Paul, firmly rooted in the saving gospel of the cross of Jesus, is (as he says in 2 Corinthians 5.18) 'entrusted with the gospel of reconciliation'. This is what it looks like in practice.

What Paul asks for is that Onesimus be accepted back into Philemon's household, both in his former job and as a brother in **Christ**. That is already, as all three of them know, far more than most owners (or slaves) would ever dream of. But he hints at something beyond, in addition. I know, he says, that you will even do 'more than I say' (verse 21). This can only refer to giving Onesimus his freedom. Like the prodigal son, who only asks to be a hired servant in his father's house, he is to be given the astonishing welcome of a son (Luke 15.11–32).

As with the prodigal son, there will no doubt be some who grumble. Why should Onesimus be rewarded for running away? What has he done to deserve it? But that's what grace is like. That's what God's love is always like. Read the gospels again and see. Then ask yourself: where in your world, in your church, in your family, at your workplace – where is the healing and restorative grace of God most badly needed? How can God's people stand in the middle of the picture, holding out their arms to people on either side, bringing together those divided by large and small gulfs, ready to be peacemakers and reconcilers in the name of Jesus?

GLOSSARY

the accuser, *see* the satan

age to come, *see* present age

apostle, disciple, the Twelve
'Apostle' means 'one who is sent'. It could be used of an ambassador or official delegate. In the New Testament it is sometimes used specifically of Jesus' inner circle of twelve; but Paul sees not only himself but several others outside the Twelve as 'apostles', the criterion being whether the person had personally seen the risen Jesus. Jesus' own choice of twelve close associates symbolized his plan to renew God's people, Israel; after the death of Judas Iscariot (Matthew 27.5; Acts 1.18), Matthias was chosen by lot to take his place, preserving the symbolic meaning. During Jesus' lifetime they, and many other followers, were seen as his 'disciples', which means 'pupils' or 'apprentices'.

baptism
Literally, 'plunging' people into water. From within a wider Jewish tradition of ritual washings and bathings, **John the Baptist** undertook a vocation of baptizing people in the Jordan, not as one ritual among others but as a unique moment of **repentance**, preparing them for the coming of the **kingdom of God**. Jesus himself was baptized by John, identifying himself with this renewal movement and developing it in his own way. His followers in turn baptized others. After his **resurrection**, and the sending of the **holy spirit**, baptism became the normal sign and means of entry into the community of Jesus' people. As early as Paul it was aligned both with the **Exodus** from Egypt (1 Corinthians 10.2) and with Jesus' death and resurrection (Romans 6.2–11).

Christ, *see* Messiah

circumcision, circumcised
The cutting off of the foreskin. Male circumcision was a major mark of identity for Jews, following its initial commandment to Abraham (Genesis 17), reinforced by Joshua (Joshua 5.2–9). Other peoples, e.g. the Egyptians, also circumcised male children. A line of thought from Deuteronomy (e.g. 30.6), through Jeremiah (e.g. 31.33), to the **Dead Sea Scrolls** and the New Testament (e.g. Romans 2.29) speaks of 'circumcision of the heart' as God's real desire, by which one may become inwardly what the male Jew is outwardly, that is, marked out

157

as part of God's people. At periods of Jewish assimilation into the surrounding culture, some Jews tried to remove the marks of circumcision (e.g. 1 Maccabees 1.11–15).

covenant

At the heart of Jewish belief is the conviction that the one God, YHWH, who had made the whole world, had called Abraham and his family to belong to him in a special way. The promises God made to Abraham and his family, and the requirements that were laid on them as a result, came to be seen in terms either of the agreement that a king would make with a subject people, or sometimes of the marriage bond between husband and wife. One regular way of describing this relationship was 'covenant', which can thus include both promise and **law**. The covenant was renewed at Mount Sinai with the giving of the **Torah**; in Deuteronomy before the entry to the promised land; and, in a more focused way, with David (e.g. Psalm 89). Jeremiah 31 promised that after the punishment of **exile** God would make a 'new covenant' with his people, forgiving them and binding them to him more intimately. Jesus believed that this was coming true through his **kingdom** proclamation and his death and **resurrection**. The early Christians developed these ideas in various ways, believing that in Jesus the promises had at last been fulfilled.

Dead Sea Scrolls

A collection of texts, some in remarkably good repair, some extremely fragmentary, found in the late 1940s around Qumran (near the north-east corner of the Dead Sea), and virtually all now edited, translated and in the public domain. They formed all or part of the library of a strict monastic group, most likely Essenes, founded in the mid-second century BC and lasting until the Jewish – Roman war of AD 66–70. The scrolls include the earliest existing manuscripts of the Hebrew and Aramaic scriptures, and several other important documents of community regulations, scriptural exegesis, hymns, wisdom writings, and other literature. They shed a flood of light on one small segment within the Judaism of Jesus' day, helping us to understand how some Jews at least were thinking, praying and reading scripture. Despite attempts to prove the contrary, they make no reference to **John the Baptist**, Jesus, Paul, James or early Christianity in general.

demons, *see* the satan

disciple, *see* apostle

Essenes, *see* Dead Sea Scrolls

eucharist

The meal in which the earliest Christians, and Christians ever since, obeyed Jesus' command to 'do this in remembrance of him' at the Last Supper (Luke

22.19; 1 Corinthians 11.23–26). The word 'eucharist' itself comes from the Greek for 'thanksgiving'; it means, basically, 'the thank-you meal', and looks back to the many times when Jesus took bread, gave thanks for it, broke it and gave it to people (e.g. Luke 24.30; John 6.11). Other early phrases for the same meal are 'the Lord's Supper' (1 Corinthians 11.20) and 'the breaking of bread' (Acts 2.42). Later it came to be called 'the mass' (from the Latin word at the end of the service, meaning 'sent out') and 'holy communion' (Paul speaks of 'sharing' or 'communion' in the body and blood of **Christ**). Later theological controversies about the precise meaning of the various actions and elements of the meal should not obscure its centrality in earliest Christian living and its continuing vital importance today.

exile

Deuteronomy (29—30) warned that if Israel disobeyed YHWH, he would send his people into exile, but that if they then repented he would bring them back. When the Babylonians sacked Jerusalem and took the people into exile, prophets such as Jeremiah interpreted this as the fulfilment of this prophecy, and made further promises about how long exile would last (70 years, according to Jeremiah 25.12; 29.10). Sure enough, exiles began to return in the late sixth century (Ezra 1.1). However, the post-exilic period was largely a disappointment, since the people were still enslaved to foreigners (Nehemiah 9.36); and at the height of persecution by the Syrians, Daniel 9.2, 24 spoke of the 'real' exile lasting not for 70 years but for 70 *weeks* of years, i.e., 490 years. Longing for the real 'return from exile', when the prophecies of Isaiah, Jeremiah, etc. would be fulfilled, and redemption from pagan oppression accomplished, continued to characterize many Jewish movements, and was a major theme in Jesus' proclamation and his summons to **repentance**.

Exodus

The Exodus from Egypt took place, according to the book of that name, under the leadership of Moses, after long years in which the Israelites had been enslaved there. (According to Genesis 15.13f., this was itself part of God's covenanted promise to Abraham.) It demonstrated, to them and to Pharaoh, King of Egypt, that Israel was God's special child (Exodus 4.22). They then wandered through the Sinai wilderness for 40 years, led by God in a pillar of cloud and fire; early on in this time they were given the **Torah** on Mount Sinai itself. Finally, after the death of Moses and under the leadership of Joshua, they crossed the Jordan and entered, and eventually conquered, the promised land of Canaan. This event, commemorated annually in Passover and other Jewish festivals, gave the Israelites not only a powerful memory of what had made them a people, but also a particular shape and content to their faith in YHWH as not only creator but also redeemer; and in subsequent enslavements, particularly the **exile**, they looked for a further redemption which would be, in effect, a new Exodus. Probably no other past event so dominated the imagination of first-century Jews;

among them the early Christians, following the lead of Jesus himself, continually referred back to the Exodus to give meaning and shape to their own critical events, most particularly Jesus' death and **resurrection**.

faith

Faith in the New Testament covers a wide area of human trust and trustworthiness, merging into love at one end of the scale and loyalty at the other. Within Jewish and Christian thinking faith in God also includes *belief*, accepting certain things as true about God, and what he has done in the world (e.g. bringing Israel out of Egypt; raising Jesus from the dead). For Jesus, 'faith' often seems to mean 'recognizing that God is decisively at work to bring the **kingdom** through Jesus'. For Paul, 'faith' is both the specific belief that Jesus is Lord and that God raised him from the dead (Romans 10.9) and the response of grateful human love to sovereign divine love (Galatians 2.20). This faith is, for Paul, the solitary badge of membership in God's people in **Christ**, marking them out in a way that **Torah**, and the works it prescribes, can never do.

Gentiles

The Jews divided the world into Jews and non-Jews. The Hebrew word for non-Jews, *goyim*, carries overtones both of family identity (i.e., not of Jewish ancestry) and of worship (i.e., of idols, not of the one true God YHWH). Though many Jews established good relations with Gentiles, not least in the Jewish Diaspora (the dispersion of Jews away from Palestine), officially there were taboos against contact such as intermarriage. In the New Testament the Greek word *ethne*, 'nations', carries the same meanings as *goyim*. Part of Paul's overmastering agenda was to insist that Gentiles who believed in Jesus had full rights in the Christian community alongside believing Jews, without having to become **circumcised**.

good news, gospel, message, word

The idea of 'good news', for which an older English word is 'gospel', had two principal meanings for first-century Jews. First, with roots in Isaiah, it meant the news of YHWH's long-awaited victory over evil and rescue of his people. Second, it was used in the Roman world of the accession, or birthday, of the emperor. Since for Jesus and Paul the announcement of God's inbreaking **kingdom** was both the fulfilment of prophecy and a challenge to the world's present rulers, 'gospel' became an important shorthand for both the message of Jesus himself, and the apostolic message about him. Paul saw this message as itself the vehicle of God's saving power (Romans 1.16; 1 Thessalonians 2.13).

The four canonical 'gospels' tell the story of Jesus in such a way as to bring out both these aspects (unlike some other so-called 'gospels' circulated in the second and subsequent centuries, which tended both to cut off the scriptural and Jewish roots of Jesus' achievement and to inculcate a private spirituality rather than confrontation with the world's rulers). Since in Isaiah this creative, life-giving good news was seen as God's own powerful word (40.8; 55.11), the early Christians could use 'word' or 'message' as another shorthand for the basic Christian proclamation.

gospel, *see* good news

heaven
Heaven is God's dimension of the created order (Genesis 1.1; Psalm 115.16; Matthew 6.9), whereas 'earth' is the world of space, time and matter that we know. 'Heaven' thus sometimes stands, reverentially, for 'God' (as in Matthew's regular 'kingdom of heaven'). Normally hidden from human sight, heaven is occasionally revealed or unveiled so that people can see God's dimension of ordinary life (e.g. 2 Kings 6.17; Revelation 1, 4—5). Heaven in the New Testament is thus not usually seen as the place where God's people go after death; at the end the New Jerusalem descends *from* heaven *to* earth, joining the two dimensions for ever. 'Entering the kingdom of heaven' does not mean 'going to heaven after death', but belonging in the present to the people who steer their earthly course by the standards and purposes of heaven (cf. the Lord's Prayer: 'on earth as in heaven', Matthew 6.10) and who are assured of membership in the age to come.

high priest, *see* priests

holy spirit
In Genesis 1.2, the spirit is God's presence and power *within* creation, without God being identified with creation. The same spirit entered people, notably the prophets, enabling them to speak and act for God. At his baptism by John the Baptist, Jesus was specially equipped with the spirit, resulting in his remarkable public career (Acts 10.38). After his resurrection, his followers were themselves filled (Acts 2) by the same spirit, now identified as Jesus' own spirit: the creator God was acting afresh, remaking the world and them too. The spirit enabled them to live out a holiness which the Torah could not, producing 'fruit' in their lives, giving them 'gifts' with which to serve God, the world and the church, and assuring them of future resurrection (Romans 8; Galatians 4—5; 1 Corinthians 12—14). From very early in Christianity (e.g. Galatians 4.1–7), the spirit became part of the new revolutionary definition of God himself: 'the one who sends the son and the spirit of the son'.

John (the Baptist)
Jesus' cousin on his mother's side, born a few months before Jesus; his father was a priest. He acted as a prophet, baptizing in the Jordan – dramatically re-enacting the Exodus from Egypt – to prepare people, by repentance, for God's coming judgment. He may have had some contact with the Essenes, though his eventual public message was different from theirs. Jesus' own vocation was decisively confirmed at his baptism by John. As part of John's message of the

kingdom, he outspokenly criticized Herod Antipas for marrying his brother's wife. Herod had him imprisoned, and then beheaded him at his wife's request (Mark 6.14–29). Groups of John's disciples continued a separate existence, without merging into Christianity, for some time afterwards (e.g. Acts 19.1–7).

justification

God's declaration, from his position as judge of all the world, that someone is in the right, despite universal sin. This declaration will be made on the last day on the basis of an entire life (Romans 2.1–16), but is brought forward into the present on the basis of Jesus' achievement, because sin has been dealt with through his cross (Romans 3.21—4.25); the means of this present justification is simply **faith.** This means, particularly, that Jews and **Gentiles** alike are full members of the family promised by God to Abraham (Galatians 3; Romans 4).

kingdom of God, kingdom of heaven

Best understood as the king*ship*, or sovereign and saving rule, of Israel's God YHWH, as celebrated in several psalms (e.g. 99.1) and prophecies (e.g. Daniel 6.26f.). Because YHWH was the creator God, when he finally became king in the way he intended this would involve setting the world to rights, and particularly rescuing Israel from its enemies. 'Kingdom of God' and various equivalents (e.g. 'No king but God!') became a revolutionary slogan around the time of Jesus. Jesus' own announcement of God's kingdom redefined these expectations around his own very different plan and vocation. His invitation to people to 'enter' the kingdom was a way of summoning them to allegiance to himself and his programme, seen as the start of God's long-awaited saving reign. For Jesus, the kingdom was coming not in a single move, but in stages, of which his own public career was one, his death and **resurrection** another, and a still future consummation another. Note that 'kingdom of **heaven**' is Matthew's preferred form for the same phrase, following a regular Jewish practice of saying 'heaven' rather than 'God'. It does not refer to a place ('heaven'), but to the fact of God's becoming king in and through Jesus and his achievement. Paul speaks of Jesus, as **Messiah**, already in possession of his kingdom, waiting to hand it over finally to the father (1 Corinthians 15.23–8; cf. Ephesians 5.5).

law, *see* Torah

lawyers, legal experts, *see* Pharisees

life, soul, spirit

Ancient people held many different views about what made human beings the special creatures they are. Some, including many Jews, believed that to be complete, humans needed bodies as well as inner selves. Others, including many influenced by the philosophy of Plato (fourth century BC), believed that the important part of a human was the 'soul' (Gk: *psyche*), which at death would be happily freed from its bodily prison. Confusingly for us, the same word *psyche* is often used in the New Testament within a Jewish framework where it clearly means 'life' or 'true self', without implying a body/soul dualism that devalues the body. Human inwardness of experience and understanding can also be referred to as 'spirit'. *See also* **resurrection**.

message, *see* **good news**

Messiah, messianic, Christ

The Hebrew word means literally 'anointed one', hence in theory either a prophet, **priest** or king. In Greek this translates as *Christos*; 'Christ' in early Christianity was a title, and only gradually became an alternative proper name for Jesus. In practice 'Messiah' is mostly restricted to the notion, which took various forms in ancient Judaism, of the coming king who would be David's true heir, through whom YHWH would bring judgment to the world, and in particular would rescue Israel from pagan enemies. There was no single template of expectations. Scriptural stories and promises contributed to different ideals and movements, often focused on (a) decisive military defeat of Israel's enemies and (b) rebuilding or cleansing the **Temple**. The **Dead Sea Scrolls** speak of two 'Messiahs', one a priest and the other a king. The universal early Christian belief that Jesus was Messiah is only explicable, granted his crucifixion by the Romans (which would have been seen as a clear sign that he was not the Messiah), by their belief that God had raised him from the dead, so vindicating the implicit messianic claims of his earlier ministry.

miracles

Like some of the old prophets, notably Elijah and Elisha, Jesus performed many deeds of remarkable power, particularly healings. The **gospels** refer to these as 'deeds of power', 'signs', 'marvels' or 'paradoxes'. Our word 'miracle' tends to imply that God, normally 'outside' the closed system of the world, sometimes 'intervenes'; miracles have then frequently been denied as a matter of principle. However, in the Bible God is always present, however strangely, and 'deeds of power' are seen as *special* acts of a *present* God rather than as *intrusive* acts of an *absent* one. Jesus' own 'mighty works' are seen particularly, following prophecy, as evidence of his messiahship (e.g. Matthew 11.2–6).

Mishnah

The main codification of Jewish law (**Torah**) by the **rabbis**, produced in about AD 200, reducing to writing the 'oral Torah' which in Jesus' day ran parallel to the 'written Torah'. The Mishnah is itself the basis of the much larger collections of traditions in the two Talmuds (roughly AD 400).

parables

From the Old Testament onwards, prophets and other teachers used various storytelling devices as vehicles for their challenge to Israel (e.g. 2 Samuel 12.1–7). Sometimes these appeared as visions with interpretations (e.g. Daniel 7). Similar techniques were used by the **rabbis**. Jesus made his own creative adaptation of these traditions, in order to break open the world-view of his contemporaries and to invite them to share his vision of God's **kingdom** instead. His stories portrayed this as something that was *happening*, not just a timeless truth, and enabled his hearers to step inside the story and make it their own. As with some Old Testament visions, some of Jesus' parables have their own interpretations (e.g. the sower, Mark 4); others are thinly disguised retellings of the prophetic story of Israel (e.g. the wicked tenants, Mark 12).

parousia

Literally, it means 'presence', as opposed to 'absence', and is sometimes used by Paul with this sense (e.g. Philippians 2.12). It was already used in the Roman world for the ceremonial arrival of, for example, the emperor at a subject city or colony. Although the ascended Lord is not 'absent' from the church, when he 'appears' (Colossians 3.4; 1 John 3.2) in his 'second coming' this will be, in effect, an 'arrival' like that of the emperor, and Paul uses it thus in 1 Corinthians 15.23; 1 Thessalonians 2.19; etc. In the **gospels** it is found only in Matthew 24 (verses 3, 27, 39).

Pharisees, lawyers, legal experts, rabbis

The Pharisees were an unofficial but powerful Jewish pressure group through most of the first centuries BC and AD. Largely lay-led, though including some **priests**, their aim was to purify Israel through intensified observance of the Jewish law (**Torah**), developing their own traditions about the precise meaning and application of scripture, their own patterns of prayer and other devotion, and their own calculations of the national hope. Though not all legal experts were Pharisees, most Pharisees were thus legal experts.

They effected a democratization of Israel's life, since for them the study and practice of Torah was equivalent to worshipping in the **Temple** – though they were adamant in pressing their own rules for the Temple liturgy on an unwilling (and often **Sadducean**) priesthood. This enabled them to survive AD 70 and, merging into the early rabbinic movement, to develop new ways forward. Politically they stood up for ancestral traditions, and were at the forefront of various movements of revolt against both pagan overlordship and compromised Jewish leaders. By Jesus' day there were two distinct schools, the stricter one of Shammai, more inclined towards armed revolt, and the more lenient one of Hillel, ready to live and let live.

Jesus' debates with the Pharisees are at least as much a matter of agenda and policy (Jesus strongly opposed their separatist nationalism) as about details of theology and piety. Saul of Tarsus was a fervent right-wing Pharisee, presumably a Shammaite, until his conversion.

After the disastrous war of AD 66–70, these schools of Hillel and Shammai continued bitter debate on appropriate policy. Following the further disaster of AD 135 (the failed Bar-Kochba revolt against Rome) their traditions were carried on by the rabbis who, though looking to the earlier Pharisees for inspiration, developed a Torah-piety in which personal holiness and purity took the place of political agendas.

present age, age to come, the life of God's coming age

By the time of Jesus many Jewish thinkers divided history into two periods: 'the present age' and 'the age to come' – the latter being the time when YHWH would at last act decisively to judge evil, to rescue Israel, and to create a new world of justice and peace. The early Christians believed that, though the full blessings of the coming age lay still in the future, it had already begun with Jesus, particularly with his death and **resurrection**, and that by **faith** and **baptism** they were able to enter it already. For this reason, the customary translation 'eternal life' is rendered here as 'the life of God's coming age'.

priests, high priest

Aaron, the older brother of Moses, was appointed Israel's first high priest (Exodus 28—29), and in theory his descendants were Israel's priests thereafter. Other members of his tribe (Levi) were 'Levites', performing other liturgical duties but not sacrificing. Priests lived among the people all around the country, having a local teaching role (Leviticus 10.11; Malachi 2.7), and going to Jerusalem by rotation to perform the **Temple** liturgy (e.g. Luke 2.8).

David appointed Zadok (whose Aaronic ancestry is sometimes questioned) as high priest, and his family remained thereafter the senior priests in Jerusalem, probably the ancestors of the **Sadducees**. One explanation of the origins of the Qumran **Essenes** is that they were a dissident group who believed themselves to be the rightful chief priests.

rabbis, *see* Pharisees

repentance

Literally, this means 'turning back'. It is widely used in the Old Testament and subsequent Jewish literature to indicate both a personal turning away from sin and Israel's corporate turning away from idolatry and back to YHWH. Through both meanings, it is linked to the idea of 'return from **exile**'; if Israel is to 'return' in all senses, it must 'return' to YHWH. This is at the heart of the summons of both **John the Baptist** and Jesus. In Paul's writings it is mostly used for **Gentiles** turning away from idols to serve the true God; also for sinning Christians who need to return to Jesus.

resurrection

In most biblical thought, human bodies matter and are not merely disposable prisons for the **soul**. When ancient Israelites wrestled with the goodness and justice of YHWH, the creator, they ultimately came to insist that he must raise the dead (Isaiah 26.19; Daniel 12.2–3) – a suggestion firmly resisted by classical pagan thought. The longed-for return from **exile** was also spoken of in terms of YHWH raising dry bones to new **life** (Ezekiel 37.1–14). These ideas were developed in the second-**Temple** period, not least at times of martyrdom (e.g. 2 Maccabees 7). Resurrection was not just 'life after death', but a newly embodied life *after* 'life after death'; those at present dead were either 'asleep', or seen as 'souls', 'angels' or 'spirits', awaiting new embodiment.

The early Christian belief that Jesus had been raised from the dead was not that he had 'gone to **heaven**', or that he had been 'exalted', or was 'divine'; they believed all those as well, but each could have been expressed without mention of resurrection. Only the bodily resurrection of Jesus explains the rise of the early church, particularly its belief in Jesus' messiahship (which his crucifixion would have called into question). The early Christians believed that they themselves would be raised to a new, transformed bodily life at the time of the Lord's return or **parousia** (e.g. Philippians 3.20f.).

sabbath

The Jewish sabbath, the seventh day of the week, was a regular reminder both of creation (Genesis 2.3; Exodus 20.8–11) and of the **Exodus** (Deuteronomy 5.15). Along with **circumcision** and the food laws, it was one of the badges of Jewish identity within the pagan world of late antiquity, and a considerable body of Jewish **law** and custom grew up around its observance.

sacrifice

Like all ancient people, the Israelites offered animal and vegetable sacrifices to their God. Unlike others, they possessed a highly detailed written code (mostly in Leviticus) for what to offer and how to offer it; this in turn was developed in the **Mishnah** (*c.* AD 200). The Old Testament specifies that sacrifices can only be offered in the Jerusalem **Temple**; after this was destroyed in AD 70, sacrifices ceased, and Judaism developed further the idea, already present in some teachings, of prayer, fasting and almsgiving as alternative forms of sacrifice. The early Christians used the language of sacrifice in connection with such things as holiness, evangelism and the **eucharist**.

Sadducees

By Jesus' day, the Sadducees were the aristocracy of Judaism, possibly tracing their origins to the family of Zadok, David's **high priest**. Based in Jerusalem, and including most of the leading priestly families, they had their own traditions and attempted to resist the pressure of the **Pharisees** to conform to theirs. They claimed to rely only on the Pentateuch (the first five books of the Old

Testament), and denied any doctrine of a future life, particularly of the **resurrection** and other ideas associated with it, presumably because of the encouragement such beliefs gave to revolutionary movements. No writings from the Sadducees have survived, unless the apocryphal book of Ben-Sirach ('Ecclesiasticus') comes from them. The Sadducees themselves did not survive the destruction of Jerusalem and the **Temple** in AD 70.

the satan, 'the accuser', demons

The Bible is never very precise about the identity of the figure known as 'the satan'. The Hebrew word means 'the accuser', and at times the satan seems to be a member of YHWH's heavenly council, with special responsibility as director of prosecutions (1 Chronicles 21.1; Job 1—2; Zechariah 3.1f.). However, it becomes identified variously with the serpent of the garden of Eden (Genesis 3.1-15) and with the rebellious daystar cast out of **heaven** (Isaiah 14.12-15), and was seen by many Jews as the quasi-personal source of evil standing behind both human wickedness and large-scale injustice, sometimes operating through semi-independent 'demons'. By Jesus' time various words were used to denote this figure, including Beelzebul/b (lit. 'Lord of the flies') and simply 'the evil one'; Jesus warned his followers against the deceits this figure could perpetrate. His opponents accused him of being in league with the satan, but the early Christians believed that Jesus in fact defeated it both in his own struggles with temptation (Matthew 4; Luke 4), his exorcisms of demons, and his death (1 Corinthians 2.8; Colossians 2.15). Final victory over this ultimate enemy is thus assured (Revelation 20), though the struggle can still be fierce for Christians (Ephesians 6.10-20).

son of David, David's son

An alternative, and infrequently used, title for **Messiah**. The messianic promises of the Old Testament often focus specifically on David's son, for example 2 Samuel 7.12-16; Psalm 89.19-37. Joseph, Mary's husband, is called 'son of David' by the angel in Matthew 1.20.

son of God

Originally a title for Israel (Exodus 4.22) and the Davidic king (Psalm 2.7); also used of ancient angelic figures (Genesis 6.2). By the New Testament period it was already used as a messianic title, for example in the **Dead Sea Scrolls**. There, and when used of Jesus in the **gospels** (e.g. Matthew 16.16), it means, or reinforces, 'Messiah', without the later significance of 'divine'. However, already in Paul the transition to the fuller meaning (one who was already equal with God and was sent by him to become human and to become Messiah) is apparent, without loss of the meaning 'Messiah' itself (e.g. Galatians 4.4).

son of man

In Hebrew or Aramaic, this simply means 'mortal' or 'human being'; in later Judaism, it is sometimes used to mean 'I' or 'someone like me'. In the New Testament the phrase is frequently linked to Daniel 7.13, where 'one like a son of man' is brought on the clouds of **heaven** to 'the Ancient of Days', being vindicated after a period of suffering, and is given kingly power. Though Daniel 7 itself interprets this as code for 'the people of the saints of the Most High', by the first century some Jews understood it as a **messianic** promise. Jesus developed this in his own way in certain key sayings which are best understood as promises that God would vindicate him, and judge those who had opposed him, after his own suffering (e.g. Mark 14.62). Jesus was thus able to use the phrase as a cryptic self-designation, hinting at his coming suffering, his vindication and his God-given authority.

soul, *see* life

spirit, *see* life, holy spirit

Temple

The Temple in Jerusalem was planned by David (*c.* 1000 BC) and built by his son Solomon as the central sanctuary for all Israel. After reforms under Hezekiah and Josiah in the seventh century BC, it was destroyed by Babylon in 587 BC. Rebuilding by the returned **exiles** began in 538 BC, and was completed in 516, initiating the 'second Temple period'. Judas Maccabaeus cleansed it in 164 BC after its desecration by Antiochus Epiphanes (167). Herod the Great began to rebuild and beautify it in 19 BC; the work was completed in AD 63. The Temple was destroyed by the Romans in AD 70. Many Jews believed it should and would be rebuilt; some still do. The Temple was not only the place of **sacrifice**; it was believed to be the unique dwelling of YHWH on earth, the place where **heaven** and earth met.

Torah, Jewish law

'Torah', narrowly conceived, consists of the first five books of the Old Testament, the 'five books of Moses' or 'Pentateuch'. (These contain much law, but also much narrative.) It can also be used for the whole Old Testament scriptures, though strictly these are the 'law, prophets and writings'. In a broader sense, it refers to the whole developing corpus of Jewish legal tradition, written and oral; the oral Torah was initially codified in the **Mishnah** around AD 200, with wider developments found in the two Talmuds, of Babylon and Jerusalem, codified around AD 400. Many Jews in the time of Jesus and Paul regarded the Torah as being so strongly God-given as to be almost itself, in some sense, divine; some (e.g. Ben-Sirach 24) identified it with the figure of 'Wisdom'. Doing what Torah said was not seen as a means of earning God's favour, but rather of expressing gratitude, and as a key badge of Jewish identity.

the Twelve, *see* apostle

word, *see* good news

YHWH

The ancient Israelite name for God, from at least the time of the **Exodus** (Exodus 6.2f.). It may originally have been pronounced 'Yahweh', but by the time of Jesus it was considered too holy to speak out loud, except for the **high priest** once a year in the Holy of Holies in the **Temple**. Instead, when reading scripture, pious Jews would say *Adonai*, 'Lord', marking this usage by adding the vowels of *Adonai* to the consonants of YHWH, eventually producing the hybrid 'Jehovah'. The word YHWH is formed from the verb 'to be', combining 'I am who I am', 'I will be who I will be', and perhaps 'I am because I am', emphasizing YHWH's sovereign creative power.

STUDY/REFLECTION GUIDE

Introducing the Study

Ephesians, Philippians, Colossians, and Philemon for Everyone is one in a series of commentaries written by N. T. Wright, noted Pauline and New Testament scholar, who intended these to be guides for readers ready to delve deeper into the scriptures. Suitable for group or individual study, Wright provides his own translation of the four Pauline letters covered in this volume. Unifying these letters is their composition during Paul's Roman imprisonment, though Wright provides his reasoning on the authorship and intended readership of each letter.

The commentary on each letter includes Wright's translation of the biblical text divided into small sections, accompanied by insights into its context and in-depth explanations of each segment. Notice that Wright provides a glossary for **key words** at the end of the volume. Your personal preparation for each session might include studying the selected texts in different translations as well as praying for guidance in understanding and relating those scriptures to your own life. Listen for the spirit's encouragement to you as you encounter the letters to believers and churches in Ephesus, Philippi and Colossae and to Philemon, and recall Wright's reminder to us in the Introduction: 'On the very first occasion when someone stood up in public to tell people about Jesus, he made it very clear: this message is for *everyone.*'

If Using the Guide for Individual Study

In addition to your copy of this book, you may wish to read Wright's translations alongside other translations, which you can find online or perhaps in a local library. Did you study a language in school? Consider finding a copy of the New Testament in that language; the additional insights coming from the unfamiliarity of that language can be spiritually revealing. Completing the questions for each text in writing (never mind complete sentences because bullet points get full marks) and completing the suggested activities as if a good friend was by your side will enrich your experience.

If Using the Guide as a Group Member

- Be prepared by reading the scripture before the sessions.
- Be on time for each session.
- Be encouraging to everyone.
- Be willing to contribute to group discussions.
- Be prayerful that great things will come from this study.

If Serving Others by Facilitating a Group

God bless you! This guide was prepared with you in mind, in the hope and prayer that spiritual blessings are abundant for you as well as those you lead. Every group is unique, so take this guide as a starting place, adapting and using the resources provided. Written for six one-hour sessions, you could adapt the length of your study to meet your needs. As an extra consideration, since these four letters are significantly different in length, this guide incorporates the study of Philemon with a culminating activity session covering all four letters.

Suggested Session Format

Opening Prayer (1 minute)
Group Opening (5 minutes)
Exploring the Scriptures (30 minutes)
Applying the Scriptures (15 minutes)
Sharing "Oh Wow" Moments (5 minutes)
Closing Prayer (1 minute)
Ticket Out the Door (3 minutes)

Readings for Each Session

Session One—Ephesians 1.1–3.21
Session Two—Ephesians 4.1–6.24
Session Three—Philippians 1.1–2.30
Session Four—Philippians 3.1–4.23
Session Five—Colossians
Session Six—Philemon

Helpful Hints for Facilitators

- Set up the room where you will meet before others are scheduled to arrive. Create expectations for learning by changing the usual appearance of the room (but be sure to get permission before making any changes).
- Ask others to lead a part of the session.

- Allow time for reflection. Silence may improve the quality of group responses.
- Involve as many persons as possible. Extend conversations by replying, 'Yes, and . . .'
- Engage the group to reset the room to its original condition, building a sense of purpose for the group.
- Pray for the members individually and as a group. The message of Ephesians will change hearts and lives, as well as churches.

SESSION 1
UNITY IN CHRIST
(PAGES 3–31)

Opening Prayer (1 minute)

King and master of our lives, use this time to reveal our magnificent life in you. Make us strong in the broken places of our relationships with you and with each other. Give us new energy and will to know and to live the purpose of our lives in Christ Jesus, in whose name we pray. Amen.

Group Opening (5 minutes)

Introduce the content and character of Paul's letter to the believers in Ephesus and to believers in all times and places using this information and any other you may discover. The primary emphasis of this letter is to explain the nature and purpose of the church as revealed in the life, death and resurrection of Jesus Christ. Wright suggests that Paul was the author of this letter, which does not include the term 'in Ephesus' in the best manuscripts currently available. He describes the letter as a 'circular letter' intended for the church in Ephesus and surrounding cities. The themes of Ephesians are far-reaching: God, Jesus, the world, the church, salvation, Christian behaviour, marriage, family and spiritual warfare. Relations between Christian Jews and Gentiles continued to be a source of division in the early church, and Paul addresses the unity of believers in Christ and in the church directly. He makes it clear that believers ought to be motivated by the death and resurrection of Jesus Christ to be reconciled to each other and so united in carrying out the purpose of Christ, the head of the church. Wright describes the view from the London Eye, at 450 feet above the ground, as an analogy to the 'God's eye' perspective presented by this letter. The message of Ephesians is 'the dynamo at the heart of the universe' in the words of Eugene Peterson (MSG, page 475).

Exploring the Scriptures (30 minutes)

These questions are intended to help you guide a group discussion of the first three chapters of Ephesians. There are more questions than time for discussion, so include those which you feel would benefit the group you serve. These questions will also guide the individual reader in study.

1. Wright describes this letter as a 'circular' to local churches. What form of modern-day communication is similar?
2. Read 1.3–14, which is a single stream of worship with a single focus: Who is this God? Why is he to be worshipped and adored in this way?
3. When Paul speaks of us as being 'in Christ', Wright explains that this means God has acted 'for us in Him (Jesus)'. Identify the nine ways God has blessed us as described in this prayer.
4. Wright chooses to translate the terms 'Christ', 'king' and 'Messiah' interchangeably. What is Wright's intent in this translation? How does it compare to other translations?
5. Why did God choose some and not others for salvation? What was Wright's explanation (pages 17–18)?
6. In 1.7–10, what event does the author identify as the Old Testament background?
7. In 1.11, we learn that we are to receive an 'inheritance'. What is it, and how is that term related to Old Testament history?
8. What, according to Wright, is the inheritance promised by God to the church?
9. What role is the holy spirit to play in our inheritance?
10. Ephesians 1.17–18 says that Paul prays for three gifts for the faithful. His prayer is that they will use those gifts to learn the _____ that goes with God's call, the _____ of the glory of his inheritance . . . and the greatness of his _____.
11. The biblical text on page 11 is titled 'Knowing the Power of the King'. 'Far too many Christians today, and, one suspects, in Paul's day, are quite unaware that this power is there and is available' (page 12). How would you describe a church that accessed the full power of Christ today?
12. When you were little, were you ever asked, 'What if everyone acted the way you did?' Paul says in 2.3 that this is the natural condition of all persons, each doing what seems the selfish best, and thus subject to God's wrath. How did God respond to our sin (2.4–7)?
13. 'If the problem is that the settled and habitual behaviour of the whole human race leads them on the fast road toward death—the

ultimate destruction of their humanness—the answer provided by God' (page 15) is given in 2.4–7: the death and resurrection of Jesus Christ!

14. According to Wright, what is the main thing Paul wants to stress about all this?

15. In pages 21–24, the author gives his explanation of 2.8–10 using deep theological concepts: salvation, justification, grace, works and faith. Imagine you were trying to explain these verses to a five-year-old. What would you say? (Don't worry if you don't feel you can do this well!)

16. In Paul's day, perhaps the central division was that between Jewish and Gentile believers, a division still all too familiar to churches. Those 'born' in the church, grounded in the customs of the church, may be distrustful of those just coming into the faith. Old ways were compared to new ones, just like in Paul's time. Wright calls these factions 'enemies', while others translate their relationship as one of 'hostility'. Not a promising start for a new faith community, is it? How did Paul explain the answer to this division?

17. Wright compares the plight of today's refugees to the church of Paul's time in the commentary to 2.17–22 (pages 21–23). Describe your response to Wright's analogy.

18. In 3.1–7, Paul describes his own role in the 'secret plan' of God—to spread the message that Gentiles are to share in Israel's inheritance. How do you imagine each segment of the church in his time might respond? What is another word for 'secret plan'?

19. Paul ends this section of Ephesians with a prayer summarizing his message to the believers who would read this letter in their churches. He pays particular attention to the realities of 'love' and 'power'. Wright asserts that 'prayer brings together love and power'. Can you relate Wright's statement to Paul's prayer in 3.14–21?

Applying the Scriptures (15 minutes)

The purpose of this time is to make practical application of our new learning to our own lives and faith communities. For this session, conduct this thought experiment: Imagine that our connection to the power of God through Jesus is like solar power. God's love provides the power to create new technology to solve old problems. Ask members of the group to rearrange themselves into two groups: the first to detail the available sources of sunlight (God's power) and the second to detail the new technology to provide the means to meet the problems and challenges the church faces today. Have each group briefly report back after about ten minutes, and then lead a discussion of your responses.

Sharing "Oh Wow" Moments (5 minutes)

Ask members to share 'oh wow' moments in their own hearts and lives from their study and this session.

Closing Prayer (1 minute)

Jesus, lover of our souls, challenge us to find the paths to your love and power which you have created for us, so that we might serve the church you embody and lead. Amen.

Ticket Out the Door (3 minutes)

Provide sticky notes or something similar for each member, including yourself. Ask each member to specify a question number or topic from today's session which intrigues them or needs more insight.

SESSION 2
UNITY IN THE BODY OF CHRIST

(PAGES 31–59)

Opening Prayer (1 minute)

Dear Jesus, healer of all relationships, we recognize our own woundedness and failures in these scriptures. Come to us now, that we may be healed to serve others and that your power and love might be revealed in the church.

Group Opening (5 minutes)

Remind the group of the 'ticket out the door' from last session and read the first of those you chose to discuss today. Continue with however many you complete in the time allotted.

Exploring the Scriptures (30 minutes)

In his concluding comments on the readings for the previous session, the author states: 'But if it's the true God we've been worshipping, we should be filled with a sense of new possibilities: of new tasks and new energy to accomplish them' (page 31).

1. What is the calling to which Paul refers in verse 1?
2. In 4.3, Paul uses the imagery of a soldier garrisoned in the church to guard its unity. Wright asserts, 'Unless we are working to maintain, defend and develop the unity we already enjoy, and to

overcome, demolish and put behind us the disunity we still find ourselves in, we can scarcely claim to be following Paul's teaching' (page 33).

3. The passage at 4.8–10 is difficult to grasp. Paul is quoting Psalm 68.18, and Wright suggests that the Jewish reader at the time the letter was written would understand this passage as a reference to Moses. How does Wright explain verse 9?

4. How does Paul explain the steps to gaining 'a mature and genuine human life'?

5. In 4.11, Paul lists the five offices of the church crucial to its first generation of believers. He lists other spiritual gifts elsewhere, but here his emphasis is on the purposes of each role. If you have access to a writing board, a visual list of roles and purposes may help.

6. In his commentary on 4.19, Wright explains how to understand those who do not know Christ: 'You won't understand where the behaviour comes from unless you understand the state of heart and mind. And you won't change the behaviour unless you change the heart and mind' (page 38). Can you tell a story about a friend whose life, heart and mind changed after 'learning Christ'?

7. 'Be renewed in the spirit of your mind' (verse 23) is the secret of Christian discipleship and Christian discipline. Free your mind and the rest will follow! Can you explain how this has worked out in your own life?

8. 'Kindness is one of the purest forms of the imitation of God', Wright says (page 40). What practical steps does Paul suggest taking to achieve this sort of kindness?

9. Paul doesn't say that we should not be angry, rather he says that we should not give anger the opportunity to settle into our hearts and lives. After all, Jesus became angry with the abuse of the temple, shouldn't we be angry also at the abuse of other people by those who are more powerful? Have you ever experienced this sort of anger?

10. We live in a world that has been sexualized to the point where nothing sexual appears to have a deeper meaning. Paul makes it clear that using others for meaningless sex is the opposite of God's intention and indeed attracts God's wrath (verse 6). Wright asserts that God's wrath is built into creation itself in this case, that misuse of sex bears the seeds of its own consequences. What is Paul's antidote for poisoned sexuality?

11. Paul is educating and exhorting believers he has never met in this passage. He doesn't claim specialized knowledge of the situations in their local cities and churches. How, then, can he help them with their problems? The passage at 5.10 says, 'Think through what's going to be pleasing to the Lord. Work it out.' What is the

relationship between a believer's thinking ability and the holy spirit?

12. In 5.11–20, Paul offers two ways for believers to stay faithful: become beacons of light, focusing your intentions on being light for others; and become a 'singing' Christian, using all the categories of music mentioned by Paul to fill and nurture your heart. We will explore the latter means in the next section of this study guide.

13. Relationships between husbands and wives, like all deep relationships, are complicated. Paul's teaching to his contemporaries is difficult to apply in the context of twenty-first century customs, but focus attention on Paul's intention and his model. He is attempting to help believers repair their own broken relations so that the optimal relationship can be developed with Christ and with his church. Nothing short of Christ's own sacrifice in love will do for a marriage relationship. Nothing less will honor Christ. Nothing less will honor the holy spirit living in each married partner. With that model clearly in mind, is it any wonder that marriage is 'work' for the best-intentioned persons, or that broken relationships cannot survive without the commitment of both partners?

14. In 6.1–9, Paul extends the teaching about marriage to relationships between parent and child, as well as masters and slaves. Paul speaks in a matter-of-fact manner about slavery, assuming its propriety for his time. He takes the extra step, however, of insisting on an attitude of mutual responsibility between all. Parents should treat their children with restraint; children should honor their parents. Slaves should do good work for masters; masters should treat the enslaved humanely. To break such relationships is to damage one's own relationship with Christ.

15. Paul assumes that living in the proper relationship with Christ will upset those with the most to lose from deviation from the status quo. Accordingly, he offers the armour of the faith, a tested strategy for holding on while being attacked. Noting that the weapons are mainly defensive, Paul's gospel of peace in Christ, the worth of all persons, and new energy in a powerful church will invite attack. What is the church to do? First, to recognize that attacks are coming; second, to learn how to put on the complete armour which God offers and third, to stand firm and undismayed.

16. As in the opening to this letter, the last section emphasizes our best and final weapon, prayer. As Wright says, no one quite knows 'how it works', but the point is that, with prayer, things we couldn't accomplish by our own effort, organization or skill, happen. Prayer is mysterious in its effect yet deeply comforting to its subjects. Nothing is as comforting as hearing the words 'I am praying for

you' from a friend. Paul's prayer is his capstone and final word for those in the church (in Ephesus).

Applying the Scriptures (15 minutes)

In his commentary on 5.19, Wright recommends the singing of spiritual songs of several kinds as a hedge against evil. As persons naturally differ from one another, couldn't other forms of worship offer the same service? For one person, film offers teaching and encouragement to focus on the Christian life; for another, paintings or sculptures may offer divine comfort. Some persons feel in the presence of God most when walking or running. The purpose of this time in the session is the sharing of personal resources for spiritual nourishment. It might be helpful for the group to work together to create a list of recommended activities, music, books and similar resources. Perhaps someone could volunteer to bring a device (phone, tablet or laptop) to create and share such a list.

Sharing "Oh Wow" Moments (5 minutes)

Ask members to share 'oh wow' moments in their own hearts and lives from their study and this session.

Closing Prayer (1 minute)

Creator and giver of all good and perfect gifts, teach us to accept your new plan for the church as well as for the relationships which define and reveal our lives. Teach us to be as kind as you, as loving as you and as willing to give of ourselves as you. Amen.

Ticket Out the Door (3 minutes)

Ask members to respond to this question on a slip of paper and give it to you on their way out of the door: Could you share a favorite Bible verse from Philippians?

SESSION 3
JOY IN COMMITMENT

(PAGES 63–85)

Opening Prayer (1 minute)

Dear Jesus, help us to be committed servants like Paul and Timothy, daring to trust you to continue the ministry you began here on earth, and looking to you as our model and guide. Bless us with energizing joy as we give our lives in serving your kingdom. Amen.

Group Opening (5 minutes)

Begin this session by asking the group to share favorite verses from Philippians, encouraging them to tell when and how they used those verses in their own lives.

Exploring the Scriptures (30 minutes)

1. Paul's letter to the church in Philippi, the first city in Europe to hear the good news of Jesus Christ, was likely written during his imprisonment in Ephesus. He is well-acquainted with this church, mentioning specific members by name by way of encouragement.
2. Wright begins his discussion of Philippians by quoting a prayer of Sir Frances Drake, who reminded us 'that it is not the beginning, but the continuing of the same, until it is thoroughly finished, that yieldeth the true glory' (page 63). Paul was confident of both his beginning and finishing his work as apostle to the Gentiles with the message of grace not because of his own abilities; rather he was confident in the ability of God. Think of God's leading in your own life, identifying how you took on the service of others in your own way, as well as noting times and events which confirmed your path as service to God.
3. In 1.9–11, Paul offers a prayer for the Philippians which previews his later teaching to them. Identify the three elements highlighted in the commentary to these verses.
4. Paul seems to have attracted trouble. In this case, he was in prison (again), and rival preachers of the gospel appeared to be using Paul's misfortunes to criticize him as a means to make themselves seem more important. The author of this book refers us to the words of Joseph to his brothers, who were afraid of Joseph's reprisals against them: 'You meant evil against me, but God meant it for good' (Genesis 50.20). Paul asserts that his imprisonment gave him an opportunity to share God's faithfulness with others, and his commitment first to Christ and the church led him to say of those who disparaged him, 'So what?' (1.18). Ask members of the group to share a time when their commitment gave them a 'so what?' attitude toward opposition.
5. Paul's own confidence in God prevents us from imagining his predicament. His own death at the hands of his captors was a certainty, more 'when' than 'if'. Ask someone in the group to read aloud 2 Corinthians 1.8–11. Note that his faith never wavered, but

his feelings included highs and lows. He admits that there were good reasons to hope for either outcome but states his motivation clearly for living: 'to help you to advance and rejoice in your faith . . .' (1.25). His joy was in his commitment to guide others to faith in Jesus. Perhaps someone would be willing to share a time when commitment to others was a motivation to persevere.

6. Wright discusses, at some length, Paul's statement that he 'would really love to leave all this and be with the Messiah' (1.23). Wright notes that the idea of 'dying and going to heaven' is nowhere discussed in the New Testament. He develops this idea at length in other books. How do you feel about this representation of death and heaven? On what do you base your opinion?

7. Paul continues in a serious vein in 1.27, exhorting the Philippians to live in a manner worthy of the gospel. Wright translates, saying 'your public behaviour must match up to the gospel of the Messiah'. What do you think that this means? Is Paul writing to the church at Philippi or the members of the church? How would the difference change your own behaviour?

8. How would you know if your behaviour is meeting the standard set down by Paul? There are two actions encouraged in 1.27, 28. How would you relate these actions to what Paul recommended in the letter to the Ephesians? Has anyone ever said to you, 'Don't let them know you are afraid!' When, and in what context?

9. At the end of this section, Wright delineates four 'gospel issues' facing the church today. He asks, 'Which gospel issues does your community face right now? Where is it important for you and your church to hold your nerve and remain unafraid in the face of opposition?' (See pages 71–72.) How would you answer him?

10. We all enjoy watching great teamwork in action. Watching the precision within the chaos backstage at a play; listening to the unison, harmony and sensitivity to the music in an orchestra or in a choir and thrilling in the single-minded purpose of a sports team are exemplars of what Paul expects from the church. As in Ephesians, the first thing to establish is the motivation for individuals to behave as a group, and for the church, that motivation is the example of Christ.

11. Wright suggests that people of the Greek world naturally thought of Alexander the Great when they thought of a great leader. In the same way, he writes that Paul and others in the Roman world would have thought of Augustus. Who in our world would be mentioned in the same way? Comparing Jesus to these, Wright asserts that Jesus is who true global sovereignty looks like and wonders if today's church knows how radically counter-cultural Paul's gospel message was. Now compare the Jesus of Philippians 2 to today's

cultural and political leaders. In what ways is Wright's question a challenge to today's church?

12. Philippians 2.5–11 is the preeminent statement of Christology in the New Testament. Wright describes it as a poem, though most scholars regard this passage as a hymn of the earliest church. Whether poetry or lyrics, this passage moves the reader to love Jesus in ways no formal theological statement ever could. Wright warns against believing that Jesus 'emptied' himself of divinity before his resurrection. How would you describe the role of Jesus in salvation portrayed in this poem?

13. Wright directs the reader to Isaiah 45.23 as the key to this passage and makes this point: God, who will not share his glory with anyone else, has shared it with Jesus. How can we have the same attitude toward serving God and others that Jesus had?

14. Who is responsible for attaining this attitude? Paul, in Wright's translation, says, 'Your task now is to work at bringing about your own salvation' (Philippians 2.12b). As we might build a home from a blueprint, stitch a quilt from a pattern or cook a five-star meal, we are to struggle to conform our lives to Christ's example. In what ways do you seek to meet this responsibility?

15. Paul proposes that the Philippians consider Timothy and Epaphroditus as examples of Christian service. Wright compares this view to having two eyes to see, enabling us to see in three dimensions, clearly discerning important features of our world. How does each example, Timothy and Epaphroditus, deepen our understanding of service?

Applying the Scriptures (15 minutes)

Wright advises that 'we are all of us, whether first-century apostles or twenty-first century converts, expected to be fully human beings, facing all that life throws at us and being honest about the results' (page 85).

He identifies three expectations: to be fully human beings, to face all that life throws at us, and to be honest about the results. Divide or allow the group to divide themselves into a group for each of these expectations, asking each group to create a list highlighting the challenges of meeting each of these expectations. Provide a means of displaying the results (dry erase board, newsprint or other). As time allows, ask each group to share its findings.

Sharing "Oh Wow" Moments (5 minutes)

Ask members to share 'oh wow' moments in their own hearts and lives from their study and this session.

Closing Prayer (1 minute)

God of self-giving love, teach us the depths of your love, the heights of your magnificence and the infinite worth that we possess in your divine gift of Jesus Christ. Amen.

Ticket Out the Door (3 minutes)

On a note card or slip of paper you provide, ask each member to share a response to an expectation in the 'Applying the Scriptures' activity that was not addressed in their own group.

SESSION 4
JOY IN THE JOURNEY
(PAGES 85–102)

Opening Prayer (1 minute)

Lord of all beginnings, guide us to a fuller practical understanding of the joyous life you created for us. Give us a vision of the prize ahead of us and the commitment to reach the finish line. Grant us the inner resolve to set aside the worries of each day in the hope of living in your peace. Amen.

Group Opening (5 minutes)

If possible, display the group activity reports from last week. Read some of the responses to the 'Ticket Out the Door' activity and add them to the responses from the week before. Ask for additional insights into the group activity.

Exploring the Scriptures (30 minutes)

1. On page 86, Wright explains the main thing Paul meant by 'the flesh' in 3.3–4. Explain to a neighbor what that concept meant.
2. Wright also identifies some secondary characteristics of 'flesh' on pages 86–87. Discuss these and then point out the specific context of this discussion of 'the flesh' as Wright explains it.
3. In verse 3.2, Paul uses the term for 'look out!' or, as Wright translates it, 'watch out', in three separate commands. What are the three groups that Paul warns the Philippians to 'be on their guard' against? What was Paul's counter-claim against these troublemakers?
4. In the 'olden days' before computers, household and business accounting was done on a large pad of specially lined paper with a column for 'debits' or expenses and another for 'credits' or income.

Creating a balance sheet of debits and credits was usually a great deal of time-consuming work. In 3.7–11, Paul explains his balance sheet in his relationship to Jesus as well as his status as a Jewish leader. If there is an accountant, bookkeeper or business owner in the group, perhaps that person could be enlisted ahead of the session to explain Wright's discussion of Paul's spiritual accounting.

5. How does Wright explain Paul's teaching on 'justification by faith' (pages 88–90)? How does Wright relate 'justification' back to the hymn in 2.5–11?

6. If there is someone technologically savvy in the group and the resources are available, playing the clip from *Chariots of Fire* about Eric Liddell would be a marvelous introduction to the next section of the text. If not, just tell the story of Eric Liddell's comeback from certain defeat to inspiring victory, illustrating how Paul has changed metaphors from accounting to athletics.

7. Wright explains that his conception of 'the prize waiting for me' may be different from what members think that prize is. Create a graph with 'similar to common beliefs' in one column and with 'different from common beliefs' heading the other, and then list the elements described in the chart on page 185.

8. Philippians 3.17–4.1 is an extended metaphor about our status as 'citizens of heaven'. Create a simple list of what it means to be a citizen of your own country, state, county and local areas, and compare that to Paul's commands.

9. In particular, examine 3.19 and note ways in which our understandings of citizenship diverge from Paul's understanding of 'heavenly citizenship'.

10. Paul's letters are not abstract documents, rather they were written at specific times for specific people in specific situations. The advice, encouragement and even warnings that Paul gives continue to have directly applicable meaning, though. In 4.2–3, he addresses a broken relationship between two faithful women of the church, publicly asking them to come to be reconciled to each other. Paul makes an appeal to a respected worker in the church to arbitrate their dispute, whether Epaphroditus or Syzygus, whose name means 'loyal companion'.

11. The author notes of verse 4 that the word most often translated as 'rejoice', a feeling inside an individual, might better be translated 'celebrate', which suggests an activity done together. What kind of public celebrations do you have in your church?

12. 'Pray about everything', Paul encourages in 4.6, 'as you pray, and make requests and give thanks as well'. What will happen to you if you follow this direction? Paul says peace will fill your heart and

life and protect you from worry, which strangles the flow of Christ's spirit in your heart. When Christ and his love for you are at the center of your life, then celebration will bubble over in your life. How can you make a place for Jesus in the center of your life?

13. Philippians 4.8–9 resounds into twenty-first century life like a blast of trumpets! Media, whether mainstream, social or broadcast, whether read, heard or spoken, has invaded our lives. How would Paul advise us to proceed in our lives? What does 'think through' in verse 8 imply? How will you apply these verses to your own life?

14. Can you imagine making the statement Paul makes in verse 9? 'Just act like I act, and God's peace will be with you!' What a burden Paul places on himself, inviting close inspection and criticism of his life by others, but even more by his redeemer.

15. Many Christians identify 4.13 as their favorite Bible verse, and it serves as the 'final answer' for this letter to the Philippians. What does Paul identify as the source of his contentment?

16. And now we come to 'the rest of the story'. Paul's warm regard for the church at Philippi was a natural result of their love for him, expressed in a financial gift to him in support of his ministry, but even more because this support was habitual, continuing throughout the course of his ministry. However, Paul was quick to address his concern about how others viewed this support. What was his concern? What metaphor did he reuse to explain his feelings?

Applying the Scriptures (15 minutes)

Use the chart below to summarize what you learned from the study of Philippians. You could work individually, in groups (one theme per group), or as one whole group. Emphasize the interrelatedness of the themes with Jesus as the center of each.

THEME	MENTIONED IN	MEANING/ DEFINITION	SOURCE/ MODEL
Joy			
Humility			
Unity			
Christian Living			

Sharing "Oh Wow" Moments (5 minutes)

What realizations/stupendous thoughts/life-changing moments did you have in these week's study and group meeting?

Closing Prayer (1 minute)

Dear Jesus, our model of service and source of all joy, fill us with your strength to meet every challenge and so be content, filled with your peace, as we live every day in you. Amen.

SESSION 5
KEEP CHRIST FIRST!
(PAGES 105–43)

Opening Prayer (1 minute)

Jesus, we thank you that you have given us a relationship with you that is whole and complete. We know that you are at the center of our world, and that our lives revolve around you. Help us to clear away everything that blocks our path to you, and in its place give us the flood of joy that is your plan for us. Amen.

Group Opening (5 minutes)

The letter to the Colossians, like those to the Ephesians and Philippians, was written by Paul when he was in jail. Paul most likely never visited the church at Colossae and had only heard about the church founded there. He heard that teachings from outside Christianity were being incorporated into the faith of the church there. Paul responded vigorously to assert the supremacy of Jesus as well as his sole sufficiency as Messiah. Though written for a church in Asia Minor around AD 61, this letter is filled with the basics of the Christian faith. The temptations of manmade religion are as attractive as ever, so Paul's encouragement to keep Christ first in our faith is as timely as ever.

Exploring the Scriptures (30 minutes)

1. How does the author connect the illustration of a garden with Colossians 1.1–8?
2. What sign does Wright identify that shows the church in Colossae is off to a good start?
3. What two lies does Wright suggest that the world often tells about God's intention for human behaviour? How does Paul use 1.6 to rebut those lies?
4. What Old Testament event does Paul have in mind for 1.13? How does Wright apply this insight to this passage?

5. In 1.12 Paul prays that the Colossians will learn to 'give thanks to the father'. What reason does Wright suggest is behind Paul's emphasis on thanksgiving in that church?

6. As in Philippians, Paul uses an early hymn to Christ as the center of his explanation of what God has done in Christ for us. In this letter, however, the emphasis is on the supremacy and sufficiency of Christ for our salvation. The church at Colossae faced challenges on several fronts from those who wished to add new elements to the Christian faith. Paul fought vigorously to combat these additions, which we will learn more about in chapter 2 of the letter.

7. On page 110, which characteristic of a Christian life does Wright suggest is a 'part' of Christian maturity?

8. If Christians are to grow as Christians, what must they 'know above all' according to Paul and the author?

9. How does Jesus hold together the old world and new? Wright says this is the turning point of the poem.

10. In Philippians, Jesus is the model for self-sacrificing love. How is Jesus the model for Christians as portrayed in this poem for Wright?

11. In Colossians 1.21–23, Wright leads us on a journey through a presentation of the meaning of reconciliation and how it is accomplished. Using the image of a map, he describes being on the map (and inside the Mall of America!) as a metaphor for reconciliation, as a result of which we 'can freely approach the living God without a stain on our character'. How is this possible?

12. Is it possible to be 'in Christ' and still be immature? How then can Christians mature, and by what means (page 119)?

13. Wright states: 'Paul then explains more particularly why, if you've already got Jesus the Messiah as your Lord, you don't need to be "completed" by any other system at all, and certainly not by a Judaism that refuses to acknowledge him' (page 124). How does Wright define the two main responses to this controversy?

14. How carefully did you read 2.15? Take a minute to read it again. Now read what Wright says about that verse on pages 126–28. What is Paul asserting about the power of Jesus?

15. Think about all of the rules that amass around religious faith: 'Every stitch that you make on a Sunday you will have to take out with your teeth when you get to heaven.' 'God helps those who help themselves.' 'Don't vote for a candidate from that other political party and still think you're going to make it to heaven.' These are real rules from real people concerned about protecting their faith, though Paul says they are misguided. When he writes, 'He

blotted out the handwriting that was against us' (verse 14). Paul was referring to the law of Moses, which no longer holds sway over us. One of the groups tormenting the church at Colossae was teaching that unless you kept a stringent set of laws, you could not be saved.

17. Wright identifies 3.9–10 as the keys to this section of Colossians. Paul, he writes, proposes two main areas of the old life that must be abandoned. What are they, and why were they chosen?

18. In 3.10, Paul writes that our new self 'is being renewed in the image of the creator', and one of the results is a 'new knowledge'. Wright understands this verse in this way: 'As so often in Colossians, it seems that, contrary to what a lot of people imagine, being a Christian means learning to think harder, not to leave your brain behind in the quest for new experiences' (page 133). How do you react to that statement?

19. Paul writes again in 3.18—4.1 on the household code for first-century believers. On pages 137–38, the author offers two interpretations of this passage by way of context. What are these aspects of the code, and how helpful are they to you personally as you seek to understand and follow these scriptures?

20. Paul returns to the subject of prayer as the letter to the Colossians winds down. Surprisingly, he asks the church and believers to pray for him. Teachers know that asking a student to participate in leading a class is a good way to involve the student in the lesson. More importantly, Paul asked the believers to pray for him because he felt the need for their support. Could you share an instance in which you requested prayer from someone and both of you benefited from that prayer?

Applying the Scriptures (15 minutes)

Find Colossians 3.12–15. Using whatever resources are available, create an explanation for each of the characteristics named by Paul as the clothes of the believer: tender-hearted, kind, humble, meek and big-hearted. As the author suggests, ask one another what actions and words will make each one come true in your life, in the life of your church and in the life of your village or town. After a time of group reflection, share your thoughts with the group.

Sharing "Oh Wow" Moments (5 minutes)

What realizations/stupendous thoughts/life-changing moments did you have in these week's study and group meeting? Don't forget Colossians 2.15!

Closing Prayer (1 minute)

Our great God, we have encountered life-challenging wisdom today. Give us the strength and wisdom to tear away our old lives and put on the lives you have prepared for us. Amen.

Ticket Out the Door (3 minutes)

Write your response on the slip of paper given to you: What topic, scripture or comment do you wish we had explored further thus far in our studies?

SESSION 6
THE LETTER TO PHILEMON
(PAGES 147–55)

Opening Prayer (1 minute)

As we have grown into new knowledge of our relationship with Jesus, O God, may we grow in service to others. Amen.

Group Opening (15 minutes)

Note to Session Facilitator: Share with the group members several of the responses to the previous 'Ticket Out the Door' activity. Lead the group in a discussion of these as long as time permits.

Exploring the Scriptures (15 minutes)

1. Philemon was the owner of the house where the church at Colossae met. A friend of Paul's, Philemon may have converted after hearing Paul preach in Ephesus, which was only one hundred miles away. The letter to the church at Colossae was sent at the same time as Philemon's letter. The central issue addressed was a slave named Onesimus, formerly owned by Philemon. Onesimus ran away from Philemon's house in the direction of the nearest large city, Ephesus. There Onesimus believed the Christian message and found his own ministry in caring for Paul's needs. Paul dealt with this difficult issue with characteristic forthrightness, sending Onesimus back to Philemon bearing a letter from Paul asking Philemon to accept his former slave back without penalty, even hinting that he should be freed. Why didn't Paul just command Philemon to free Onesimus?
2. The key sentence in this passage, the author says, is verse 6; in his prayers, Paul often tells us the inner meaning of the letter when he

tells us what it is that he prays for. How does that insight apply in this case?

3. What is the first step Paul takes in persuading Philemon to accept Onesimus?
4. What appeal does Paul use to ask Philemon for this response?
5. What is Paul's relationship with Onesimus?
6. Wright describes Paul's appeal to Philemon to accept Onesimus as a 'living example' of what?
7. In your own life, is there someone with whom you need to seek reconciliation? What barriers stand in the way of any reconciliation between persons?
8. The author offers a valuable word of caution on page 154 about how to react to a person who tells you that they are 100 per cent certain that you should do something as God's will. What is that advice, and have you ever had occasion to take it for yourself?
9. Wright declares that 'Jesus hung with arms outstretched between heaven and earth, making a bridge upwards and downwards between God and the human race, and from side to side between all the warring factions of earth' (page 154). How does Paul use this concept when coming between Philemon and Onesimus?
10. What happens, according to Wright, when believers follow that pattern in their own lives?
11. Wright compares the situation between Philemon and Onesimus to which parable of Jesus? What objection did people raise then that likely would be raised today? Today, how can we carry out the mission of reconciliation in our own lives modeled by Jesus and Paul?

Applying the Scriptures (25 minutes)

Today's session is largely an opportunity to bring together all that we have learned in this study, so here are several activities to lead the group in that direction. You will not likely have time to complete them all, so choose among them as the Spirit leads, as interest is shown, and as time permits.

1. What are the themes common to the New Testament books we examined in this study? As a starter, here are a few, but make your own list and share with the group: Paul in prison, Jesus (many aspects of), unity, and Christian living.
2. 'The Christian ideal has not been tried and found wanting; it has been found difficult and left untried.'[1] Perhaps you wondered as

---

1. G. K. Chesterton, *What's Wrong with the World*, https://www.gutenberg.org/files/1717/1717-h/1717-h.htm.

you studied this book why your own experience in faith has been so different from what Paul describes. Take into account the difference in time and social context, and describe your Christian experience with reference to Chesterton's quote.

3. If you wish to complete an activity alone, try this. Write a letter to your pastor, a loved one or a close friend describing what you have learned in this study as well as how it has changed your understanding of what it means to be a Christian.

4. Which of the themes in the first activity is closest to your heart and most connected to your own spiritual gifts? Consider, and make a list of, what actions you could take to join the leadership of your church in guiding your church toward the path of that theme.

Sharing "Oh Wow" Moments (5 minutes)

Do you have a new favorite Bible verse as a result of this study? Take a moment to share it with the group!

Closing Prayer (1 minute)

Thank you, Holy God, for the divine gift of the scriptures. May your energy help us to complete your work within us, transforming our minds, our lives and our thoughts to be our acceptable gifts to you. Amen.